SCHUTZHUND

SCHUTZHUND

THEORY
AND
TRAINING METHODS

Susan Barwig
and
Stewart Hilliard

HOWELL
BOOK HOUSE
New York

Howell Book House

Published by Wiley Publishing, Inc., New York, NY

For general information on our other products and services or to obtain technical support please contact our Customer Care Department within the U.S. at 800-762-2974, outside the U.S. at 317-572-3993 or fax 317-572-4002.

Wiley also publishes its books in a variety of electronic formats. Some content that appears in print may not be available in electronic books.

Library of Congress Cataloging-in-Publication Data:

Barwig, Susan.
    Schutzhund : theory and training methods / by Susan Barwig and Stewart Hilliard.
      p.   cm.
    Includes bibliographical references.
    ISBN 0-87605-731-8
    1. Schutzhund dogs—Training. I. Hilliard, Stewart. II. Title.
    SF428.78.B37 1991
    636.7′3—dc20   90-37408
                                                   CIP

Manufactured in the United States of America.

20 19 18 17 16

Contents

Preface

When Susan Barwig published the first edition of this book in 1978, she meant it to be a basic introduction to the sport, an answer to the question "What is Schutzhund?"

In 1978, Schutzhund was a little-known and arcane discipline practiced by a few hundred devotees across the United States. They were regarded with suspicion and even horror by many American dog fanciers. In the United States there was no old and accepted tradition of working dogs, as there was in Western Europe, and twelve years ago Americans tended to associate any sort of biting-dog training with shady characters in greasy overalls who fed their dogs gunpowder in order to make them mean.

In 1978, advertisements for German Shepherd Dogs mentioned side gait more often than working ability, and not many people considered a pedigree full of German Schutzhund III dogs a selling point for a litter of puppies.

In 1978, animals with AKC Companion Dog titles were advertised as "working" dogs. Much has changed in twelve years.

Dog World is now crammed full of ads for German Shepherds, Rottweilers and Doberman Pinschers imported from Germany, all of them proudly announcing the animals' titles and accomplishments in Schutzhund sport. The United Schutzhund Clubs of America have even instituted a controlled-breeding program (modeled after that of the German Shepherd Dog Club of Germany) which emphasizes not only selection for correct conformation but also the deliberate promotion of character and working ability.

We are becoming acquainted with a new vision—the idea that dogs should be admired for more than pretty ears, a handsome coat, a correct topline and a perfect tail.

Now many of us look for *character* in our dogs rather than just conformation and beauty. We admire a fine working animal—and call it fine—for its courage, its spirit and its power. In short, it is formidable rather than just adorable. Instead of doting on it and spoiling it as we invariably seem to do with beauty dogs, we respect this animal for its power, love it for its devotion to us and keep and train it responsibly because of our respect for it.

Now more Americans than ever are asking "What is Schutzhund?" This book, like its predecessor, is designed to answer this question, giving the reader a feeling not just for the mechanics and ritual of a Schutzhund trial, but also for the theory and the atmosphere of the sport.

However, much more than its predecessor, it is also designed to convey a good general understanding of Schutzhund training and also many specific techniques for teaching the dogs. We think that *Schutzhund: Theory and Training Methods* will prove fascinating not only to novices getting their first introduction to the sport, but also to seasoned trainers looking for a new perspective.

The Requirements chapters describe what the dog must do in a trial—much more simply and readably than in a rule book.

The Overview chapters give the reader general information about, and also hopefully some insight into, each of the three phases of Schutzhund and the demands that they place on the animal.

The training chapters break all of the exercises which the dog must learn down into simple steps designed to be easily grasped by the animal, and also arrange them into meticulous *progressions* (the careful layerings of skills and concepts that eventually evolve into polished exercises).

For reasons of space, we were unable to describe the schooling of *all* the exercises in Schutzhund in full detail in this introductory volume. We were forced to be selective, especially in protection training, which is very complex.

We give a reasonably detailed picture of the theory and methods of *drive work*, because basic agitation is the foundation upon which all other training is based. Because the *hold and bark* and the *out* are by far the two most important skills of control, we treated them in some detail. With respect to those two exercises, we hope that we have succeeded in conveying a rich understanding of our methods to the reader and imparted information and ideas that can actually be used on the training field.

On the other hand, our methods for the *blind search* and what we call *obedience for bites* are subtle and complicated, and to describe them in detail would have required another volume.

Throughout the book we have employed the pronoun "he" to refer to the handler and also the agitator and the assistant in training. No sexism is implied. We fully recognize that there are many extremely capable female dog trainers in the sport. Our decision to use the masculine pronoun was prompted by stylistics, not chauvinism.

About the Authors

Susan Barwig holds master's degrees in both education and psychology, and currently teaches in the Graduate School of Education at the University of Colorado.

Ms. Barwig's hobby for many years has been dogs, and she is involved in all kinds of training, having enjoyed great success in training dogs for tracking, obedience and protection. She has entered her own dogs in international Schutzhund competitions for three consecutive years, traveling as a member of the American team to Belgium, Italy and Hungary.

In addition to working with her own dogs, Ms. Barwig is the author of *Schutzhund* (which in its original version won the Dog Writers' Association of America's ''Best Technical Book of the Year'' award), and the editor of *The German Shepherd Book*. She is also the editor of *The German Shepherd Quarterly*. As the founder and president of Canine Training Systems, Ltd., she produces specialty dog training videos on a variety of dog sports.

Steward Hilliard began training working dogs in 1980. He has taught a number of seminars across the United States on canine behavior, Schutzhund and Ring Sport, as well as police and protection dog training.

From 1984 to 1989 he served as training director of the Rampart Range Working Dog Association of Denver, Colorado. That training program produced many handler–dog teams titled in Obedience, Tracking, Schutzhund, Ring Sport and United States Police Canine competition, including two world championship Schutzhund competitors.

He received his bachelor's degree in psychology from the University of Colorado at Denver and is studying for his doctorate in biopsychology and animal behavior at the University of Texas in Austin.

The canine training techniques described in this book are not intended for any canine or specially bred canine whose genetic lineage or environmental experiences have pre-disposed him to unlawful, illegal, or indiscriminately attack-oriented behavior. All training techniques described in this book have been developed over long periods of time by recognized canine training experts. However, neither the Publisher nor the Authors shall be liable for any claim made by any person, trainer or dog owner for any injury or loss of property which arises out of the use or implementation of any of the various training methods contained in this book. Protection training, particularly, can be dangerous and should be attempted only be experienced, adult trainers who are well aware of the risks involved and who accept these risks without reservation.

Acknowledgments

We wish to express our appreciation to the following people for their help in the preparation of this book.

To the following trainers whose excellence in their field has been most helpful:

Charley Bartholomew	Jack Lennig
Janet Birk	Jurgen Lorcher
Bernard Cornet	Rudi Muller
Johannes Grewe	Helmut Raiser
Walter Koch	

In addition, our thanks to our extended family—the members of the Rampart Range Working Dog Association of Denver, Colorado, many of whose fine dogs appear in the photographs in this book.

Photographers

    Rick Williams (Captured Moments)
    Betsy Duffner

Illustrations and Figures

    Stewart Hilliard
    Richard Holley

Editorial Helpers

    Elizabeth Hilliard
    George Hilliard
    Teresa Brashear

"Joy in work, devotion to duty and to master. . . docility and obedience, teachableness and quickness to understand."—Max von Stephanitz

1

What Is Schutzhund?

THE IDEAL DOG possesses certain inherent qualities of character. It is a friendly, good-natured family member; an alert, courageous protector and an obedient, reliable companion. These qualities are not only the products of its upbringing and how it was taught to behave. They are also the result of its genetic endowment—the quality of its parents, its grandparents and their parents, too.

Schutzhund is a sport whose purpose is to evaluate a dog's character by giving it work to do, and then comparing its performance with that of other working dogs. In German, the word *Schutzhund* means literally *protection dog*, for that is what a Schutzhund is meant to be. The sport evolved in Germany around the turn of the twentieth century as a means of testing and preserving the character and the utility of working dogs.

During the late eighteenth and early nineteenth centuries, Western Europe was well populated with many types of rural shepherd dogs. These animals herded sheep, cattle and other livestock for their masters. They also guarded livestock at night and gave warning of the approach of strangers to innumerable small farms and hamlets. Shepherd dogs were an indispensable part of the farm economy.

These dogs did not belong to breeds per se. Rather, their size, build, coat and color conformed to *types* that were traditional in various regions, and blended smoothly from one region to the next. At this time, ownership of actual *breeds* of pedigreed dogs was primarily a privilege of the noble and the wealthy, who devoted themselves mainly to sight hounds, trail hounds and other dogs of the chase. In contrast, rural shepherd dogs were kept and bred by generation after generation of peasants and farmers. People of means and wealth had as little regard for peasant dogs as they did for peasants, and in comparison to a noble hound of St. Hubert, a shepherd dog was little more than a cur.

It was not until some time later, near the end of the nineteenth century, that some members of the leisure class who had both the time and money to keep and breed dogs simply for pleasure took an interest in the common farm dogs of the countryside. For perhaps the first time these animals were viewed as altogether more valuable than the livestock they guarded, and in various areas of Europe certain unusual men began to take steps to preserve and develop them.

One of these was an aristocratic young German cavalry officer named Max von Stephanitz who in 1899 founded the German Shepherd Dog Club of Germany (called the SV). The importance of von Stephanitz in the establishment and development of the German Shepherd cannot be overestimated. Almost single-handedly he built the breed. He presided over the club, began the stud book, wrote the standard of the breed and appointed the judges who would select the most worthy specimens. He also organized training contests for the SV. Well before von Stephanitz's time, numerous informal contests were conducted in small villages all over Europe, but it was he who formalized these competitions under the auspices of the SV and structured them to include tests of performance in tracking, obedience and protection. These training contests became the sport we know today as Schutzhund.

Von Stephanitz was totally committed to the idea that the German Shepherd is, and must stay, a working animal whose worth is derived from its utility. He strongly encouraged the use of dogs by the German police and military. There was a great need, he felt, for an animal that possessed a "highly developed sense of smell, enormous courage, intrepidness, agility and, despite its aggressiveness, great obedience." Von Stephanitz was a man of vision. From its founding in 1899, the SV prospered for thirty-six years under his absolute control. In addition to building a prosperous and effective organization, he also put in place a system of strict controls that guided the breeding of the German Shepherd in Germany during the first half of the twentieth century.

Today the SV is the largest and most influential breed organization in the world, and it continues much in the tradition of von Stephanitz. The system he put into effect decades ago still serves to preserve and develop the best physical and temperamental attributes of the breed, and Schutzhund is an integral part of this system. Among the SV's regulations for controlled breeding, the most basic requirement for breed worthiness is the Schutzhund examination.

A German Shepherd Dog in Germany cannot receive official registration papers unless both of its parents have passed a Schutzhund trial. Furthermore, unless the dog itself also passes a Schutzhund examination, it cannot be exhibited in conformation shows; it is not eligible for the coveted V rating (for *Vorzüglich*, excellent) in beauty and structure; it may not compete for the title of *Sieger* (Champion) of Germany; it will not be recommended for breeding by a *Körmeister* (breed master).

By ensuring that a dog will only be used for breeding if it has the necessary

Nineteenth-century German farm and herding dogs. *Top,* two smooth-coated shepherds photographed circa 1880. *Right,* a rough-coated shepherd from Württemberg. (From von Stephanitz, *The German Shepherd Dog,* 1923.)

An early SV-registered German Shepherd: Hussan v. Mecklenburg, a son of the 1906-1907 German *Sieger* Roland v. Starkenburg. (From von Stephanitz, *The German Shepherd Dog,* 1923.)

character and working attributes to pass a performance test, the Germans have guaranteed a long legacy for the German Shepherd as a working animal.

The Schutzhund trial is a day-long test of character and trainability; it is an evaluation of the dog's stability, drive and willingness. The animal must be a multitalented generalist that can, in the space of one day, compete successfully in three entirely different phases of performance: tracking, obedience and protection. Schutzhund I is the most elementary title awarded, while Schutzhund III demands the most challenging level of ability.

The tracking test assesses the dog's perseverance and concentration, its scenting ability and its willingness to work for its handler. The animal must follow the footsteps of a tracklayer, finding and indicating to its handler objects, called *articles*, that the tracklayer has left on the track. With each category (Schutzhund I, II or III), the length and age of the track are increased.

Obedience evaluates the dog's responsiveness to its handler. The obedience test involves a number of different situations in which the dog must eagerly and precisely carry out its handler's orders. It must be proficient at heeling at its handler's side, retrieving, jumping and performing a variety of skills.

The protection phase gauges the dog's courage, desire for combat, self-reliance and obedience to its handler under very exciting and difficult circumstances. This phase involves searching for and warning its handler of a hidden "villain," aggressively stopping an assault on its handler and preventing the escape of the villain, among other skills.

The trial is presided over by a recognized judge. It is understood that the judge will be a fellow trainer, a person who has years of experience with working dogs. He must have "feeling" for the animals and be able to look at the whole picture of what a working dog represents. The judge is expected to have the ability to watch a dog work for a little while and then know what is in its heart—what it has inside.

The judge's job is ostensibly to determine a winner. But possibly more important, his job is to promote those animals that display outstanding quality of character so that they will be used for breeding (providing they also meet a number of other requirements for beauty and physical soundness), and to weed out those animals that are deficient or unsound in character. Accordingly he can, and will, disqualify a dog at any point during a trial if the animal shows a severe temperamental flaw.

The Schutzhund trial is sanctioned and organized by a local Schutzhund club, which is part of a large Schutzhund organization. Although there are some professionals who make their living through the sport, Schutzhund breeding and training are meant to be amateur pursuits, and a reputable club is strictly a nonprofit group.

In Germany, the two largest Schutzhund organizations are the SV (the German Shepherd Dog Club) and the DVG (the German Alliance for Utility Dog Sports). The trial rules and regulations of both organizations are essentially identical. However, the emphasis is slightly different in each. While the SV is a breed club dedicated to the promotion of the German Shepherd Dog, the DVG

The ideal dog is a friendly, good-natured family member, an alert, courageous protector and an obedient, reliable companion. (Andy Barwig and Susan Barwig's "Uri," Schutzhund III, UDT.)

The German Shepherd Dog Club of Germany's system of regulating breeding. In addition to fulfilling a hip X-ray requirement and passing a Schutzhund trial and a breed survey examination, the dog must also complete without difficulty a twelve-mile endurance test before being eligible for breeding. (V Jasmine v. Forellenbach, Schutzhund II, with Dr. Nancy Cole.)

America in international Schutzhund competition— Leo Muller and "Argo" representing the United States at the World Championships in Italy.

is a training club that accepts a number of other breeds besides the German Shepherd in competition. The SV emphasizes the character test and breed worthiness aspects of Schutzhund, and the SV judge looks not only at the training of a dog in trial but also at its quality, asking himself if that dog should be used to produce other German Shepherd Dogs. The DVG emphasizes the sport and competition aspects of Schutzhund, and the DVG judge looks primarily at the dog's training and how well its handler presents the animal in trial.

Normally small and friendly, each local club is part of the larger Schutzhund community. A Schutzhund enthusiast from just about anywhere can expect a nice reception at a club in another province, or even in another country.

The club serves a social function as well, especially in Europe. Families and friends get together on training days to eat, drink, laugh and tell tales in the clubhouse and around the field as the dogs run through their routines. The closeness and team spirit of a good club are in evidence. Because everyone is nervous, all the competitors and club members support and encourage one another.

Through its commitment to Schutzhund and its uncompromising insistence on strictly controlled breeding practices, the SV has succeeded in producing the best German Shepherd Dogs in the world. As a result, German-bred German Shepherds are exported by the thousands to places as far away as Japan and Hong Kong. Along with their dogs, Germans have also exported their dog sport. Schutzhund trials have spread to countries throughout the world, including Africa, Australia, South America, North America and even Soviet bloc countries. In many countries stadiums fill with people and brim with excited anticipation when Schutzhund contests take place. In Europe, for example, approximately 40,000 German Shepherds participate in 10,000 trials each year. Besides German Shepherds, many other breeds of dog now compete, including Boxers, Doberman Pinschers, Giant Schnauzers, Bouviers des Flandres, Rottweilers and Belgian shepherds (Groenandael, Malinois and Tervuren).

Despite its longtime popularity in Europe, Schutzhund has only recently come to the United States. The first Schutzhund-type trial on American soil was organized in June 1963 by the Peninsula Canine Corps of Santa Clara, California. The Peninsula Canine Corps was formed in 1957, and boasted as its prime mover Gernot Riedel, a German emigrant who has been an important figure in the American dog sport ever since. The trial was not officially sanctioned, and did not even include tracking, but it was a beginning.

As we seem to do with many newly introduced competitive sports, Americans grew to prominence in Schutzhund with a speed that astounded the skeptics. In 1969, six years after the initial competition in California, the first SV-sanctioned trial on American soil took place in Los Angeles under the leadership of Henry Friehs, another German emigrant. In the same year Alfons Erfelt (of American Temperament Test Society fame) and Drs. Preiser and Lindsey formed the North American Schutzhund Association (NASA).

In 1975, a large group of American Schutzhund pioneers, including Phil Hoelcher, Gernot Riedel, Bud Robinson and Mike McKown, convened in Dallas to try to reconcile the ambitions of the dozen or more local Schutzhund clubs that existed at the time. The result was the founding of the United Schutzhund Clubs of America (USA) under the chairmanship of Luke MacFarland. Scarcely two years later the USA fielded its first team at the World Union of German Shepherd Clubs' European Schutzhund III Championship (consisting of Phil Hoelcher with Cliff vom Endbacher Forst, Wayne Hammer with Nikko von der Ruine Engelhaus and Gernot Riedel as team captain).

Around 1978, an early American branch of the DVG called Working Dogs of America (WDA) dissolved in some dispute. DVG America was obliged to limp along only until the next year, when a sharp and acrimonious conflict of policies and personalities resulted in the expulsion from the USA of seven influential trainers, including Phil Hoelcher, Tom Rose, Laddy Nethercutt, Pat Patterson and Mary Coppage. They immediately went over to the DVG, and with their help DVG America quickly burgeoned, becoming especially important in Florida, one of the hot spots for the dog sport in the United States.

In 1983, the German Shepherd Dog Club of America (GSDCA) allowed some of its members to form an adjunct to the club, which they called the German Shepherd Dog Club of America Working Dog Association (GSDCA/WDA) and which was somewhat nebulously associated with its parent organization. It had to be done this way because of the GSDCA's fear of displeasing the American Kennel Club, which has frowned upon Schutzhund since the beginning. (Earlier, in 1973 and 1974, the GSDCA had conducted a brief flirtation with Schutzhund, sponsoring trials and scheduling judges provided by the SV, but the GSDCA disavowed the sport in 1975 primarily because of AKC objections.)

Today, Schutzhund is firmly established on American shores. Although DVG America is thriving, and the GSDCA/WDA is still on the scene, the USA is the largest and most important organization in the States, boasting approximately two hundred clubs. Recently, the USA has even taken steps to adopt a regulated breeding system for German Shepherd Dogs much like the SV's, issuing its own pedigrees and so forth. However, while the USA's primary emphasis is upon promoting the German Shepherd, the organization welcomes all breeds in its competitions.

American Schutzhund enthusiasts have traveled a rocky road. Organizations and personalities have come and gone, and there have been a lot of fireworks on the way, but today American teams have become a powerful force in the international Schutzhund community. For the last several years teams fielded by the GSDCA/WDA and the USA have consistently placed high in the World Schutzhund III Championships, and in both 1988 and 1989 Jackie Reinhart of Florida won the German DVG Schutzhund III Championships outright.

There are a variety of reasons that account for the rapid growth of Schutzhund in this country. Many dogs trained in Schutzhund are now used by police forces and the military, as search and rescue dogs, as personal protection dogs and as companions in private homes. Growing fear of personal assault and the need to protect property, as well as the desire for a trustworthy, outgoing family pet, have all contributed to the popularity of the Schutzhund concept.

Doberman Pinscher. (Linda Tobiasz's "Kristoff," Schutzhund I.)

Giant Schnauzer.

German Shepherd. (Susan Barwig's V "Ajax," Schutzhund III, FH.)

Belgian Malinois. (Charley Bartholomew's "Utha.")

2

Selecting the Schutzhund Dog

Although many individuals within a particular breed may be suitable for the rigors of Schutzhund, generally dogs from the following breeds are most consistently able to perform the work.

Airedale Terrier

Airedales were used extensively for police work in England and Europe before World War II.

Belgian Groenandael, Tervuren and Malinois

Belgian shepherds were used extensively as messenger dogs, ambulance dogs and security dogs during World War I. Today the Malinois especially is favored by many working dog trainers of France, Belgium and the Netherlands, and the breed is rapidly becoming more common in Schutzhund trials both in Germany and America.

Bouvier des Flandres

The Bouvier was often used for police work in Europe. Today, the greatest number of working-quality Bouviers are bred in the Netherlands, and at least one police department on the Eastern seaboard of the United States has imported several of these animals.

Boxer. (Richard Tomata's and William Scolnik's Ch. Happy Ours Fortune de Jacquet.)

Belgian Groenandael. (Charley Bartholomew's Gillian de Loup Noir, Schutzhund III, Ring I.)

Rottweiler. (Kathy Jo Megan's "Diego.")

Belgian Tervuren.

Boxer

At one time the Boxer was second in popularity only to the German Shepherd Dog in German Schutzhund clubs. They are used as guide dogs and also in the West German police and military.

Doberman Pinscher

Dobermans have seen much service with both the police and military worldwide. They are quite popular in Schutzhund in the United States, and the Doberman Pinscher Club of America was one of the early supporters of American Schutzhund.

German Shepherd

German Shepherds are used extensively by the military and police and as guide dogs for the blind. They are the most popular breed worldwide for Schutzhund as well as most kinds of service work.

Giant Schnauzer

Although comparatively rare, the Giant has been used a great deal in Europe by police departments and Schutzhund enthusiasts as well.

Rottweiler

Probably the oldest of the working breeds, the Rottweiler dates back to the Dark Ages. They are used in both police and military work and in the last few years have become exceedingly popular in the United States.

Other dogs that should not be overlooked for use in Schutzhund work are the Australian Shepherd, Chesapeake Bay and Labrador Retrievers, Bull Terrier and Staffordshire Terrier, as well as some of the giant breeds.

It is not the breed of the dog that is important, it is its character. Von Stephanitz summarized the qualities of the ideal working dog and noted the following requirements: "Joy in work, devotion to duty and to master, mistrust and sharpness against strangers and unusual things, docility and obedience, teachableness and quickness to understand."

SELECTING THE RIGHT SEX

Deciding on a female or male is a personal decision. Each sex has its own merits. Von Stephanitz preferred bitches. He felt that the female had a greater sensitivity to her handler and was more amenable to training. He felt she was "more independent, more reliable and more careful in nature and work." He continued, "It is easier to train her, she grasps more quickly, her memory is more retentive, and she will, at least with an understanding leader, work more willingly and more carefully than a dog. A good bitch can be keen and sharp like a dog." He stresses that both sexes work sheep equally well, a job that demands hardness and sharpness.

Others consider the male to have greater independence and self-reliance. The United States Air Force dog program uses only males. William Koehler, a noted former army dog trainer and author, emphasizes concentrating on obtaining the best prospect for protection work whether it be male or female.

We have observed that, in general, it is more common to find males with the strength of character for Schutzhund than it is to find females of equal quality. This is one reason that a truly good bitch is so seldom for sale. However, a powerful male can sometimes be a difficult animal to live with and train, whereas even an extremely good bitch is normally a little sensitive to her handler and therefore relatively easily controlled.

In Germany the SV demands that *all* German Shepherd Dogs used for breeding, regardless of sex, pass at least a Schutzhund I or a herding test.

GETTING THE BEST PUPPY PROSPECT

When selecting a puppy for use in Schutzhund we must evaluate it both on its own merits and on those of its bloodlines. Perhaps the best indicator of what kind of dog it will grow into is what kind of adults its parents and grandparents are. In the United States it is not easy to obtain this type of information, but it is strongly recommended that the prospective puppy buyer evaluate the puppy's parents for stability, responsiveness and courage. In Germany this information is easier to obtain since every German Shepherd Dog must have a Schutzhund degree or herding title in order to be used for breeding, and both Schutzhund trial scores and breed survey results are readily available.

In addition to inspecting pedigrees for working quality bloodlines one should also look carefully at the individual puppy before agreeing to buy it. The pup must be bold, alert and willing if it is to grow into a responsive and courageous adult.

Preliminary research conducted by Dr. Michael Fox, a veterinarian and expert on animal behavior, indicates that basic temperament characteristics of young pups remain with them throughout life. Although not fully developed in the dog until around eighteen months of age, the animal's general character can be clearly assessed by six to eight weeks of age. With this in mind it is evident that the prospective Schutzhund puppy can be selected with more confidence by using some simple temperament tests.

One American who did a great deal of work on puppy temperament tests was Clarence Pfaffenberger. Combining years of work training dogs with an appreciation for scientific research, he was able to translate technical data obtained from research into very useful information on the working dog. Today he is considered a pioneer because of his work with Guide Dogs for the Blind. At the beginning of his search for the ideal working dog for the blind only 9 percent of the dogs who started training could be trained as responsible guides. By implementing the results of his studies, 90 percent of the dogs starting the program were later graduated. Pfaffenberger's program stressed two main factors: using only dogs with proven working abilities for breeding, and early socialization of all prospective guide dog puppies. As a result of his research, he eventually came to the conclusion that future brood bitches and stud dogs could be selected with confidence by the age of twelve weeks.

Pfaffenberger's data on his attempts to produce the ideal guide dog puppy are relevant to the topic of selecting and raising the Schutzhund prospect. It is especially interesting to note that Pfaffenberger recorded a high correlation between natural retrieving behavior and success in guiding the blind. As a result of our experience with working dogs, we believe that natural retrieving behavior is absolutely essential in the Schutzhund for two reasons: because it provides a ready source of motivation and energy and because retrieving normally goes hand in hand with willingness and responsiveness. In short, natural retrievers are most often willing to please.

In order to develop his successful breeding and training program, Pfaffenberger conducted years of research, much of it in association with Drs. John Paul Scott and John L. Fuller of the Jackson Memorial Laboratory in Maine. Scott and Fuller performed a number of landmark studies on behavioral genetics and the development of behavior in five different breeds of dog. They concluded that growing puppies undergo *critical developmental periods.*

Because of poorly developed sense organs, the puppy shows little learning before the twenty-first day of life, although the ability is doubtless there. However, the period between the twenty-first and twenty-eighth days is critical. During this time the "puppy can become emotionally upset and it will have a lasting effect upon its social ability." Others have called this the *fear-imprint period.* The period between the fourth and sixteenth weeks is the time when social attachments are formed. This has been called the *socialization period.* According to Scott and Fuller, by the end of the sixteenth week the dog's character is essentially formed.

We must note that most authorities on Schutzhund training do not believe that the die is cast at four months. Rather, Schutzhund theory emphasizes the importance of *all* the dog's experiences up to and past a year of age for the development of its ultimate character. Furthermore, most working dog trainers will testify to the capacity dogs show for radical changes in overall behavior (for the better *and* the worse) anytime during their first twelve and even eighteen months of life.

The findings of Pfaffenberger, Scott and Fuller have many implications for the rearing of a puppy intended for work. A summary of them includes:

1. Character traits are inherited and can be effectively evaluated in a puppy at an early age.
2. A puppy should stay with its litter until the seventh week. If it is removed too soon, it will develop abnormal relationships with other dogs. If it remains too long, it will not form appropriate attachments to people. For the best human–dog relationships, the period between the seventh and twelfth week is the best time to remove a puppy from its litter and bring it home. However, this time can be somewhat delayed if appropriate individual socialization is given regularly to the dog while in the kennel.
3. A puppy needs much individual attention to establish its self-importance as an individual.

Pfaffenberger's puppy evaluations are fascinating. He first listed the behaviors undesirable in puppies being trained as guide dogs. His list included dogs who were lacking spirit, too sensitive to noise or correction, fearful, stubborn, unaware of the environment and lacking in stability. He utilized a number of tests to evaluate these behaviors in the dogs. He exposed the puppies to new stimuli, such as a flashlight or an object waved in front of them. He felt curiosity was a sign of intelligence. He blew a whistle and observed the pup's reaction to it. A puppy that was frightened by the approach of a two-wheeled cart or moving vehicle was not further considered for guide work. Pfaffenberger thought that one of the best overall tests for character is simply observing the puppy's natural attitude toward people. He believed that a pup should pay attention and show friendliness at the approach of a stranger. Other training tests involved teaching the dog to heel, sit and fetch, and he evaluated willingness and trainability during these exercises.

Pfaffenberger conducted his tests over a five-week period in order to get a good sample of each pup's behavior. Young puppies are extremely dynamic, and they will seldom test out the same way on two different occasions. It is therefore advisable for the prospective Schutzhund puppy buyer to observe and examine the litter on many different occasions, spread out over as long a period of time as possible. In this way, a buyer may be able to take note of developmental trends.

Of course, some of the qualities Pfaffenberger sought in his guide dogs are not those we desire in a Schutzhund prospect. For example, aggression is discouraged in the guide dog. However, in both types of training the animal must possess a high level of responsiveness and intelligence, and we can gain much by reading Pfaffenberger's work.

For the breeder of a litter, early record keeping can provide valuable clues to the potential of each puppy. For example, vigor and competitiveness in nursing can indicate a more dominant, aggressive character.

Konrad Most in his writings stressed the value of instinct in selecting at birth the puppy best suited for the rigors of Schutzhund work. He preferred the

It is not the breed of the dog that is important; it is character. Many dogs of breeds not traditionally used for police-style work have been successful in Schutzhund. Above, Dr. Gerry Pasek schools "Shadow" in the early stages of protection training. "Shadow" went on to become one of only a handful of Schutzhund III Labrador Retrievers in the world.

The ideal puppy prospect greets a friendly stranger with confidence.

Social response. The puppy is left alone in a pen. A stranger enters the pen and squats down near the puppy. The ideal Schutzhund prospect is friendly and sociable.

This puppy shows interest and moves to investigate a can filled with stones dropped directly in front of it. (Officer Jack Lennig's "Seth.")

16

puppy that actively seeks out its mother and sucks vigorously. This type of puppy continues, Most said, to be active and competitive as it grows.

To assess the character of a six- to eight-week-old pup a wider variety of tests can be administered. Confidence, alertness, intelligence, sociability, competitiveness, aggressiveness and stability are all highly desirable qualities in a Schutzhund dog. Dr. Michael Fox suggests a variety of situations to evaluate some of these qualities in a puppy:

1. *Response to a Unique Stimulus*. The puppy should be placed alone in its pen. A new toy (visual stimulus) can be placed in with it. The puppy's confidence and interest in the new object are recorded. A similar record of the dog's response to a loud sound (auditory stimulus) can be recorded as well. Ideally, the puppy expresses interest in the novel stimulus and shows a desire to investigate it.

2. *Response to Isolation*. The puppy is left alone in its pen and its responses are noted. The most desirable pup will show a great deal of exploratory behavior.

3. *Response to People*. Again the puppy is evaluated while left alone in its pen. A stranger enters the pen and then squats near the puppy but remains silent. The degree of anxiety or caution that the pup shows in approaching the person is noted. Is the puppy indifferent to the person or does it seek attention? After remaining still for a short time, the handler should stand up and walk around the pen. Does the puppy respond by following or is it instead very timid or retiring? The ideal puppy is friendly and gregarious.

4. *Competitive Spirit*. An aggressive play situation can be set up easily. The handler wiggles a strong piece of cloth or a rag in front of the puppy and initiates a tug-of-war game with it. A strong biting and pulling response is *extremely* desirable in a Schutzhund prospect. It is interesting to note the reaction of the pup when the handler shouts or beats the ground during the tug-of-war. Does the puppy fight more strongly for the possession of the rag, or does it begin to nervously chew and shift its grip on it? Does it let go altogether and retreat from the handler? The ideal puppy is so caught up in the fun of biting and struggling for the rag that it is virtually oblivious of anything that the person does. At the end of the game it is important to surrender the rag to the puppy so that it feels as though it has won.

5. *Intelligence and Problem Solving*. The puppy can be placed behind a barrier of chicken wire, sixteen feet long and four feet high. The handler then calls the pup from the opposite side. The degree of desire to get to the handler as well as the dog's persistence in finding a way around the obstacle is noted.

While the selection of a puppy can be made with some reliability based on puppy tests administered during the six- to eight-week-old age level, according to Dr. Fox it is important to understand the problems involved in the selection of the adolescent dog. Many dogs experience a period of vacillation and instability during the adolescent phase (roughly from four through eighteen months of age). For this reason character tests can be administered again with a higher degree of confidence after the puppy's adolescent stage.

Another important person in the field of working dog character evaluation is Dr. Bodingbauer, an Austrian Doberman enthusiast. He was a professor of veterinary medicine in Vienna and wrote extensively discussing character and temperament in the working dog. He utilized the research of many notables, including Scott and Drs. Rudolf and Rudolfine Menzel, animal psychologists at the University of Haifa. Bodingbauer employed a number of tests in order to look closely at the temperament of the potential working dog. His tests served as the core of the Doberman Pinscher Temperament Evaluation Program under the leadership of Vic Montelion and the American Temperament Testing Society. The German Shepherd Dog Club also adopted some of Dr. Bodingbauer's tests.

Courage is a quality that is highly desirable in the Schutzhund dog. Dr. Bodingbauer spent considerable effort in his book discussing what courage is and is not, and how it can be evaluated. First he differentiates between courage and fearlessness. He stresses that the fearless dog is not afraid. Therefore this animal will react indifferently or impassively in the face of danger because it does not recognize the danger. This can be because the dog has a poorly developed self-preservation instinct or because of insufficient reaction preparedness (in Schutzhund we call this dullness). Bodingbauer taught that the courageous dog is fully aware that it is in danger, and that the essential quality of courage lies in the dog's willingness to confront a threat to its handler with disregard for its own safety. The courageous dog faces a threat even though retreat from the situation is possible.

In contrast to this somewhat romantic view of canine courage, we observe that Helmut Raiser, an important modern working dog theorist and trainer, defines courage simply as "a high threshold for avoidance behavior."

Dr. Bodingbauer describes the most common canine responses to stress by picturing the reactions of three different dogs to gunfire (see illustration opposite). The dog at the bottom has an extremely high level of awareness for its environment and a very low threshold for auditory stimuli. It will react either by behaving aggressively or by fleeing. In contrast, when the same stimulus is applied to the dog with an extremely high threshold, no reaction takes place. The animal has a very low level of awareness and potential danger is often ignored.

Each of these extremes—very low nervous thresholds as well as very high nervous thresholds—are undesirable in nearly any sort of working or companion dog.

By contrast, the middle dog is alert and aware of all events taking place around it. It takes note of the gunfire, but is neither frightened nor made hostile by it. This sort of stability is one of the most important characteristics of a Schutzhund or protection dog, and therefore the nervous threshold level is an important consideration in selecting a dog for work.

Inherited, inborn characteristics, Bodingbauer believed, can be evaluated

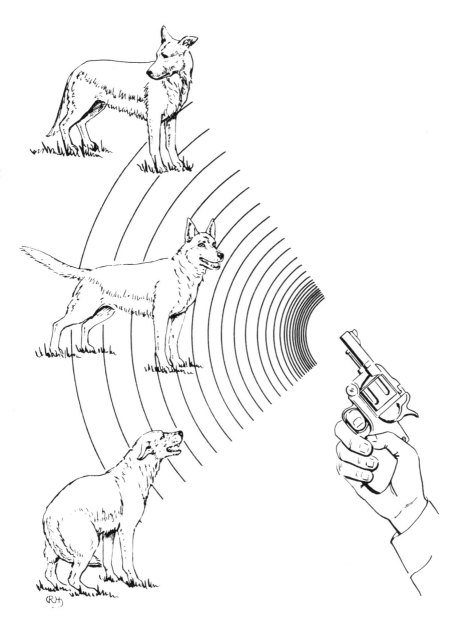

In response to a strong auditory stimulus, a particular dog may react in an oblivious or unaware manner *(top),* in an alert, curious manner *(middle)* or in a hypersensitive manner *(bottom).* The ideal Schutzhund prospect reacts to gunshots alertly and curiously but without fear or aggression.

with the help of several tests administered to the young dog. During the testing, however, there are several important considerations. First, the age of the dog must be taken into account. A response that is developmentally normal in a dog of one age can be either extraordinarily advantageous or even extraordinarily disadvantageous in a dog of another age (for instance, very defensive or aggressive behavior may be acceptable or even desirable in a dog of eighteen months, but it is a very bad sign in a puppy of four months). In addition, the test should be performed on territory that is unknown to the dog. Some animals will respond confidently or favorably when on their own territory but will not have adequate character to react equally well elsewhere. At the conclusion of the evaluation the dog receives a ranking of its potential for work of "very promising," "promising," "less promising" or "unpromising." The following are some of the tests that Bodingbauer employed.

The first test that he used involves five-week-old pups. A motorized toy is set off in front of them. The more courageous ones go resolutely forward to investigate, while the less bold ones wait. A noisy chain can be tossed loudly in front of the pups and their reactions noted to this stimulus as well. By inviting puppies of this age to bite a leather strap or piece of cloth, he received clues to their fighting spirit. He noted that particularly talented dogs are so enthusiastic in their zeal that they often can be lifted off the ground while still holding fast to their bite.

Scenting potential for tracking work can be ascertained early as well. The tracking test is conducted by having the dog's owner engage in light play with the pup. Then he runs abruptly to a hiding place (a hedgerow or large tree, perhaps). When he is hidden from the dog's view, he prepares a scent pad. He lays down a strong scent by treading down a surface about a yard square. After a minute or two on the scent pad the tracklayer sights on a second hiding place and walks in a straight line to it. The wind should be at his back. He then returns on exactly the same path back to the scent pad, and then once again retraces his steps to the hiding place. Thus the track has been walked on three times. When the dog's handler has reached his hiding place, the dog is led to the beginning of the scent pad and encouraged to find its master. The evaluator observes whether the dog uses its nose or its eyes during the search. Did it pick out the scent at the pad and attempt to follow the scent? Did it complete the track quickly and with concentration or slowly and with disinterest? When it finds its master the dog should be praised enthusiastically and rewarded with a piece of food.

Other characteristics regarding the dog's trainability and temperament can also be assessed. Willingness can be observed by watching the rapport between dog and owner. However, it is important to recognize possible incompatibility between the temperaments of the handler and dog. A mismatch can prevent a good dog from realizing its potential.

The dog's confidence and nerves can be evaluated under a number of situations. Its reaction to sounds can be evaluated by rattling pot lids while the source of the sound is not visible. The following reactions are possible:

1. **The dog shows interest and moves toward the sound.**
2. It ignores the noise.
3. It pricks up its ears but remains stationary.
4. It is frightened.

Another sound test involves firing a blank pistol at a distance of about ten paces. The following reactions are possible:

1. **The dog is not frightened.**
2. It is very sensitive and reacts aggressively.
3. It is timid and backs away.

The dog's reaction to visual stimuli can be noted as well. An umbrella is opened abruptly at a distance of approximately five feet from the dog. Possible reactions are the same as those for noise, above.

In all the auditory and visual tests, it is extremely important to evaluate how the dog recovers from stress. If it reacts strongly and adversely to a stimulus but then adjusts quickly to the situation, this is a very positive indication. It is unrealistic to expect either a puppy or an adult to be completely brave. At one point or another in their lives, all dogs will experience fear. Our main concern is how they deal with it.

The final test of confidence involves the approach of two strangers. The first is friendly to the handler and the dog. From this encounter we can draw certain conclusions. If the dog is friendly to the stranger, it indicates self-confidence. On the other hand, if it retreats from a harmless stranger, we can conclude that it lacks boldness. Next, the second stranger approaches the dog in a threatening manner, appearing as suspicious and ominous as possible. If the dog becomes alert and threatens the stranger, the stranger retreats. This test is only performed on older puppies of at least twelve months. It is important to note that a hysterically aggressive reaction is as undesirable as dullness or outright fear. We prefer the dog that surges forward into the leash, possibly barking, and shows a strong desire to make physical contact with the hostile stranger.

One of the most commonly used tests of a dog's fighting spirit is the Henze courage test, modified by the Menzels, which proceeds as follows: ''The agitator runs away quickly. As soon as he has run some fifty paces the dog is set loose and encouraged to 'get' the fleeing man. Right before the dog reaches him, the agitator turns and threatens the dog with a stick and by yelling at it.'' Fighting spirit is seen in the dog that flies into the agitator without slowing down and bites as hard and as full as it can (the agitator wears a sleeve).

This test is one of the integral parts of the Schutzhund examination. Although very revealing in many cases, the Henze courage test must be interpreted in light of the dog's past experience. A dog that performs a creditable courage test without any previous experience in bite-work training would rate as extraordinarily powerful in nearly anyone's book, an example of an exceptionally good genetic endowment. However, we must look differently at another dog that has its Schutzhund III and that has already received a great deal of training in bite

The umbrella test. The tester opens an umbrella suddenly at an approaching dog. This animal is frightened and recoils violently.

The umbrella test. This puppy exhibits a touch of apprehensiveness in response to the pop of the umbrella, but does not recoil and shows willingness to approach it.

work. When this animal bites well during the courage test, its performance is not so much a demonstration of good character as of good training. To put it another way, its character is *masked* by its training and will only be more fully revealed in a situation that is more unusual for it.

The final part of the courage test, which is called the "double stimulus" test, serves to unmask those dogs that bite because they have been trained to bite the sleeve rather than because they desire to protect their handler. After the dog is engaged in a fight with an agitator wearing a sleeve, the agitator then stands motionless. An unprotected assailant (no sleeve and no protective clothing to "key" the dog) then attacks the dog's handler. It is fascinating to observe whether the dog will continue to guard the agitator with the sleeve, or if it will defend its handler from attack. (The dog is on leash and wears a leather muzzle during this test.) Interestingly enough, normally the more formal bite-work training the animal has undergone, the more preoccupied it will be with the sleeve and thus the less likely it will be to defend its handler. On the other hand, few untrained dogs will have the nerve to try to bite either person when muzzled like this.

Many of these evaluative tools have now become part of police dog tests in Germany and elsewhere.

To summarize, the very promising Schutzhund dog will:

1. show both interest in searching for its handler and also a tendency to immediately use its nose in order to do so
2. be very interested in playing with and retrieving objects thrown for it
3. be either undisturbed by the approach of a friendly stranger or overtly friendly toward him
4. show both an eagerness to follow its handler and stay near him as well as a tendency to go off exploring on its own
5. be frightened by very little, and when it *is* frightened by something it will soon lose its fear and forget the incident
6. immediately and vigorously bite any object like a burlap sack that is moved rapidly past it and be oblivious of any attempt to frighten it
7. move very strongly toward a menacing stranger (when the dog is at least one year old), trying to make physical contact with him, but not exhibiting any signs of hysterical or fear-motivated aggressiveness.

In protection, it is not only the handler who trains the dog—the decoy plays a vital role. While it is often possible to successfully train a dog using a good decoy and a bad handler, it is usually impossible to train a dog using a good handler and a bad decoy. Accordingly, in addition to all of the special skills and abilities peculiar to a skilled decoy, the person who agitates the dog must have integrity, intelligence and self-discipline. (Janet Birk and Chesapeake Bay Retriever "Jason," Schutzhund III, working on Stewart Hilliard.)

"Mucke" works happily for handler Barbara Valente because Barbara has taught the dog a perfect understanding of all skills and a lively pleasure in accomplishing them.

24

3

An Overview of Schutzhund Training

ALTHOUGH TECHNIQUES OF DOG TRAINING have evolved rapidly since the early days of Schutzhund, the basic philosophy of the sport has not changed dramatically in many years. The flavor of von Stephanitz's writing from the 1920s expresses our attitude even today. He reflects, "This training, then, must know how to awaken the inborn capacities, and to develop them, and must in addition tone down what is superfluous, strengthen what is weak and guide what is erring into the right path."

The meaning of this passage is apparent. The role of the trainer is to develop the innate behavior and tendencies of the working dog. In tracking he develops the animal's natural urges to follow scent and to eat. In obedience he exploits the dog's need to interact with and "belong to" other social beings. In protection he intensifies and makes use of the dog's most volatile and powerful urges, those of an aggressive predator.

A working dog must bring with it to training a number of qualities of character. In the previous chapter we discussed briefly how the handler can select the right dog for the work. However, at all times the dog and handler are a team. Good results are the product of both their personalities. What a pity that a fine young working dog is not also in a position to select whom *it* will work with, to test its handler for character!

THE TRAINER

A good dog trainer is patient. He understands that training takes time and is willing to spend the time. He is intelligent, and he thinks clearly about what effect his actions will have upon the dog. Also, he has "feeling," an accurate intuition for what makes dogs do the things that they do. He is decisive—fast-handed and effective in all that he does. He is not dogmatic, but flexible—always ready to reexamine his beliefs and methods and adapt them to the particular nature and endowment of his pupil.

A good trainer is emotionally disciplined and has an even disposition. He is not prone to temper tantrums and can administer both praise and punishment appropriately. When he physically punishes the animal, he does so impartially—he punishes as the result of a thoughtful decision to use force in order to get results, rather than from wrath and the desire to relieve some of his frustration by taking vengeance upon the dog.

The trainer must have integrity, in the sense that he is his own person and does not depend upon his dog's behavior or performance to give him a sense of worth, identity or importance.

Finally, the good dog trainer has a worldly understanding of his pupil, and knows it for a dog and only a dog. He realizes that the animal does things for its own reasons and does not necessarily live its whole life in order to please its trainer. He accepts that sometimes his dog will be less than completely brave, that the animal has no sense of fair play or honesty, that it does nothing for spite and that its basic nature is that of an opportunistic predator.

The trainer must respect his dog not just as an asset or possession, or as a way of gaining recognition by winning trophies, but as a living, breathing and utterly unique product of nature. After all, each and every dog is an event of biology that will never happen again.

From the trainer's respect for his dog should arise the capacity to self-examine. Let the trainer examine himself when his dog makes a mistake or does not understand an exercise, and ask himself, "Where am I at fault?"

THE METHOD

Whomever shall find the answer to the question "How shall I say this to my dog?" has won the game and can develop from his animal whatever he likes.
—Max von Stephanitz

The fundamental task in Schutzhund training, indeed in any form of dog training, is getting the animal to understand what it is we want from it. Successful trainers *are* successful because they make their dogs understand what is asked of them. Those who are not successful do not.

One of the basic tools for making a dog understand what we want from it is *consistency*. If we set for the animal a rule, a limit on its behavior, then that rule must remain invariable. For example, if we decide that after the command

"Out!" the dog will be allowed two seconds in which to release the sleeve before we will correct it, then we must always expect no more and no less from it. The dog must be able to *predict* what we will do in any given situation so that it can make a sensible decision about what to do. If we are inconsistent, then we are unpredictable. Unpredictability confuses the dog, and confusion makes it weak.

Practice, simple repetition, is another way that we make the animal understand what we desire. A dog is a creature of habit. If we can induce it to do something correctly several times, then we begin to form in the dog the habit of always doing it that way. This provides us with the opportunity to praise and reward the animal so that it will begin to understand precisely which actions bring it reward and which do not.

But if we allow the animal to practice a skill incorrectly, habit can also be our enemy. For example, if the dog begins to quarter while tracking (weaving back and forth across the track instead of following it closely), we must immediately find a way to modify what it is doing so that it stops quartering and begins tracking correctly. Otherwise quartering can become its habitual strategy for working out a track. Similarly, if the animal is allowed to come around the jump instead of over it or to bite the agitator during the hold and bark, these faults can become habits, even if they occur only occasionally.

It is not that practice on an activity makes perfect, but that perfect practice makes perfect.

Last, and most important, we get the dog to understand what we want by breaking what we have to teach it down into small, easily comprehensible pieces. In education this practice is called *task analysis*, and it involves analyzing each lesson to be learned, dividing it into "key" ideas or movements and then teaching these concepts or skills one at a time. Throughout this book we have made a task analysis of all the exercises that the dog must perform in order to pass Schutzhund I, II and III and broken them down for the reader into "Goals" and "Important Concepts for Meeting the Goals."

This approach is progressive, involving small steps, and is pyramidal in its effect. Each concept builds upon what the dog has learned from the preceding one, and each concept must be fully mastered before moving on to the next. Furthermore, if the dog is experiencing confusion or making errors on a particular task, it is the responsibility of the handler to once more break that task into concepts and skills and begin instruction again at the specific point where the dog is having difficulty. He must ensure that the dog is successful and confident in each of these lower steps before he returns to the original task.

The job of making the dog understand what we want from it is best accomplished without the use of force. Not only are we concerned that it understands its work, but also we want the dog to enjoy its work. Therefore, in the initial stages of training the animal for a particular skill, we avoid if possible the use of any kind of pain, correction or intimidation. We call this no-force phase of training the *teaching phase*. If, during the teaching phase, we must employ force to introduce a skill (as we often must do in protection work), then we take great pains to use the least force that we can.

Only once we are absolutely certain that the dog knows what we want from it will we begin the *correction* or *training phase*, in which we use some kind of force or compulsion to punish or prevent the animal's errors.

Throughout this book we use the term *correction* for this compulsion. A good correction serves two purposes. First, it punishes the dog for doing something that we do not want it to or prevents the dog from doing it. Second, a good correction encourages or even forces the dog to do what we want it to do. Thus, when the dog ignores a "Sit!" command, a slap on the rump both punishes it for refusing to sit and also causes it quickly to assume the desired position.

Corrections can be made with the hands, feet or leash, or in a number of other ways. However they are accomplished, corrections should always be administered quickly—in close association with the undesirable behavior—and sharply enough to make a definitive impression on the dog. Nagging the dog with many light corrections is detrimental because it perpetuates the animal's errors.

We must take care that training does not become abusive, both for ethical reasons and because abusive dog training does not bring the best results. Therefore, corrections must not be made too strongly or out of anger. For each handler, each dog and each particular error, there is a suitable level of intensity of correction that discourages the animal from repeating its mistake, but does not damage its spirit and its basic love for the work.

In addition, abusiveness should not be defined solely by how strongly the handler corrects his dog, but also by *whether the dog understands what it did to bring the correction and how it can avoid another in the future*.

Our main concern is to employ force effectively when we have to, but without having it show in the dog's attitude toward its work. In training we seek to create a spirited and useful companion, not a cringing slave. The German general Erich Ludendorff said in reference to soldiers, "The training of men should not kill, but strengthen character." Much the same principle applies to dogs.

Therefore, the more strongly we are obliged to correct a dog in order to bring about a desired result, the more strongly we must reward the animal when it finally does it correctly. There are two main secrets to the use of force without diminishing the dog's character:

- The animal understands what it must do in order to avoid being corrected a second time.
- When it readily does as we ask, thereby avoiding the correction, we enthusiastically give it something that it wants very much—praise, play, a run after the ball, a bite on the decoy, etc.

According to Konrad Most, a service and military dog trainer of von Stephanitz's era,

With a powerful form of compulsion we must also ensure that the initial discomfort subsequently turns to pleasure. We have no wish to see a panic-stricken slave doing what we want in fear and trembling, but a dog that enjoys life and is happy in his work, putting all his heart into it. Just as the art of human education is to substitute desire for obligation, that of an animal training requires a disagreeable activity to be changed into an agreeable one. This aim is achieved, in the first place, by the limitation of compulsion already prescribed: it must stop the very instant the act required begins. Secondly, it is essential that as soon as the disagreeable experience ceases, an agreeable one follows immediately, as a regular consequence. The result of this liberation from the pressure of compulsion is that the dog quickly learns how to escape from his disagreeable experience and, in addition, finds that the act, though in itself disagreeable, is soon transformed into an agreeable experience. This causes him to develop an amazing zest for his work.

The final phase of training is *proofing*. At this level we check for understanding and increase the strength of the dog's habit by asking the animal to perform in unusual circumstances that are actually far more difficult than those it will face in a trial. In doing so we cause the dog to generalize the lessons it has learned on the training field to other situations.

Dogs are context-specific learners. Skills and concepts that we teach them tend to be unique to a certain set of circumstances. For example, if a dog is taught to track in a grassy pasture and indicate leather articles, it is likely that the animal will be unable to perform when asked to work in a weed-covered field and indicate cloth articles. Similarly, just because the dog bites well on a decoy who wears a leather sleeve and bulky protection pants, we cannot be sure that the dog will bite in an actual street situation in which the assailant wears no sleeve or protection pants.

Therefore, once we have *taught* the exercises and then *trained* them, we take great pains to *proof* them in all manner of bizarre situations. We perform obedience routines in busy parking lots, run tracks with a noisy crowd of people walking along with the dog as it works and perform hold-and-bark exercises in the beds of pickup trucks, inside houses and closets or on the tops of haystacks. When we have proofed our dog extensively in these demanding situations, anything it might see on trial day will seem elementary.

In all fields of endeavor, people seek the best, the most ideal approach. Unfortunately, there is no ideal approach to Schutzhund training. There are as many different ways of creating a competitive animal as there are trainers and dogs. *All* methods and ideas that produce results have some merit and can be drawn upon to supplement the program chosen to train the particular dog.

Whatever the approach, it should take into account three points. First, the program selected should consider the way that animals learn—initially by pleasant and unpleasant experiences and then by repetition. Second, the training program must provide a means of soliciting both motivation and repetition. Third, the approach should be progressive and pyramidal in its effect—each step in training should develop from the previous one.

"Every dog has a nose, that is to say, every dog has a sense of smell and without it, he could not live at all . . . but it is something quite different when this dog knows to turn his powers of scent to good account for us."—Max von Stephanitz

4

Tracking:
Requirements
of the Trial

TEMPERAMENT TEST

Before the tracking test each dog in Schutzhund I, II or III is closely examined by the judge for stability and impartiality. Impartiality refers to an aspect of the dog's character which is neither hostile nor fearful of strangers. Every judge has a slightly different way of evaluating temperament. Most judges insist on touching the animals and watching their behavior while walking on a loose leash amid a group of people. If the judge detects a sign of shyness, timidity or any indication of inappropriate aggressiveness, he will disqualify the animal in question from further participation in the trial.

SCHUTZHUND I TRACKING TEST

The handler reports to the judge with two articles in hand. The articles should be neutral in color and approximately hand size. At the judge's direction he lays a track approximately 300 to 400 paces long. The pattern of the Schutzhund I track is rectangular, as shown in the illustration on page 34.

The handler begins laying his track by placing a stake on his left and then stamping out a scent pad approximately one yard square. He then proceeds in a straight line in the direction indicated by the judge. At the judge's command (a wave or a blast on a whistle) the tracklayer makes a right-angle turn and then continues in a new direction. Again at the judge's command, and without slowing down or hesitating, he drops the first article directly on the track. He continues walking until the judge signals again, at which point he makes another right-angle turn and begins the third leg. The handler finishes laying the track by dropping the second article at the judge's command.

The dog may not watch while the handler lays the track. It is normally left to wait in a car.

After twenty minutes have passed, the handler returns with his dog and reports to the judge, giving both his name and the name of the animal. The judge asks the handler, "Will the dog point out or pick up?" The handler responds by telling how his dog will indicate the articles on the track. He need not be more specific than to say, "Point out," despite the fact that the dog has three possible ways of indicating an article—sit, stand or down.

At this point the handler puts the tracking harness (if he is using one) on the dog, leads it to the scent pad and commands it to track. If he is not using a harness, the handler must attach the long line to the dead ring of his dog's chain-link collar. (The use of a tracking line is optional in Schutzhund and some dogs work their tracks "free," although this is not a common practice.)

The animal is allowed as much time as necessary to pick up the scent and, as it moves forward, the handler must remain on the starting pad until all thirty feet of the tracking line are played out and the dog has clearly committed itself to the direction of the track.

When the dog finds the article, the animal should either pick it up and retrieve it to the handler or point the article out. The dog who points out may sit, stand or drop near the article. The only requirement is that it indicate both articles in the same fashion. It is most correct if the animal makes its indication in such a way that the article is placed between its front feet. The handler drops the lead, goes to the article and holds it up for the judge to see. He then puts the article in his pocket and restarts his dog.

Many judges prefer that the handler return all the way to the end of the long line before restarting the dog. It is more common to pick up the line where it lies next to the animal and then to let it play out through the hands as the dog moves down the track.

Points are deducted for the following:

10 points—missing an article
1 to 4 points—faulty start, circling on turns, working carelessly or refusing to work continuously
1 to 8 points—tracking impetuously or urinating during the track

Home free. The joy of finding the last article on the track and holding it up for the judge to see. (Susan Barwig and her "Uri," Schutzhund III, UDT.)

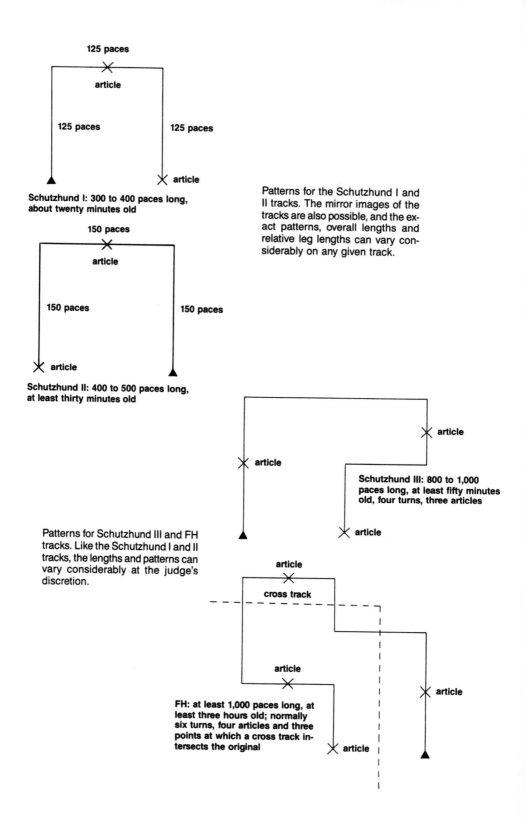

125 paces

article

125 paces   **125 paces**

article

Schutzhund I: 300 to 400 paces long, about twenty minutes old

Patterns for the Schutzhund I and II tracks. The mirror images of the tracks are also possible, and the exact patterns, overall lengths and relative leg lengths can vary considerably on any given track.

150 paces

article

150 paces   **150 paces**

article   article

Schutzhund II: 400 to 500 paces long, at least thirty minutes old

article

article

Schutzhund III: 800 to 1,000 paces long, at least fifty minutes old, four turns, three articles

article

Patterns for Schutzhund III and FH tracks. Like the Schutzhund I and II tracks, the lengths and patterns can vary considerably at the judge's discretion.

article

cross track

article

FH: at least 1,000 paces long, at least three hours old; normally six turns, four articles and three points at which a cross track intersects the original

article

article

SCHUTZHUND II TRACKING TEST

The requirements for the Schutzhund II test are somewhat more difficult. The track is both longer and older. It is approximately 400 to 500 paces, laid by a stranger, and is aged at least thirty minutes. However, all other conditions are the same as in Schutzhund I.

SCHUTZHUND III TRACKING TEST

The Schutzhund III track is more difficult still. The track, again laid by a stranger, is from 800 to 1,000 paces long, has at least four turns and is at least fifty minutes old. The tracklayer drops three articles along the track. Although the pattern can vary, it generally follows the one shown in the illustration opposite. All other conditions are the same as in the Schutzhund I and II tests.

FH (THE ADVANCED TRACKING TITLE)

To be eligible for the FH title a dog must be sixteen months old and have a Schutzhund I title or a Traffic Proof Companion Dog title (VB).

The FH is the most difficult of the Schutzhund tracking tests, corresponding in difficulty to the American or Canadian TDX. The track, always laid by a stranger, is at least 1,000 paces long and three hours old. It contains a minimum of six turns. There are also three places where another stranger's track crosses the original track, and there are also changes in the terrain—variations in elevation and vegetation and even dirt roads cutting the track. The tracklayer leaves four articles on the track that the dog must either point out or pick up.

As in Schutzhund I, II and III, the handler may work the dog with or without a long line. Points are deducted for the following:

4 points—faulty start
7 points—missing an article
4 points—indicating a wrong article

SCORING

To pass the Schutzhund tracking tests the dog–handler team must earn a minimum of seventy points out of 100. The point-total ratings are as follows:

96 to 100 points Excellent (*Vorzüglich*)
90 to 95 points Very Good (*Sehr Gut*)
80 to 89 points Good (*Gut*)
70 to 79 points Satisfactory (*Befriedigend*)
36 to 69 points Faulty (*Mangelhaft*)
 0 to 35 points Insufficient (*Ungenügend*)

German army ambulance dogs on active service, presumably before or during World War I. (From von Stephanitz, *The German Shepherd Dog*, 1923.)

An ambulance dog in training, taking the *bringsel* in its mouth on discovering a "wounded" man. (From von Stephanitz, *The German Shepherd Dog,* 1923.)

5

An Overview of
the Tracking Phase

THE USE OF SCENTING DOGS in the service of humans has a long history. The ancient Greeks are known to have used dogs for tracking criminals and runaways, and the great Athenian playwright Sophocles even recorded the escapades of such dogs in his satire *The Tracking Dogs*.

In more recent times dogs have been used to search out the lost and injured on battlefields. In 1893, the German imperial army established an ambulance corps that used dogs trained to sweep an area looking for wounded soldiers. When the dog discovered a victim, it would find an article of clothing and return with it to its handler. The handler would then follow the dog back to the injured man. The dog sometimes had great difficulty in locating an appropriate article to take back to the handler, so eventually a device called a *bringsel* was introduced. The *bringsel* dragged from the animal's collar on a short cord as it searched the battlefield. When it found a wounded man, it would take the *bringsel* in its mouth and retrieve it to its handler, signifying that it had discovered a casualty.

During World War I, in the mud and carnage and chaos of the trenches, ambulance dogs rendered great service to wounded soldiers of both German and Allied armies alike. The immortal Rin-Tin-Tin was reportedly a son of one of these ambulance dogs. Born under fire in the trenches of World War I (to a bitch said to have been captured from the Germans), he was taken home by a returning American soldier and finished his days in Hollywood as a film legend.

Later, during World War II and the Vietnam War, the United States Army made extensive use of the scenting powers of scout dogs in the Pacific islands and Indochina. These animals led patrols at night through the dense jungles, helping to locate enemy units and warning of ambushes.

For many years, search and rescue dogs have been used to find people lost in remote areas. More recently avalanche and disaster dogs have been trained to detect bodies buried under many feet of snow and debris. Search dogs have received international publicity in the last few years as a result of three enormous disasters. In the first, the eruption of Mount St. Helens in the Northwest, dogs went into the ash-covered and barren quake area to locate bodies. After the Mexico City earthquake in the mid-1980s, dog teams from around the world, including Schutzhund-trained animals from Germany, were sent to find survivors and bodies trapped under crumbled offices, hospitals and apartment buildings. Most recently search dogs received headlines again when they searched out victims of the Armenian quake, which killed 20,000 people.

Modern military and police organizations worldwide use dogs trained in scent work to locate narcotics, weapons and bombs. In America, hundreds of law enforcement agencies employ police service dogs. Every night in cities and towns all over the United States criminals hoping to escape detection are found and apprehended through the scenting powers of police K-9s.

Officer Jack Lennig of the Lakewood, Colorado, police department shared two of his favorite nose-work stories with us: The first occurred one night while Officer Lennig was cruising his beat. He saw a young man in an alley who fled the moment he saw the police car, disappearing into the rabbit warren of alleys and lots behind a major red-light district. On the assumption that anyone who ran like that had something to hide, Officer Lennig started his dog Beau on the man's track. The animal led him perhaps a quarter of a mile through backyards and trash-choked lots, and across a four-lane highway. Finally, Beau turned a corner onto a major thoroughfare and followed the sidewalk a short distance to the door of a bar. Officer Lennig went inside and described the man to the bartender, who said that the fugitive had just been there and bought a drink, but left by the back door without finishing it. Officer Lennig started his dog again out back, and another quarter of a mile of alleys and asphalt parking lots later, the dog led him to the front door of a residence. The officer knocked at the door and the suspect answered it, protesting that he had been asleep in bed and hadn't been out all night. Officer Lennig made a call on the radio, found that the man had several outstanding warrants and arrested him on the spot.

A more violent situation involved a woman walking home from work. A man jumped out of the bushes, dragged her to a nearby field and raped and robbed her, taking her diamond ring off her finger. Panicked by her screams, he pitched the ring into the field and ran off. The woman managed to flag down a Lakewood policeman and they returned with a K-9 unit to the field. The dog tracked the suspect down, finding him hiding in his nearby home. Then the dog was cast out into the field to search for any additional evidence. Unbelievably, after a few minutes of intense searching, the dog returned to its handler and spat out the diamond ring that had been lodged deep in the grass of the field.

Officer Lennig has enough anecdotes of this sort to fill a book of his own. Like any experienced K-9 officer, he is absolutely convinced of the value of a good scenting dog in law enforcement.

Officer Kenny Mathias of the Raleigh, North Carolina, police department, an authority on the subject, told us how a Dutch police tracking dog solved the famous Heineken kidnapping in Holland, in which a member of this wealthy beer-brewing family was abducted. When the kidnapping vehicle was found, the police still had no suspect. So they laid a piece of gauze on the driver's seat of the car, left it there for twenty-four hours, and then sealed it in a jar. The gauze rested in the jar for two years while investigators developed a suspect. The Dutch police then performed a scent lineup, in which the suspect and four others impregnated sections of steel pipe with their scent, and the dog compared the scent of the gauze with that of the pipes. The dog matched the suspect's pipe with the gauze and, confronted with the evidence, the man confessed to the kidnapping.

This anecdote amazes the authors and probably the reader as well. Two additional pieces of information are equally remarkable.

Glen Johnson, a well-known expert on tracking, trained dogs to search out gas leaks on the Canadian pipeline. One of his dogs detected a wooden clothespin impregnated with gas odorant (used for training) that had lain buried underground for three weeks. The chemistry department of the University of Windsor, where Johnson teaches, estimated the odorant remaining on the clothespin at less than one part per trillion.

Search and rescue dogs are sometimes used on searches for victims of drowning. The animals are rowed back and forth across the water in small boats, and indicate their finds over the side. These dogs have discovered bodies in dozens of feet of water.

The inevitable question that arises is: How do the dogs do it? The authors have no idea how they do it, and we note with some amusement that the experts in olfaction do not know either. In fact, the physiological basis of scenting is simply not fully understood. Scientists are amazed at the diversity and the sensitivity of even the human nose.

> Unlike taste, which is divisible into only four modalities (sweet, sour, salty, bitter), many thousands of different odors can be distinguished by people who are trained in this capacity. . . . The extreme sensitivity of olfaction is possibly as amazing as its diversity—at maximum sensitivity, only one odorant molecule is needed to excite an olfactory receptor. (Stuart Fox, *Human Physiology*, 2nd edition. Dubuque, Iowa: William Brown Publications, 1987.)

Fox makes these comments in relation only to the human nose. We can only guess at the rich experience of the world that a dog's nose gives it, because a dog's nose is so different from a human's. A human being's nose contains approximately five million olfactory receptor cells dispersed across about one square inch of area. In contrast, the average German Shepherd Dog possesses

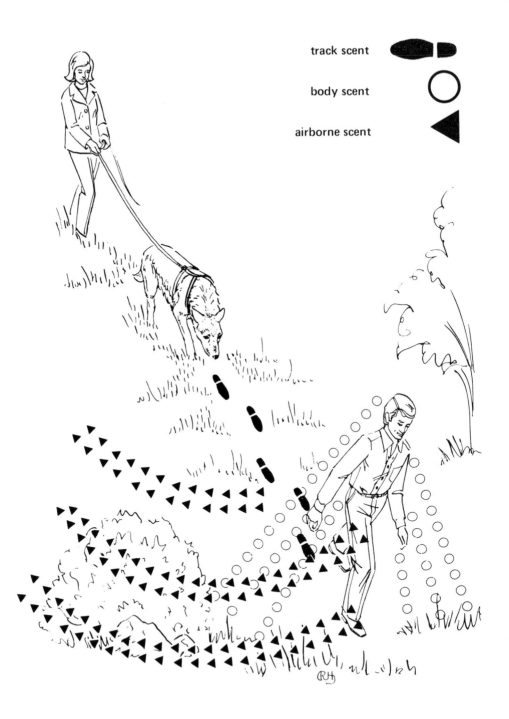

track scent

body scent

airborne scent

approximately 150 million olfactory receptor cells distributed in about six square inches of nasal epithelium (Pearsall and Verbruggen, 1982).

Not only is the nature of the dog's "smell" experience different from ours, but it is behaviorally far more significant to it. In humans, primates who began eons ago as tree dwellers, the primary aims of behavior are accomplished visually. Primates use their eyes to locate food, avoid contact with predators and motivate sexual activity, whereas dogs rely to a great extent upon their noses for the same purposes. Yet a human can differentiate among some 4,000 different odors (Pearsall and Verbruggen, 1982). Only our observations of scent-detection dogs give us any conception of the unimaginable abilities of a dog in this realm.

Since the exact physiological mechanism of olfaction is unknown, much of the process of tracking is still a mystery to us. We are not exactly certain what it is that the dog follows when it tracks a human. According to Pearsall and Verbruggen in *Scent*, a track is:

> the imprint we leave whether traveling through a room, a field or over a road. The track is influenced by such variables as wind, temperature, humidity, rain, snow, terrain, grasses and trees. Our track also is affected by the immense variety of living creatures that share the world with us.

There appear to be two ways that a dog is able to follow a track. First, it can follow the *body scent*. This scent is the unique aroma that each person or animal emits. The components of this unique aroma in part include skin particles, perspiration, oils and gases and also, in animals, scent glands. This scent follows the individuals and is carried in the air currents around where they have walked. Noted obedience and tracking trainer Milo Pearsall describes scent as "slightly-heavier-than-air gas, very easily blown about by the wind, yet sticking tenaciously in part to everything it touches." Some of this odor settles in a corridor around the footsteps while another part remains airborne.

Because smoke particles are approximately equal in size to those particles shed by the human skin, some of the most interesting evidence we have about the dissipation of scent comes from watching the discharge of smoke bombs. Even on a calm day with minimal air movement, visible smoke takes on a life of its own. It attaches to bushes and rocks, springs upward along the sides of inclines or buildings and lingers in depressions and areas of long grass. When the ground is cool, smoke clings thickly to the earth. When the ground is heated by direct rays of the sun, the smoke expands, thins and dissipates upward.

The second type of scent is the *track scent*. This is the odor that a person, animal or object leaves behind after coming in contact with the earth's surface. It appears that this contact with the ground changes the scent of the disturbed area in some way. Track scent dissipates very slowly in comparison with body and airborne scent.

Which kind of scent should the dog follow? That depends upon what sort of tracking you are doing.

The normal criterion for success in police scent work and search and rescue is simple: Does the dog find what we are looking for or not? In service dog work we are not concerned with style or appearance, only with efficiency and results. Therefore, tracking dogs that are used for police work and search and rescue are trained to *trail*—encouraged to use both air and track scent. They follow the track rather loosely and will freely cast about for body and airborne scent, exploiting it in order to draw nearer to their goal.

Schutzhund is a competition. In the tracking phase points are awarded, and there must be a winner. One dog must track better than the rest, and in Schutzhund this means more exactly, more precisely on top of the footsteps of the tracklayer. Because body scent is widely dispersed and blown easily about by the wind, a dog that searches for body scent will quickly take to *quartering*. It will zigzag back and forth, working the fringes of the scent path, much the way blind people feel their way down a hallway by touching first one wall and then the other. Air scenting therefore leads to very inexact tracking.

In addition, air scent appears to be transient. Depending upon conditions and terrain, some fifteen to forty-five minutes after the tracklayer has passed, his body scent has lifted and become so dispersed or discontinuous that a dog cannot easily follow it. Because the track scent lasts far longer and because it is much less affected by wind conditions than body scent, it is therefore more reliable and much more closely associated with the actual track itself. This is the scent we must teach the Schutzhund dog to follow.

An exquisitely trained competition dog actually *footstep tracks* in good conditions. This animal follows the track as if it were on rails, making geometrically precise turns, its head weaving from side to side across a six-inch area as the dog locates and checks each of the tracklayer's footsteps.

Because of the importance of track scent, the type of terrain and vegetation strongly affects how the dog will track. Hot sand, frozen ground, asphalt and stone are all difficult and nearly impossible for the dog to follow a track across. However, the veteran tracking dog eventually must be able to adapt to virtually any type of terrain and all weather conditions.

For teaching Schutzhund tracking, tracks on short, pastern-length grass or soft dirt are the most suitable, as they retain the scent well. Tall grass retains odor all along its blades and the dog therefore tends to practice tracking with a high nose. Tall grass also shelters body scent from the wind and sun, so it dissipates slowly. When in an area of knee-high grass, the tracklayer's body scent will remain for a surprisingly long time dispersed in a wide area about the track. The resulting low-hanging cloud of air scent among the grass stems will greatly confuse the novice tracking dog. Thus it is a good idea to avoid this type of vegetation during training sessions.

Hills can also have a pronounced effect on the dog's performance because of the gentle uphill and downhill air currents that distract the animal from the track scent.

By causing the scent to drift, wind also affects the dog on the track. For example, if the animal is tracking into the wind toward a turn, it will tend to make its move before the actual turn. When the wind is at its back, the dog will

Trial day for Phil Hoelcher and his Kazan v. Anger, Schutzhund III.

Dick Gasaway's puppy "Zeus v. haus Barwig" demonstrates the two most important prerequisites for competitive Schutzhund tracking: concentration and a deep nose.

turn slightly past the turn. Because of these and other factors we spend much time encouraging the competitive tracking dog to utilize primarily the track scent.

The age of the track affects the dog's performance as well. On a fresh track where there is a great deal of body scent, many dogs do extremely well. (We conjecture that police dogs are often highly effective in following fresh tracks because of the intense aroma emitted by a frightened fugitive.)

Under normal weather conditions the track scent and body scent are approximately equal in intensity at about thirty minutes of age. After that time, however, the track scent begins to dominate.

The amount of time the track retains body and airborne scent varies with the weather and terrain. Any extremes in these conditions can cut down on the tracking dog's effectiveness, but none of them need totally defeat its ability to perform.

Contrary to popular lore, the shape of the dog's head has little effect upon its ability to track. Bloodhounds, for example, do not excel in tracking and tailing because of any special anatomical equipment they possess, and theoretically a Boxer has as much absolute ability to detect scent as a German Shepherd. The difference between an outstanding tracking dog and a mediocre one is not physical but behavioral—an innately greater desire to track and a gift for concentrating single-mindedly upon a task for long periods of time.

Therefore, the most critical aspect in the success of a particular dog in tracking appears to be its motivation to track at the time its handler desires. Apathy, lack of concentration and refusal to work are all usually indications of incentive problems rather than an inability to perform. While we cannot easily change the style of a dog's tracking, we can increase its incentive to do it. A slow tracker can become a slow, methodical worker. An overexuberant tracker can become a controlled, eager worker.

Basically there are three ways of motivating the dog to begin tracking. The most traditional method makes use of what old-time German trainers called the dog's *pack drive*—the animal's desire to be with its master. Because of this desire, when its handler is hidden the dog will actively search him out. Von Stephanitz, and more recently Davis, as well as many police dog trainers have used this approach to training. With a highly motivated dog that has a natural talent for tracking, this method can be highly effective.

For a dog possessing less natural incentive, food often proves helpful. Some Germans do their training with a smelly piece of meat dragged behind the tracklayer to encourage the dog to put its nose to the ground and track. Glen Johnson, a well-known Canadian authority on tracking, uses a food-drop approach to begin all the dogs he trains. He uses the food drops to increase the dog's motivation to track and to provide a reward for it when it is correct—when the dog is right on top of the track. It is also an excellent way to teach the dog to take scent in each footstep. However, the food drops are not intended to be continued indefinitely. They are eventually phased out.

We use a third type of motivator with a dog that is a natural retriever. In this dog's training program its reward for tracking is finding an article or toy at the end of its track.

A fourth type of incentive is used infrequently. It involves motivating the animal by allowing it to find and bite an agitator at the end of the track. This bite-motivation method is only effective with a small percentage of dogs. The most instructive reason for its effectiveness is the phenomenon of *too much motivation*.

The Yerkes-Dodson law of psychology states that the most effective level of motivation for a task will depend upon the difficulty of that task. As expected, animals or people engaged in simple tasks profit by very high motivation. However, the performance of animals engaged in complex or difficult tasks is actually disrupted by very high motivation.

Because tracking is a very complex task depending upon concentration, and because bite work produces intense motivation, we should not be surprised that bite motivation usually disrupts performance in tracking.

The question of bite motivation illustrates an important point. The best tracking dogs are calm and methodical while they work. Not only is this the style that produces the most reliable, precise tracking, but also it is the style that will most favorably impress the judge. The emphasis in much of tracking training is therefore to slow the animal down and get it to concentrate, and the trick is to motivate it well but not too well. The Yerkes-Dodson phenomenon also helps explain why attempts to train dogs for tracking by forcing them are so often ineffective, because fear can be thought of as the most intense motivator of all.

However, all the abovementioned training styles can and do work. The important thing is to select the right incentive for the particular dog.

The now classic method for training competitive tracking dogs combines two of these incentives—retrieving and food. Most Schutzhund trainers use a more or less modified Glen Johnson food-drop approach to teach the animal to make use of track scent. In addition, they invariably associate the end of the track with a ball or some other retrieving toy such as a kong (an irregularly shaped and erratically bouncing dog toy), either by leaving the ball at the end of the track where the dog can find it or by simply pulling it out of a pocket when the animal has finished its task.

It should be clear that the dog has little innate motivation to arbitrarily follow any trail of disturbed ground. It does, however, have powerful innate desires for food and for the ball. The central concept the dog must learn in tracking is that the seemingly unrelated odor of track scent will guide it from one food drop to another, and ultimately to the ball, and win for it its master's praise.

It is fascinating to note that von Stephanitz, in the early 1900s, had already realized that bite work should seldom be joined with tracking. In many ways this man was a visionary, and he espoused a training philosophy that is still adhered to today. He was a strong advocate of starting a dog in tracking work when young in order to "form and sharpen its mind through nasal experiences." He insisted upon the use of a leash in training as a way to correct the dog's faults and to teach it correctly. And it was he who suggested starting the dog's schooling on its handler's track and then switching to strangers' tracks. As a final suggestion he stated:

> In the development of the use of the nose, care must always be taken that everything is done in love and kindness, without any perceptible constraint. The track dog itself must, however, be trained very carefully and must be continually worked, for it is an artist, and an artist can only retain prominence when practicing and continually trying to improve on past efforts.

Many of von Stephanitz's ideas have formed the basis for modern training practices. However, beyond his broad generalities there has been relatively little literature written on the art of training the tracking dog. One useful book on the subject is Glen Johnson's *Tracking Dog: Theory and Methods*. It must be noted that the method presented in his book is geared to passing an AKC or CKC tracking test (TD), rather than to teaching the animal to use its nose in actual police or search and rescue situations. However, Johnson's progression is systematic and discussed in a thoughtful, easy-to-follow format and can be adapted for Schutzhund tracking.

Tracking plays a critical part in the success or failure of the dog in a Schutzhund trial. As in the other two phases of sport, obedience and protection, a failure in tracking (less than seventy points) means no Schutzhund title. However, proportionately more dog–handler teams fail the tracking test than any other phase.

Frankly, tracking can be baffling. In addition to good methods, the trainer also needs a feel for tracking. In addition to feeling, he needs a little luck. As if it were some arcane act, or a kind of black magic, some people seem to have the touch and some do not.

The uncertainty of tracking breeds superstition, and sometimes unusual behavior. At the trial, handlers often wear lucky jackets, boots or gloves, or use lucky tracking lines without which they would not dare to compete. They engage in rituals, arranging their lines just so, or preparing their dogs just so, as if to appease some capricious and ill-tempered god who reigns over the tracking field.

The difficulty of tracking is that the animal must work on its own. The handler can give his dog only a minimal amount of help during a tracking test—particularly in Schutzhund II and III—and he is forced to rely entirely on the animal's desire as well as its ability.

Tracking therefore requires a great deal of good, consistent training time; if good scores are desired in competition one must spend a disproportionate amount of this time initially in the basic teaching phase of tracking. We know that almost any dog can track regardless of even extreme adversity. Whether or not it actually does is a function of the training it has received and its motivation to do so. It is the handler's responsibility to give the dog a series of tracks it can learn on as well as the incentive to learn.

The degree of similarity between an AKC tracking test and a Schutzhund tracking test is high. A dog ready to compete for its Schutzhund III degree is also ready for its TD. Both require that the dog track a stranger approximately 800 paces through a few turns. The advanced Schutzhund tracking test, the FH, is approximately equal in difficulty to a TDX. Both tracks are very long and well aged, and laid on difficult terrain with obstacles.

Whether training a dog for an AKC title, a CKC title or a Schutzhund degree (or schooling a tracking dog for actual service work) similar training techniques are required. Each desired behavior on the part of the dog must be scrutinized in detail. Each small part of the task must be taught to the dog until the animal has mastered it. Just as we would not expect a young child to know how to read a book simply upon being given one, neither would we expect a dog to know how to track because we have taken it to a scent pad and told it "Track!" It is not that the untrained dog does not yet possess the ability to detect and differentiate scents—in truth its skills are phenomenal in this area. However, this animal does not yet know what it is that we expect it to *do* with a scent. It is here we begin our instruction.

In some respects human beings and dogs learn tasks similarly. Both need to have what is taught them broken down into small increments. In this book, remember, we have organized Schutzhund exercises into increments for the reader and called them "Goals" and "Important Concepts for Meeting the Goals." Just as in the obedience and protection sections, we have built them into the tracking section, breaking each skill required for the Schutzhund tracking test down into a series of goals and concepts. Each concept requires much practice. Each must be fully mastered before moving on to the next, and for each concept that the dog is in the process of learning, the animal will need success and reinforcement.

Just like the other two phases of a Schutzhund trial, tracking is not just a competitive training event but also an examination of character. On the day of the trial, before it is allowed to track, each dog is examined by the judge for its nervous stability. The animal must be steady, neither timid nor inappropriately aggressive. It may be friendly or it may not, but above all it must not be unreliable or dangerous.

Every judge, it seems, has a different way of examining the dogs. Some touch the animals, some just observe the dog's behavior in the midst of a group of people. If any dog entered in a trial shows a sign of a severe flaw in temperament, it will not have the chance to track. Instead, it will be eliminated from the trial on the spot.

In addition, completely apart from the temperament test, by watching the dog on the tracking field an astute judge can evaluate the dog's nerves and its bond with its handler, as well as its desire to work independently. He can gauge the animal's confidence in itself and its work, its ability to concentrate and, very importantly, its drive to perform the task. It is during the tracking phase that the judge forms an initial opinion about the quality of the dog as well as the value of the training it has been given by its handler.

The following list contains some general considerations in training the tracking dog.

1. A large number of practice sessions should be provided for each concept, and each of these concepts must be mastered before proceeding to the next.
2. Beginning tracks should run into the wind so that the smell of the track will blow directly to the dog. Avoid crosswinds on beginning tracks.
3. Beginning tracks should be laid on flat surfaces away from large objects in order to keep the scent and thus the dog's nose in the footsteps.
4. Only when the dog is confident on the track and really understands the concepts of tracking should the wind, terrain and other environmental conditions be made adverse to its performance.
5. Tracking sessions should be kept positive. Avoid reprimanding the dog and using harsh obedience commands while preparing or running the track. This does not mean that the dog should never be corrected, but that a command such as "No!" should be said in such a way that the animal understands without feeling intensely pressured.
6. The dog should always find an article or reward at the end of the track. Even if the animal overruns or misses the original one, a substitute can be pulled from the handler's pocket and thrown onto the track. The dog must always be successful.
7. Once the dog has passed its Schutzhund I, occasionally use a variety of tracklayers, both male and female, as well as tracklayers of varying weights. They should be encouraged to wear an assortment of footgear. Of course, it is still possible and even advantageous for the handler to hone the dog's skills by laying his own tracks, even at an advanced level.
8. If using a harness, it should be used only for tracking. Put it on the dog a few feet before the tracking stake and remove it immediately at the conclusion of the track so that the animal associates the harness with its work.
9. During the teaching phase it is necessary to help the dog find the track whenever necessary. Therefore it is absolutely crucial to know the *exact location of the track*. This can be accomplished by marking the track with flags, mapping it or learning the knack for remembering exactly where one has walked.
10. Only one variable should be manipulated at each tracking training session. For example, if we are changing the age of the track, we must keep the distance, type of terrain and wind conditions constant.
11. One should attempt a tracking session only when in a pleasant mood. Do not go tracking in an irritable, agitated or angry mood, and if things suddenly go wrong during training, put the dog in the car and go home, even if a track is already laid.
12. In order to give the dog additional encouragement, a time for play with the ball or a run in the field should always follow a tracking training session.

EQUIPMENT NEEDED FOR TRACKING

Tracking Harness (optional)

The harness should be soft and comfortable, preferably with adjustable buckles on the chest and girth. Two kinds of harnesses are commonly used. The nonrestrictive harness is perhaps more desirable in that it does not restrict or interfere in any way with the dog's shoulder movement. The second type of harness, the restrictive harness, is often used by military and police organizations. A puppy harness can be cheaply made by using cotton webbing and stitching it on a regular sewing machine.

A tracking harness is not required for a Schutzhund trial, and many dogs compete in just their chain collars.

Thirty-foot Tracking Lead (ten-yard-long line)

A ⅝-inch webbed lead is readily available commercially and works well. However, if a lighter material is desired (for smaller dogs or for more lead sensitivity), a lead can easily be made from light cord. It is helpful with some types of leads to put a knot at fifteen feet.

Tracking Stakes or Location Markers

Tracking stakes are used for the benefit of the handler, not the dog. They aid the handler in remembering the exact location and direction of the track, so that he can either help the dog back to the footsteps or correct it back to them.

For this purpose, ⅜-inch dowels that are approximately thirty-six inches long are readily available in hardware stores and building supply outlets. A small bright piece of fabric or tape can be tied to the top of the stake to make it more noticeable in weedy terrain. The end of the stake can also be sharpened in a pencil sharpener to make penetration into the ground easier. Children's arrows or surveyor flags also make good tracking stakes.

Old-fashioned clothespins, sprayed a bright color, also can be clipped to vegetation on long, difficult tracks to indicate turns and direction.

Articles

The articles should be hand size or smaller, and a variety of fabrics—including leather and cloth—should be used. Old socks that are knotted work well, as do gloves. In many trials, the articles given the tracklayers by the organizing club are simply small flat squares of leather. For the purposes of training, leather scraps are available from shoe repair or craft shops.

The articles used for training should be about the same value (lightness or darkness of color) as the vegetation, so that the dog does not learn to search them out with its eyes instead of its nose.

Von Stephanitz strongly advocated the use of police tracking dogs as "detectives" that could track a human away from the scene of a crime and even identify that person among a group of others. (From von Stephanitz, *The German Shepherd Dog,* 1923.)

Clipboard, Graph Paper and Pen

Once flags are no longer used in training, it will be necessary to map out the tracks. All practice tracks are a learning experience for both dog and handler, and adjustments must be made if the dog inadvertently loses the track. Therefore, it is absolutely necessary for the handler to know where the actual footsteps are at all times. This can best be done by sketching a quick but accurate map immediately after laying the track.

Reward

At the completion of the track one of the dog's favorite toys should be produced and a big production made of a few minutes of play. If the dog is not interested in chasing a ball or toy, another reward should be used, such as food or a romp on the tracking field. If the dog becomes too excited and eager to reach the end of the track for the toy, a less stimulating reinforcer must be utilized.

6

Tracking:
Roles of the Handler
and Tracklayer

COMPARED TO obedience and protection training, tracking is relatively uncomplicated. A good tracking trainer is not successful because he employs some complex or mysterious technique. He is successful because he spends the time to develop a rapport with his dog on the tracking field—training religiously four, five or even six days a week.

Most of all he is successful because he enjoys the work. He regards tracking training as an opportunity to spend time with his dog. Early every day the two can be found alone together on the tracking field, enjoying the morning and each other.

GOAL 1: The handler must have the ability to progressively teach his dog the skill of tracking.

Important Concepts for Meeting the Goal

1. Motivating the dog to track
2. Teaching the dog to footstep track
3. Handling the long line
4. Reading the dog when it indicates loss of track or a change in direction
5. Planning a progressive training program

1. Motivating the dog to track

During the initial stages of training, the handler never scolds or corrects his dog on the tracking field. Tracking must be a lighthearted, enjoyable occasion for the animal.

The handler must provide the dog with strong incentives to track. The reward system we use varies with the characteristics of the particular dog and is designed to mesh with the animal's strongest and most dependable drives. Regardless of the type of motivation used, the teaching progression remains basically the same (that is, first straight tracks, then turns and articles and last proofing and problem solving).

If the dog is started by using its natural desire to seek its handler out, an assistant is needed. The assistant holds the dog while the handler walks away, calling to the animal and encouraging it with, "Come! Come on! Let's go!" After just a few paces, the handler steps out of sight behind a building, hedge or fence. There, hidden from the dog's sight, he begins laying a track. Using stakes or flags to show the assistant where he has gone, he scuffs the ground heavily and walks perhaps fifty or seventy-five yards in a new direction and then hides himself among some bushes or trees or even lies prone behind a tall clump of grass.

The assistant then puts the dog on its handler's scent, walking around the barrier to the beginning of the track and encouraging it with, "Seek! Seek!" Some dogs will immediately fall to using their nose in this situation, and begin to drag the assistant off up the track toward the handler's hiding place. The assistant walks with the animal on a short line, encouraging it to stay right on top of the handler's track, pointing to the handler's footsteps with his hand and preventing any circling or exaggerated quartering. When the dog finds its handler, its reward is a joyous reunion and a play session.

This method is a very old one, and seldom used nowadays. Because the track is so fresh (only a minute or two old) the dog tends to depend on drifting body scent to take it to its handler. In this way it learns to air scent rather than actually track footstep by footstep. This is especially true because of its generally high level of excitement, and the fact that it tends to search with its eyes for its master as it goes, which keeps its head up. Both of these factors interfere with the sort of head-down, slow work that we desire.

Therefore, we commonly use this method only as a way of starting very young puppies in tracking. The purpose is not so much to teach the pup to track as it is to teach it to rely upon and believe in what its nose tells it, and also to teach it that scent work is great fun. Accordingly, we normally perform this hide-and-seek game only with a puppy that is from ten to fourteen weeks old, and the assistant simply turns the pup loose once its handler is well hidden. The puppy is allowed to work its way to its handler any way that it can, and the assistant just walks along with it to make sure that it does not travel in entirely the wrong direction.

As we have already pointed out, for teaching competitive tracking most trainers now use food to motivate the dog. Some trainers advocate introducing the animal to tracking by having the tracklayer pull a drag of smelly meat. A drag can easily be made by using an old pair of hose. The food (overripe herring or tripe is used in Germany) can be put in one toe and the tracklayer trails it behind him as he lays the track. At first the drag is used throughout much of the track, then gradually just a few feet at a time, and eventually not at all. To reward it for following the track, the dog finds a substantial quantity of food at the end (*not* the drag meat, which is by then a little worse for wear, but its regular food or some favorite treat).

Glen Johnson describes in his book an excellent structured program using food drops as the dog's reward. The method can easily be adapted to Schutzhund tracking, and is especially useful with a dog that is not a natural retriever (not ''ball crazy''). The animal is taken off its normal daily ration of food. One-half of the quantity of food normally given to it in a day is instead fed to it on the track in evenly divided amounts and at specified intervals along the track. Every seventh day the dog receives a healthy portion of food and the handler does not take it tracking. It is important, of course, that the food given on the track be nourishing and of high quality.

The now classic method of training competitive Schutzhund tracking dogs involves combining the use of food and a retrieving object—like a ball or a kong. The method is similar to Johnson's, and might be called a modified food-drop approach. However, the food drops (or *baits* as we call them) are more numerous, much smaller and placed at irregular and unpredictable intervals along the track.

We begin a young dog or puppy by placing bait in virtually every footstep of a very short track. At the end of this track the puppy finds a large food drop and also its ball or some other toy, and the handler spends time playing and romping with it after every tracking session.

Through this method, the dog gains a strong desire to track, and yet learns the habit of methodically searching out each and every one of the tracklayer's footsteps.

For these baited tracks, no assistant or tracklayer is necessary. The handler does all the work himself, leaving the animal tied up or crated, laying the track and dropping baits, and then returning to his dog and running the track with it.

In order to maintain the animal's desire and enthusiasm for tracking, the dog is always brought to the tracking field keenly hungry. The handler takes it out of the car or truck and ties it up or puts it in a crate where it can watch the track being laid. While the handler lays the track he calls to the dog and teases it. In addition, before he goes to lay the track he untangles and spreads out the tracking line and harness so that he can quickly put them on the animal when he returns, as any sort of delay at the start of the track can diminish the dog's enthusiasm.

2. Teaching the dog to footstep track

Much of the work of teaching the dog to footstep track is accomplished by laying short tracks with a small piece of bait in each footstep. However, the handler also plays a great role by maneuvering the dog down the track in such a way that it works the whole distance from footstep to footstep. Footstep tracking does not just automatically happen. Because the dog is excited, it tends to be too headstrong and, rather than carefully checking each footstep, it will rush off down the track, missing most of the baits in the process. The handler's job is to prevent this by walking very close to the animal, holding it gently back and using his hand to point out each footstep and bait to the dog so that the animal moves slowly and does not miss even one.

As soon as he possibly can, the handler stops pointing out the baits and the footsteps, and lets the dog practice locating them on its own. However, he still remains very close to the dog, keeping a short leash (two to three feet) and using it to guide the animal straight down the track and also to keep it moving slowly, steadily and exactly on top of the footsteps.

When he begins to reduce the bait on the track he does so very slowly and gradually, taking great care to ensure that the dog still takes scent in every footstep.

3. Handling the long line

It is important that the dog begin working on its own as quickly as possible. If it learns to follow a track by letting its handler show it every step, the dog will never develop the ability to work out a track on its own. Instead it will, as many dogs do, learn an amazingly clever way of reading its handler in order to tell where the track is. These animals track very well as long as their handlers *know* where the track is. When they do not, as in Schutzhund II and III, the results are disastrous.

As soon as the dog begins to show a good understanding of tracking, the handler should begin to give it a little more leash, and thus the opportunity to work on its own and solve the track independently. However, the handler must make sure that the dog solves it the way we want it to: by tracking precisely from footstep to footstep. The handler can accomplish this by working carefully with the line. When the animal begins to veer away from the footsteps, he increases his resistance on the line, so that it is harder for the dog to move forward. When the animal comes back onto the track the handler decreases resistance, so that the animal finds it easier to move forward when it is tracking correctly.

The handler should be in no hurry to move back away from his dog to the end of the thirty-foot long line. Many trainers advance with their dogs to the point that the animals are correctly working full-size Schutzhund III tracks before they ever use anything longer than a six-foot leash for training sessions.

However, when he does judge that it is time to move back from the dog and let more line out, the handler must do so very gradually. Also, he does so

We begin a young dog or puppy by placing a bait in virtually every footstep of a very short track. This very close association between food and the tracklayer's footsteps will lead to footstep tracking.

The handler should be in no great hurry to move back away from the dog to the end of a thirty-foot line. This handler works on about twelve feet of line—long enough to make the animal work on its own but short enough so that the handler can step forward and help the dog at any time. (Photo by James Pearson.)

55

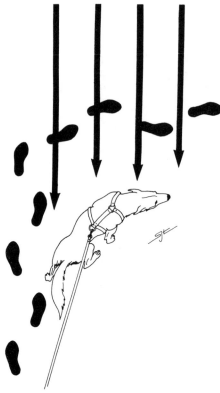

Air scent drifts with the wind, and a dog tracking into the wind tends to make the turn early, or "undershoot."

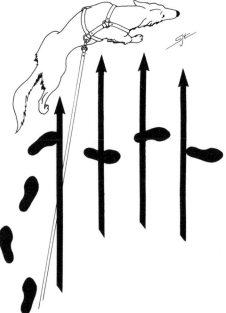

A dog tracking with the wind tends to make the turn late, or "overshoot." It is therefore important to teach the dog to footstep track, relying upon track scent rather than air scent.

dynamically. For example, he might let the dog go out twenty feet ahead on an easy leg of the track. But later, when he anticipates a challenging change in terrain or some other difficulty he will gradually work his way back up the line so that, if the dog has any difficulty, he will be close by to help the animal.

In order to make it easier to keep track of how much line he has given the dog to work on, the long line can be knotted at fifteen feet. When working the dog on twenty or thirty feet of line, the handler should keep the line taut to keep the animal moving forward, to improve his sensitivity in reading the dog and to keep the animal from entangling itself in the line.

4. Reading the dog when it indicates loss of track or a change in direction

In Schutzhund II and III tracking tests, the track is not laid by the handler, but by a tracklayer designated by the hosting club. In spite of this, the handler will sometimes have a sketchy idea of where his track goes. Sometimes he will even be able to see footprints. However, quite frequently in competition the handler will not have the faintest idea where the track leads—whether the first turn is to the left or the right, whether the second leg is 100 yards long or 300, etc.

This does not mean that the handler cannot do anything to help his dog. On the contrary, how he chooses to follow the dog will make all the difference in terms of whether or not the animal *commits itself* to the track. For example, when the dog is having trouble on a turn, the first thing that it will do is *indicate loss of track*. Then it will begin to cast about for the new direction of the track. If the dog moves off uncertainly in the wrong direction, showing in every line of its body that it is making a guess, and the handler blithely steps off after it, the handler will soon find himself being taken for a walk. On the other hand, if the dog commits itself confidently and surely to the correct direction, but the handler refuses to budge—stops it with the line because he lacks trust in his dog or is unable to read the animal's indication that it has found the track—then the animal will quickly decide that it must have been wrong, that the track must lie in the other direction. This will not only result in failure of the track, but it will also harm the dog's track sureness and confidence in its ability. Therefore, it is vital that the handler be able to *read* his dog, that he have the ability to see unmistakably when the animal is on the track and also to recognize when it is lost.

During training for turns, the handler should take notice during each practice session of how his dog indicates loss of the track. The most common indicators are: tail raised or wagged, nose and head elevated suddenly, obvious confusion or circling, etc. When he returns to his vehicle after a training session, the handler should make written notes in a tracking journal about how the dog made its indications of loss of track or changes in direction. These observations will become essential when the animal begins working unknown tracks and the handler must rely entirely on his dog's capabilities in order to get it through to the end of the track.

5. Planning a progressive training program

In tracking training one idea is paramount: The dog must always be successful. It must always obtain gratification (by completing the track *correctly* and then receiving its reward). Furthermore, the dog must rely entirely on itself to solve the track, rather than depending upon its handler to get it through any difficulty.

Therefore, the handler must carefully monitor the dog's progress. He must accurately evaluate what the dog is capable of doing today and also predict what it will be able to do tomorrow. Each time that he takes the dog out to track it should be with the specific purpose of improving their performance as a team. Sometimes he does this by laying a track that the dog can easily manage, so that the animal practices tracking perfectly and gains confidence. On other occasions he improves performance by preparing a problem for the animal, some small change in one of the variables that determine the difficulty of the track—wind direction, frequency of the baits, age, changes in terrain or vegetation, etc. However, the handler must accurately predict what the dog is capable of doing on any given day so that the animal is neither discouraged nor forced to depend upon its handler to get it to the end of the track. The challenge is to plan each track in such a way that it is difficult enough to teach the dog something, but not so difficult that the animal cannot solve it itself with minimal intervention by its handler.

For this reason, it is often useful to keep a tracking journal. The handler records in it the conditions, length, age and general difficulty of the track, and then also records exactly how the dog negotiated it. By looking back through his journal the handler can take note of trends and important changes in performance, and also identify specific problems he might not otherwise notice. For example, the journal might reveal that the dog has difficulty with tracks over thirty minutes old in temperatures above 75°F, or that whenever it is on a particular medication its performance drops markedly.

GOAL 2: The tracklayer must lay well-designed tracks and then remember exactly where they lead.

In much of the training, the handler acts as his own tracklayer. Later on, in the advanced stages of training, the tracklayer will be a training partner who lays mystery tracks so that the handler can practice relying upon and trusting his dog.

The tracklayer has much responsibility for the success of a dog–handler team in both training and in competition. He must be able to lay all sorts of imaginative and ingenious tracks for training, exploiting natural features and vegetation to educate the dog. He must also be able to lay a series of regular and consistent regulation Schutzhund trial tracks.

When track markers are not used, he must be able to map out and/or remember exactly where the track leads. This way the handler training his dog knows when he can say "Good dog!" and when he must say "Phooey!" And in trial the judge also must be able to depend upon the tracklayer to correctly answer the question, "There, where the dog is going now, did you walk right there or not?"

In Schutzhund I competition, in which the handler lays his own track, he can obviously be of immense help to his dog if he has the knack of remembering exactly where he has walked.

Important Concepts for Meeting the Goal

1. Laying straight tracks
2. Laying a clean track
3. Mapping and remembering tracks
4. Laying regulation tracks

1. Laying straight tracks

It is only when we begin teaching a dog to track that we realize how difficult it is to walk in a perfectly straight line without sidewalks, fences or roads to guide us. In order to do so, the tracklayer must pick out not just one landmark toward which he will walk, but two. These objects should be noteworthy and memorable and separated by as great a distance as possible—a tree near the end of the track and a barn in the distance, for example. The tracklayer lines them up with each other somewhat like the sights of a rifle and then, as he walks, he keeps them in the same relation to each other. He will know he is beginning to curve when one of the objects begins to change position relative to the other.

The importance of perfectly straight legs to the overall track is that, if we have two flags marking each end of a leg, and if the tracklayer traveled a perfectly straight line between them, then we always know exactly where to find his footsteps. If, on the other hand, he curved as he walked, we can be wrong by as much as six or seven yards on a long leg.

2. Laying a clean track

The tracklayer must take great care that he leaves behind him a well-defined and uncontaminated path of track scent for the dog to follow. For this reason, he makes a "jump start"—leaping to the place where he will make the scent pad so that the track leads only away from it. By the same token, when he has finished laying the track, he should leap away from it. This way the track will finish cleanly at a dead end, with nowhere else to go, so that a dog who tracks very precisely is not confused by being stopped when the track has not yet ended.

When he walks back around to the starting pad from the end of a track he has just laid, the tracklayer should walk well clear of his track, and also downwind of it if at all possible, so that the dog will not be confused by scent blowing to it from upwind. The tracklayer must keep in mind that he lays a track coming back as well as going out, and take care not to contaminate the training track he has just taken such trouble to prepare.

It goes without saying that no one should cross or ''cut'' the track before the dog works it, and also that it is best that the piece of ground used for training be empty of all traffic for twenty-four hours beforehand, or even longer in lush or wet conditions.

3. Mapping and remembering tracks

Before he even begins to lay a track, the tracklayer surveys the ground available to him and, keeping the dog's ability and stage of training in mind, he picks landmarks and sketches out in his mind the path he will walk. He does *not* simply begin to lay the track and hope to find landmarks along the way at about the right places and the right distances for the dog's ability. Instead, he plans his legs and turns in advance so that they will be recognizable and distinct and conform to the dog's level of expertise.

As he walks the track, he may or may not mark his path with tracking stakes or flags, depending upon the length and difficulty of the track and also the availability of landmarks. It is always best to use as few flags as possible, because the dog soon learns their significance and uses them to help it navigate instead of relying entirely upon its nose. For the same reason, the tracklayer should be a little subtle in his use of flags. For example, rather than marking all his turns with one flag right at the apex of the turn, he should instead use two. He places one well before the turn, and one well after, with a small clump of grass or an anthill marking the exact location of the turn itself. Otherwise the dog will soon begin to make a turn anytime it encounters a flag.

Color-coded clothespins or pieces of ribbon can also be used to mark the track by clipping or hanging them in the vegetation, but only if the vegetation is well up off the ground. Because these markers are impregnated with the track-layer's scent they are essentially articles, and if they are merely dropped on the ground or hung in the grass, a well-trained dog should indicate every one of them.

As he walks the track the tracklayer should make mental notes and rehearse the track over and over in his mind. He should be able, before he starts his dog, to close his eyes and summon up a mental picture of every turn and leg of the track and the landmarks and flags that mark them. It is helpful for the tracklayer to sketch a quick map of the track once he is finished laying it, especially if the track must age for an hour or so before the dog will begin to work it.

It is also advantageous to occasionally lay tracks in soft dirt, heavy dew or light snow so that every footstep is visible to the handler as he handles his dog down the track. This kind of track is our best opportunity to run proofing problems in which we ask the dog to negotiate extremely demanding bends and curves and even spirals.

Laying the track itself is at least half the work of teaching the dog to track.

Dr. Adel Zohdy and "Dolf," Schutzhund III, begin their day with an early morning tracking session.

4. Laying regulation tracks

In trial, a stake is used to indicate the beginning of the track. To the right of the stake the tracklayer makes a scent pad by trampling the ground in an area approximately one yard square. He then proceeds to lay the first leg of the track in a straight line. When he reaches the location of the first turn, he pivots 90 degrees right or left (according to the judge's instructions) and proceeds without hesitation in the new direction. The tracklayer should walk the track at a normal pace and with his normal step. He is very careful to drop the articles directly onto the track. In a trial, the judge normally indicates where he wants the articles dropped and where the turns are to be.

We make the search game more difficult by moving out into the yard and scattering the baits across an area of short but dense grass. (Andy Barwig and "Dux.")

Susan Barwig walks "Quella" carefully down the length of the track, holding the pup to a slow pace and using a hand to point out each footstep.

The importance of the start on the track cannot be overstated. Here Shirley Stadjuhar's dog begins to work slowly and surely.

7

Tracking: Schooling the Dog

THE PRIMARY GOAL in Schutzhund tracking is to teach the dog to footstep track. Only a dog that puts its nose into each footstep and works carefully and determinedly can receive the full 100 points in competition. Accordingly, we must teach the dog to follow track scent, not air or body scent. We do this by associating the tracklayer's footsteps, and thus the track scent, with small bits of food.

GOAL 1: The dog will work a short, straight track slowly and precisely.

The first step is to teach the dog to follow a straight track. We break this skill down into a number of simple concepts.

The vast majority of Schutzhund dogs begin their schooling in tracking when they are still very young, at perhaps ten to twelve weeks, and therefore much of the following information is described in terms of puppy training. However, the reader should be aware that we use almost exactly the same techniques to begin older pups and adult animals in tracking.

Important Concepts for Meeting the Goal

1. Searching on command
2. Taking a full scent at the start of the track

3. Taking scent in each footstep of the track
4. Correcting the dog back to the track

1. Searching on command

The first lesson in tracking can be taught at home, first inside the house and then later in the yard. The handler will need five or six small pieces of the puppy's favorite treat (cheddar cheese and small slices of hot dog are usually well received). While the puppy watches (normally an assistant holds the puppy for the handler), the handler distributes the bait randomly throughout a small area perhaps eighteen inches across. He has his assistant release the puppy and, with a gentle but enthusiastic "Seek!" command, points the tidbits out to the animal, encouraging it to find them and gobble them up. The handler repeats this procedure perhaps three times each training session.

Once the puppy makes an association between the "Seek!" command and food, so that it drops its head and begins to search avidly upon hearing it and seeing its handler point to the ground, we make the game more difficult by moving it out into the yard. We pick an area with short but dense grass, so that the tidbits will not be visible and the puppy will have to search them out by sniffing among the blades of grass.

Once the puppy is eagerly snuffling out every one of the baits, we begin to increase the size of the search area where they are hidden, giving the pup more ground to cover and teaching it to be very persistent in searching out food. The handler ensures that the pup finds every one of the baits by directing it across the entire search area with his hand and the command "Seek! Seek!"

Each time the youngster finds a piece of food, its handler reinforces it with soothing praise words and gentle petting.

2. Taking a full scent at the start of the track

The impact of the *start* of a track cannot be overstated. Very often, the way that the Schutzhund dog starts will be typical of its entire performance. If the dog starts slowly, surely and with intense concentration, we can usually be assured that we are about to witness a fine track. On the other hand, if it rushes away from the starting pad without really taking the scent, or if it does not show strong motivation and drive by searching the scent pad eagerly, we can conclude that the dog will be lucky to finish its track.

After a week or two of careful work at home, our puppy has a clear understanding that "Seek!" means that if it drops its head and scours the area indicated to it, it will be rewarded. Searching a scent pad is only a minor extension of something that it already does enthusiastically.

While the pup watches from a crate or from the arms of an assistant who restrains it, the handler stamps out a scent pad on the tracking field about one yard square. He puts in a tracking flag or stake at arm's length to the left of it, and scatters five or six small baits across it. As he "kicks in" the scent pad the handler talks to his puppy, encouraging and teasing the pup in order to excite it.

Then, when all is ready, he returns to his puppy and walks it on leash to the scent pad, commands it to "Seek!" and directs it across the pad with his hand. While the pup searches out and eats the tidbits, the handler praises and pets it calmly.

The handler repeats this drill three or four times for several training sessions, at the same time gradually reducing the number of baits on the pad until finally there are only three, placed at the corners of a triangular scent pad. During this stage of training, the puppy makes the additional and useful association that it will be rewarded by searching to the right of a tracking flag.

3. Taking scent in each footstep of the track

Once the puppy thoroughly scours a scent pad on command, we are ready for the handler to proceed to tracking proper.

All the initial training, up to and including turns and articles, is done in optimal conditions. The tracks are laid on flat ground in evenly distributed grass that is about instep high (ankle high at most). The handler does not age the tracks any longer than it takes him to prepare them and then ready his dog for the start, nor does the handler work his novice tracking dog in very windy or inclement weather.

After laying a triangular scent pad with food in each corner, the handler departs from the apex of the triangle and slowly, with very small steps, walks perhaps ten or twelve feet. As he goes, he leaves a small bait in the middle of each footstep, and at the end of the short track he also places a food drop—a pile consisting of a handful of the bait.

Then he goes back to his puppy, walks the pup up to the scent pad and commands the pup to "Seek!" as before. The handler uses a finger to direct the puppy over the entire scent pad and then, before the pup lifts its head, out onto the first footstep of the track. Slowly and carefully, he walks the youngster down the length of the short track. He holds a very short leash to keep the puppy right on top of the footsteps and also to prevent it from rushing down the track. Gently, he holds the young dog to a slow, steady pace. He walks bent over beside the pup, running his finger along in the grass directly in front of the youngster's nose, so that the pup works the track all the way to the end without ever lifting its head. When the animal reaches the food drop and begins to eat, the handler praises it enthusiastically.

Meanwhile, the assistant comes forward and takes hold of the pup; when the puppy looks up from eating the last of its food drop, it finds the handler already laying another short track a few feet away. The handler runs the puppy through three tracks like this in a row, and then plays with the puppy for a while on the field afterward. It is very important that the young dog understand that the end of the track means play and "quality time" with its master.

Assuming that it is tracking four or five times per week, the puppy continues working at this short distance for perhaps two weeks. Of course, each dog learns at its own rate. What is most important is that the pup completely master the scent pad and the short track before proceeding.

At this point the handler begins to increase the length of the tracks. He also begins to walk more and more normally as he lays the tracks, so that now his footsteps are separated by the usual distance rather than lying heel to toe. He increases the length of the track very gradually, and he still leaves a bait in every footstep. Only when the youngster works a fifty-foot track continuously and with intense concentration does the handler begin to reduce the number of food drops.

Up to this point in training, the young dog has probably taken little notice of either the track scent *or* the air scent left wafting about in the breeze by the tracklayer. Instead it has been single-mindedly preoccupied with sniffing for and finding the food scent. Now we must teach it that, although the food will no longer be distributed evenly all along the track, the key to getting from one bait to the next is following the track scent.

At first, when the handler is laying a track, he just omits a bait every now and again, so that the pup occasionally finds footsteps without food. Progressively and very carefully, the handler omits the bait more and more often, and the puppy begins to use the empty footsteps to guide it from one bait to the next. Now the young animal is beginning to learn the most important lesson that we have to teach it about tracking: It must search for and follow the track scent.

Gradually, we ask the puppy to work a longer and longer distance between baits. However, and this is the important point, the distribution of the baits along the track is *random*, meaning that the pup can never predict how far it will have to travel in order to reach the next bait. For example, a beginning track will have food at footsteps one, three, four, nine, eleven, twelve, fifteen and so on, while a more advanced track will have food in footsteps one, seven, twelve, twenty-one, twenty-two, thirty-five, thirty-nine and so forth. Because the puppy does not know whether the next bait is three paces away or sixteen, it keeps its nose down and searches intensively.

Over a period of several weeks, both the overall length of the tracks and the distance between the food drops gradually increase, until the puppy is tracking a distance of perhaps seventy-five paces and in the process finding only two or three baits.

We may still work the puppy on three tracks each training session, but only one of them is as much as seventy-five paces long. The other two are very short, and intended mainly for practice on the start and a few feet of very intense tracking. This too we randomize, running the short tracks and long ones in different order, so that when the pup starts a track it never knows whether it will end in ten feet or 150 feet.

Each track ends with a large food drop that rewards the pup for its work. Because we are depending upon food to motivate the youngster it must, of course, be brought to the tracking field keenly hungry. If for some reason it has little interest in tracking on a particular day, we immediately take it away from the field. We do not feed it that day (it can have water, of course), and we repeat the same track the next morning. We leave more than the usual amount of food at the end of the track, and if it does fine work we feed it well.

At this, the teaching stage of tracking, absolutely no corrections are made. The young dog is not scolded, physically punished or corrected or even told ''No!'' Instead, the handler helps and encourages the puppy in every possible way to understand what he desires. In short, *the teaching phase of tracking concerns itself with preventing rather than correcting errors.*

4. Correcting the dog back to the track

By the time that the dog has mastered straight tracks of about seventy-five paces, tracking exactly and with concentration from footstep to footstep, it will usually be old enough (six to seven months) and well motivated enough so that light corrections will harm neither its character nor its delight in tracking.

The handler now begins to give the youngster a little more leash as it works. Rather than walking hunched over right on top of the animal and meticulously guiding it down the track, ready to point to the footsteps with his hand any time the puppy veers a few inches downwind, he walks upright directly behind the pup on several feet of leash.

Whenever the dog deviates from the footsteps, the handler tells it "Phooey!" and pops the line gently. (We do not use the word "No!" because it is too strong and inhibitory in nature for tracking training.) At the same time he steps up next to the animal's head and uses a finger to direct it back into the footsteps. The instant the dog recovers the track and moves forward exactly on top of it, the handler praises it soothingly and moves back behind it again.

GOAL 2: The dog will follow the track precisely through turns, without casting or circling.

Next the young dog must learn that the track will turn, and that it can turn with it and follow it in the new direction. This concept is difficult for both the dog (who has become quite certain that tracks always travel perfectly straight) and the handler (who must learn the knack of letting his dog solve a problem on its own but without allowing it to practice faulty tracking). The dog, for its part, must indicate loss of scent immediately so that it does not overshoot the turn and lose the track. And for his part, the handler must learn to read the signals that his dog gives when it detects that something has changed in the track.

Many trainers teach turns gradually, beginning with curves so slight that the dog scarcely takes notice, and continuing until the dog is making acute turns of more than 90 degrees.

But turns can also be taught as a "loss of track" exercise in footstep-to-footstep tracking. In this sort of exercise we expect the dog to negotiate a 90-degree turn right from the start. We prefer this method because, in order to make precise turns, the dog must learn to *stop* when it can no longer smell a footstep directly in front of it and check with its nose to its left and its right until it finds whether the track has ended or merely set off in a new direction. It is very important that

- the dog realizes within a foot or two that it has lost the footsteps
- it signals clearly and unambiguously that it has lost the footsteps

Over a period of several weeks, both the overall length of the tracks and also the distance between baits increases. Here an assistant holds the dog while the handler lays a track. Note how the handler lays the track near the boundary line of a soccer field so that the location of the track will be unmistakable.

In the initial stages of training on turns, the handler helps her dog by stepping up close on the inside of the turn and guiding the animal through it. (Barbara Valente and "Mucke," Schutzhund I.)

By the time straight tracks of about seventy-five paces are mastered, the dog will usually be old enough and well motivated enough so that very light corrections may be administered without harming character or delight in tracking. (Anne Weickert and her Blitz v. Haus Barwig.)

- its handler recognizes its loss of track signal, praises and encourages the animal to carefully check all around it for the new direction of the track

Otherwise the dog will often fail to stop the instant it overruns the turn. Its loss of track indication will become indistinct, and it will learn the habit of overshooting turns and circling back to find them again.

Of course, if we have not already taught the dog to footstep track slowly and meticulously, it will "blow past" his first 90-degree turn and not indicate puzzlement or loss of track until several yards further on. In this case the handler can always stop the dog with the line, in order to prevent it from overrunning the turn, but *then it is the handler who signals to his dog that the track is turning rather than the reverse.*

Therefore, we must not begin work on turns until the young dog is tracking very exactly and confidently.

Important Concepts for Meeting the Goal

1. Baiting all the way through the turn
2. Baiting after the turn
3. Repeating the turn

1. Baiting all the way through the turn

Our first task is to make the dog realize that tracks often change direction. However, in the process we must avoid having it circle or practice faulty tracking in any way.

The handler lays three short tracks of about fifty to seventy-five paces each. All three have normal, well-laid and well-baited scent pads, but two of them turn one direction—right, for example—and one of them turns the other direction. The handler baits every single footstep through the turns, beginning about two yards before the turn and ending perhaps two yards after it. Each of the tracks ends with a food drop, and after the end of the last one the handler romps and plays ball with his dog for a while.

He starts his dog on the first track, keeping it on a very short leash, and makes sure that it is moving very slowly and carefully when it encounters the baits lying before the turn. As the dog moves along from footstep to footstep eating each of the baits, the handler steps up very close to it on the inside of the turn. It if has been well prepared and has learned to footstep track accurately, the dog should easily follow the turn around. But in the event that it begins to overrun the turn or go in the wrong direction, the handler is right there to help it by stopping it with the leash and then pointing out the new direction of the track with his hand.

The handler works his dog through the last two tracks in just the same way, and then plays with it and takes it home.

The next day he reverses the directions of the turns on the three tracks, so that now two of them turn left, and one turns right. As always, he is ready to help the dog *before* the animal gets into any difficulty.

As the days pass, the handler continues training on these series of short tracks with continuously baited turns, until the dog follows them steadily and precisely. However, the handler constantly varies the lengths of the legs of the tracks and he begins to increase their length as well, so that the animal never knows whether it will encounter a turn within three yards or thirty. In addition, the handler also occasionally picks a day to throw in a long, straight track of 150 or 200 paces in place of the normal series of three short tracks with turns in order to gain some length and add variety to training.

2. Baiting after the turn

Up to this point we have used bait on the track to signal to the animal that the track was about to change direction and to help it follow through the turn. Now we must begin teaching the dog to recognize the change in direction itself and to find the second leg of the track on its own without the help of food in each footstep.

As before, the handler lays three short tracks with turns, but he does not bait the turns continuously. Instead, he leaves a food drop perhaps six or seven paces after the turn.

The first few training sessions that he performs this routine he can also *double lay* the turns in order to call his dog's attention to the change in direction. He walks around the turn once, stops, turns around and walks directly on top of his footsteps back through the turn to a point about two yards before it; he then stops again, retraces his footsteps (so that he has actually walked through the turn three times) and recommences laying the new leg.

As he approaches the turns with his dog, the handler again moves up very close to the animal on the inside of the turn in order to help it if necessary. His task is a ticklish one. He must give the dog every opportunity to work the turn out itself, but at the same time he must be ready to intervene and help the animal before it overruns the turn or goes in the wrong direction.

The instant the animal picks up the new leg of the track and begins to follow it, the handler encourages it with praise and, when the dog comes upon the food drop six paces after the turn, the handler pats and praises it enthusiastically.

3. Repeating the turn

After several weeks of practice, the dog should be cleanly making turns to both the left and the right. However, the dog has not yet really learned the skill of following a turn in a track, for two reasons.

First, the handler is still indicating to his dog both the turn in the track and also the direction of the turn by moving up close alongside it on the inside of the turn. Second, he is intervening so quickly that the dog never loses the track for a moment. Thus the animal makes no loss of track indication and does not stop moving forward on its own. Instead it makes a turn *when its handler signals it to make a turn.*

We now have no alternative but to allow the dog to lose the track. We must stop warning *it* that the track is turning and instead begin letting it warn *us* that the track is turning.

The handler lays three short tracks with turns, as before, and leaves a food drop six paces after each turn. As he approaches the first turn with his dog, the handler gives no indication to the animal. One of three things will happen:

1. The dog will make the turn cleanly, going around it as if it were on rails.
2. The dog will stop within a foot or two after overrunning the turn, indicate loss of track, and then check carefully about it for the new leg and follow it.
3. It will overrun the turn by two or three feet or more without any loss-of-track indication. Then it may give every sign of continuing off over the horizon, *or* it may begin to cast wildly about for the scent.

It is, of course, ideal if the dog goes around the turn cleanly. We would like it to track this way always. However, no matter how good the animal is, sooner or later it will lose the track. Knowing this to be true, and recognizing that the dog will probably lose the footsteps momentarily several times on every track it ever runs, we must be sure of one thing: that it never "lies." If the animal has not got the track exactly, we must encourage it to:

1. Indicate clearly that it has lost the footsteps.
2. Stop before it wanders any further from the track, and then cast carefully about for it.

If the dog makes the turn cleanly, wonderful! The handler praises it and lets it discover the food drop, feeds and plays with it at the end of the track and ends the session on that note. It cannot get any better.

If the dog indicates loss of track immediately after it overruns the turn, stops and begins to search carefully for the new leg of the track, still wonderful! The handler praises it softly for the indication and quietly encourages it to rediscover the track. On the second and third tracks the dog will probably make the turn more cleanly.

If, on the other hand, it overruns the turn and keeps going—without a strong indication of loss of track and without stopping—the handler tells it sharply "Phooey!" and then calls its name. He backs up a few feet along the track, calling his dog to him. When the animal arrives, the handler immediately restarts it on the track a few yards before the turn. If the dog overruns again, the handler again tells it "Phooey!" and then calls it back and restarts it.

He will not allow the animal to proceed past the turn or go any farther until it negotiates the change of direction somewhat cleanly—either follow it as if it is on rails or stopping immediately when it overruns it and then searching carefully for the new leg.

Several attempts will probably be required, but eventually the dog will negotiate the turn correctly. The handler must be careful to praise it for any loss-of-track indication and to enthusiastically pet it when it discovers the bait after the turn.

The dog should do better on its second and third turns that day, and within a few weeks it will probably be making most of its turns cleanly. At this point the handler begins laying only one track per day, with two to three turns, instead of three tracks.

The handler must be careful not to give the turns away to the dog with any action or word on his part as he approaches them with the animal, or by too obviously staking or marking them when he lays the track. Also, he should vary the lengths of the tracks and the lengths of the legs so that the dog cannot ever predict where the next turn will be. This will keep the animal turning when its nose tells it to rather than when it thinks it is time.

GOAL 3: The dog will indicate the articles on the track by lying down upon them.

In Schutzhund I and II, the tracklayer leaves two articles on the track. In Schutzhund III there are three, which account for twenty-one of the 100 total points available in the tracking phase. It is therefore imperative that the dog locate all three articles and indicate them cleanly. If the dog is a good, exact worker, the articles seldom pose any problems for it. As it proceeds down the track, footstep by footstep, it will run directly into them.

If the animal is not a precise tracker, it is even more important to motivate it for the articles, so that it is *eager* to find them. Then, if it is far off the footsteps when it nears an article, the article's presence and the scent cone it gives off downwind may bring the dog back to the track. Therefore, the articles in Schutzhund tracking are somewhat of a blessing rather than a training problem. They often make a difficult Schutzhund III track easier, because if the handler can depend upon his dog to find the articles, then it has three places in the field where it *knows* without a doubt the tracklayer has been. The articles can thus serve as vitally important reference points.

The dog is free to indicate the article in any one of three ways—sitting, downing or standing on it—or it may even pick the article up and retrieve it to its handler. The only stipulation is that it must indicate all the articles in the same way. However, it is almost universally agreed that the best method is to teach the dog to lie down upon the article, and it is therefore quite rare to see a dog in competition that has been trained to do otherwise.

The skill of finding the articles is quite different than tracking. It is perhaps more similar to a scent discrimination exercise, because the dog frequently comes upon objects while tracking that *might* be articles, and it must then determine whether or not they have been touched by the tracklayer. It is therefore possible to teach the articles as a separate exercise from tracking proper. Indeed,

The fruits of careful proofing: Steve Thompson leaves the tracking field with his Caiser v. Haus Barwig, Schutzhund III, after a ninety-nine-point track in blizzard conditions.

The articles in Schutzhund tracking can be a blessing rather than a difficulty, because they remotivate the dog and serve as important reference points to the exact location of the track.

73

it is even desirable to do so, because we will employ compulsion with the articles in order to make the dog absolutely reliable.

Important Concepts for Meeting the Goal

1. Lying down upon the articles
2. Indicating the articles on the track
3. Restarting the dog after an article

1. Lying down upon the articles

Because we will use compulsion in association with the articles, we do not introduce them on the tracking field. Instead, we introduce them as an obedience exercise, and we often simply do it at home in the backyard.

The handler downs his dog and leaves it. He walks out a few yards in front of the animal and scatters about on the ground several leather articles that he has impregnated with his scent by carrying them inside his shirt or clamped under his arm for a minute or two.

He returns to his dog and takes it on leash to each of the articles in turn. He points each one out with his hand, so that the dog smells it, and then he commands the dog to "Down!" Once the dog is down, the handler kneels with it and, picking up the article, he makes a great production of showing it to the animal and praising it in association with the article. At the same time he slips a bait from his pocket and feeds it to the dog.

Over a period of several weeks the handler does this again and again, walking the dog up to an article impregnated with his scent, downing the dog upon it and then feeding and praising the animal. His goal is to associate finding the article with food and praise.

It might seem far simpler to use a leather object such as a glove, and place the bait inside the glove. This method will certainly have the dog eagerly searching for articles and downing on them in short order. However, by doing so, we can create two training problems.

First, the dog does not learn to find and indicate an object impregnated with the handler's scent. It is simply searching for food, as it has done during much of its early tracking training. This means that at some later date the handler may have trouble getting it to search out the kinds of articles that are used in Schutzhund III competition, which are flat and small and definitely do not smell of food. The dog may eventually overrun an article or two at an unanticipated and inconvenient time (that is, on a very difficult track during which it has done everything right, except the articles), and the handler will be forced to correct the dog for it.

Second, when a dog is taught to indicate articles by using gloves containing food, it invariably mouths and chews at them. This often results in the habit of mouthing the articles. If the dog is an extremely proficient tracker, scoring in the high nineties, his scores will be hurt by mouthing, especially in major trials where the judging is severe.

After several training sessions, the dog will automatically and happily lie down when it finds an article. However, at this stage the handler must ensure that the dog also feels a sense of obligation where the articles are concerned. Therefore he begins to pressure the animal a little bit, perhaps even slapping it on the back with the leash if it does not down quickly enough (we assume that we are dealing with an adult dog that already knows basic obedience). It is far better to get the issue of the down settled here in the backyard, rather than be forced to correct the dog later in the midst of an actual track because it is reluctant to lie down on an article.

Once the dog is down on the article, the handler spends thirty seconds or a minute with it, praising it softly and feeding it, so that the articles come to represent for him a haven from stress, a place to relax. The handler also practices picking the article up, holding it above his head as though he were showing it to the judge in a trial, walking around the dog, adjusting its collar and so forth while still keeping the animal down.

2. Indicating the articles on the track

Only once the down on the article is completely taught does the handler begin to combine this skill with an actual track. He lays a long, straight track with perhaps three articles. The track ends in a food drop some fifteen or twenty paces past the last article. He makes sure that the track is very easy, and also that the ground cover is short so that it will not hide the articles.

At each article the dog will automatically down, and then the handler spends thirty seconds or a minute with it praising and petting it and giving it a piece of food from time to time.

Previously, the dog worked its way down the track simply to find the food drop at the end and all the baits along the way. Now, it will work its way down the track in order to find the articles as well, because they have come to represent relaxation, reassurance and pleasure.

3. Restarting the dog after an article

Obviously, every time the dog stops and lies down on an article, it must start the track again. We consider each of these restarts almost equal in importance to the original start from the scent pad. It is vital that the dog put its nose to the ground and carefully move off down the track from footstep to footstep.

In competition, it is quite common to see dogs become excited by finding the article and therefore charge away from it when restarted, requiring anywhere from three to fifteen yards before they really begin to work again. If a difficult piece of terrain happens to lie right after the article, this habit can result in disaster.

Therefore, when the handler starts the dog from the articles, he takes great pains to make sure that the animal is calm and quiet, and puts its nose immediately to the ground. If necessary, he can also lay the track in such a fashion that the dog will find a small bait or two within the first twenty or thirty paces after the articles. The result should be that the dog will pick up the habit of tracking very carefully away from them.

Only when the dog is reliably finding all the articles and indicating them correctly, and also starting off from them in good style, does the handler begin to combine both turns and articles on the same track.

GOAL 4: The dog will complete tracks at least an hour old and approximately 1,000 yards in length without difficulty.

Up to this point in training, the handler has designed training tracks for his dog solely according to the lesson at hand. They have normally been rather short and simple, and seldom more than ten minutes old. Now, however, we have the trial regulations to worry about.

Our problem is to increase both the length and the age of the training tracks to comply with Schutzhund III regulations. (Ambitious trainers do not train for Schutzhund I and II, they train for Schutzhund III and pick up I and II on the way.) Furthermore, we must do it without detracting from the dog's precision and performance.

Important Concepts for Meeting the Goal

1. Increasing length
2. Aging the track

1. Increasing length

We increase the length of the track very gradually. Also—and this is very important—we increase it *randomly*. For instance, one day the dog will have a short track with one turn, the next day a very long track with three turns, and on the third day it will have a short, complicated track involving four turns. Month by month, the average distance the dog must cover increases, but on a particular day it has no way of knowing if its last article and food drop lie 100 paces away or 1,000. The result of this uncertainty is a very intense, yard-by-yard search of the entire length of the track.

In addition, when deciding on the length of a training track, we also consider conditions of weather and terrain. For instance, a 1,000-yard track in a light dusting of snow is one thing, and a 1,000-yard track in a wheat field on a ninety-degree day in June is something else again.

2. Aging the track

When we advance the age of the track past the ten- to fifteen-minute mark for the first time, we manipulate only this one variable. We do *not* experiment with different lengths, terrains or conditions while we are teaching the dog to work older scent. Instead, we lay fairly stereotyped tracks of about Schutzhund I length and difficulty.

The handler increases the age of the track very gradually from one day to the next, five minutes at a time. He spends at least several days at each increment (twenty-five, thirty, thirty-five, etc.). Depending upon conditions, the "hump" —where the predominant scent on the track changes from air to ground— should occur somewhere between twenty and forty minutes, and the handler should expect his dog to have some difficulty in this interval. He works close to his dog, handling it carefully, and helps it past any problems.

GOAL 5: The dog will learn to work its way confidently through difficulties encountered on the track.

Because handlers involved in organizing a competition want to see high scores in their trials, sponsoring clubs normally make every effort to provide optimal tracking conditions for the day of competition. Our club invariably uses a turf farm for trials. However, it is often not possible to arrange for the use of such a large piece of lush, green real estate. Especially in some of the more arid regions of the United States, American Schutzhund trainers regularly compete in tracking conditions that appall the German judges who are often brought in to officiate at the events. Sometimes the organizing club will make a special effort to provide very demanding conditions in order to find out whose dog "really tracks." This was the case at the GSDCA/WDA Europameisterschaft Qualification Trial in Colorado in 1984, when the organizers tried to make absolutely sure that any dog that qualified for the WDA team would acquit itself well in the tracking phase of the European championships.

Other sorts of challenges will crop up unintentionally, as happened one day to a Schutzhund III competitor from New Mexico that was halfway through its tracking test when it was discovered that the spectators had been standing for a quarter of an hour on top of the last leg of its track.

Incidents of this sort are a reminder that luck plays a role in Schutzhund. There is nothing we can do to change our luck, so instead we try to teach our dogs to cope with the unexpected.

Thus far, we have performed the vast majority of our training in optimal conditions. Our dog has learned all its basic skills in short, regular, green grass with little wind. Now we must add difficulty to its work by exposing it to all sorts of adversities, including drastic changes in terrain and vegetation, roads and ditches and cross tracks cutting its track and the dog's having to refind the track once it has lost it. However, we must do this in such a fashion as to *increase* the animal's skill and its confidence in its ability, rather than the reverse.

Proofing in this manner improves not only the dog's skill, but also its intensity and concentration. By proofing the animal we systematically teach it to *calmly* solve problems.

In many parts of the United States tracking conditions are not ideal. However, experience has shown that a well-schooled dog can follow a track even in very dry or barren terrain. Here, Salynn McCollum's Sartan v. Haus Barwig shows a deep nose and fine style in the desert outside of Sante Fe, New Mexico.

Training in optimal conditions. April Sanders' "Ben," Schutzhund III, works with a deep nose in a dirt field. Footprints are visible in freshly plowed fields.

Important Concepts for Meeting the Goal

1. Negotiating changes in terrain
2. Crossing over an obstacle and then relocating the track
3. Recovering the track after losing it
4. Tracking surely despite adverse weather or ground conditions
5. Ignoring cross tracks

1. Negotiating changes in terrain

Several years ago, one of the best and most consistent tracking dogs in the United States landed a spot on the American team that was to compete at the world championships. While out on its track the day of the championships, its handler was appalled when this excellent dog suddenly and unequivocally stopped tracking at a point where the terrain changed abruptly from field grass to corn stubble. It appeared as if the dog had run into a brick wall. It simply would not pass from one field to the next. Despite outstanding scores in the other two phases of competition, its handler went home a bitterly disappointed man.

What the dog clearly understood from its training was that one does not go where there is no track. Because of lack of experience, the dog concluded from the drastic change of terrain that when the track scent changed, its track ended there at the edge of the grassy field.

In order to avoid problems like this, handlers can systematically train the dog to track confidently across all sorts of changes in terrain—from dirt to short grass, from wheat stubble to alfalfa, and so forth.

Whenever he can take advantage of such changes, the handler lays relatively simple tracks across them, always leaving some sort of reward (an article or a food drop) on the track ten or twenty paces past the zone of difficulty. At first the handler helps the dog carefully across the border between the two types of terrain, staying close to it and pointing out the track to it if it becomes uncertain. Later, the handler stays back a few feet on the long line, and obliges the dog to work through the transition in track scent itself.

As a result of just a little methodical training, the dog can gain great skill and confidence in tracking from one type of terrain into a vastly different type.

2. Crossing over an obstacle and then relocating the track

Many times the authors have encountered unusual obstacles while tracking. One of us was once obliged to shinny over a huge fallen tree in the midst of an FH track. The dog scrambled across and immediately recovered the track and set off down it. Even in Schutzhund III competition, dogs are not infrequently required to track across dirt roads, ditches or sharp inclines. It is best that we carefully teach our dog how to negotiate these small disturbances in track scent *before* it encounters them in a trial.

The handler lays his track across the obstacle (a dirt road, for instance) very carefully, leaving distinct footsteps all the way up to it, heavily scenting the road itself, and even laying a bait right in the middle of it. A few feet on the other side of it, he leaves an article.

The first few times that he takes his dog over such an obstacle, he helps the animal across and makes sure that it finds the article easily. Once the dog shows an understanding of its task, the handler simply gives it a lot of line. He lets the dog cross the road, cast about on the other side until it recovers the track and then follows it down to the article.

Soon the dog will develop a useful strategy for crossing obstacles without losing its composure, even when they are virtually devoid of scent.

3. Recovering the track after losing it

It is a fact of life that the dog will, on occasion, completely lose the track. When this occurs in competition, the experience is nerve-wracking for the handler, as he watches his dog cast for the track and listens behind him for the blast on the judge's whistle that will tell him that his day of competition is over. Much of the stress of having the dog go wide of the track can be reduced if we know that the dog has a strategy for recovering it.

Losing the track is expensive in terms of points, especially if the dog has to cast across a wide area to refind it. But, if it *does* recover the track and follow it out to the end, the judge will take note of its persistence and, during his critique, comment favorably on the dog's ability to work independently.

We begin teaching the dog by using a heavily baited straight track. Somewhere along it, the handler simply takes a giant step off to the right or the left and then continues parallel to his original path, again baiting each footstep as he goes.

When the dog comes down the first leg of the track to the dead end, it will indicate loss of track, and then begin to cast about. The baits on the second, parallel leg will help it to locate it easily. In addition, the handler stays close by its side to keep it from circling or casting too far back and forth. Ideally, the animal will search slowly and carefully, so that it covers the area immediately about it very efficiently and without a great deal of wasted movement that will cost it points in the trial and possibly get it even more lost than it was originally.

After the dog has learned to search efficiently, the handler gradually reduces the amount of bait on both legs of this "step-over" track. It is absolutely essential that the handler know exactly where both legs begin and end. Therefore, he should always lay his own step-overs, rather than employ a tracklayer.

One of the most useful benefits of this type of proofing is that the dog will not become stressed or anxious when it loses the track during a trial, because rather than being punished for its error, it has learned a way to rectify it.

4. Tracking surely despite adverse weather or ground conditions

Proofing for bad weather and terrain means going out to track in unpleasant conditions such as strong wind, rain or very high or low temperatures. It also means laying tracks on sandy, rough or hard-packed surfaces and in dead or newly mowed grass.

The important thing is to help the dog a great deal initially so that it can negotiate these conditions successfully and meet them without losing its composure.

In Hungary in 1985, the competitors in the world championships had been promised lush tracking fields, so everyone worried far more about the obedience and protection phases. No one in Hungary expected weather in the high 90s in late September. Neither did they expect cornfields seared by the sun. That year the dogs worked in terrible heat on dead, brown vegetation. Competitors who finished with a passing score breathed a sigh of relief, and undoubtedly they passed because they had prepared their dogs well for such adversities.

5. Ignoring cross tracks

Few of us have the opportunity to work in fields that are absolutely clean. The vast majority of available tracking sites are chronically contaminated by mice, other dogs, and scurrying rabbits, joggers or schoolchildren taking shortcuts. For this reason it is important to proof the dog on cross tracks, so that it will ignore them and continue following the tracklayer's footsteps.

Again, the handler lays a straight track for the dog, and then arranges to have a number of different types of cross tracks "cut" it—a bicyclist, a person on foot, a car, etc. It is best if, in the beginning, these cross tracks are greatly different in age than the handler's track. A few yards past the point where each cross track will cut his footsteps, the handler leaves a reward for the dog—an article or a bait.

As the dog passes over each cross track, it is allowed to, and even should, acknowledge it. However, it if begins to commit to it in any way, the handler gently stops the animal and redirects it back to the track without scolding or punishing it. As soon as the dog is back on the original footsteps, he encourages the animal to continue tracking.

Once the dog has had extensive practice and shows an understanding of the task, the handler can correct it if it commits to a cross track. A quiet "Phooey!" and a light slap on the back with the tracking line should be sufficient.

SUMMARY

To summarize our philosophy of tracking training:

First we *teach* the animal, supporting and encouraging while it learns the concepts and skills that we present. Then we *train* it, presenting problems and correcting the dog if it errs, in order to make it clear exactly what the job is. Lastly we *proof* it by presenting problems that are far harder than those it will encounter in trial.

"Joy in work, devotion to duty and to master . . ."—Max von Stephanitz

8

Obedience: Requirements of the Trial

SCHUTZHUND I OBEDIENCE TEST

Heeling on Leash (fifteen points)

The dog begins the pattern sitting at heel position. With the command "Heel!" handler and dog move forward approximately forty paces and then turn around and come back. The dog walks at its handler's left side, working with its shoulder approximately even with its master's knee. The animal will be penalized for forging ahead, crowding, lagging behind or going wide. The judge may direct the exercise, but more often the handler executes his own heeling pattern. Each pattern must contain movement at a normal, slow and rapid pace (the handler may command the dog to "Heel!" at each change of pace), and each pattern must contain a right and a left turn, an about-turn and also a halt. The about-turn is made to the left, moving directly into the dog. When the handler halts, the dog should automatically sit straight and square with its front legs even with its master's knees. After the structured heeling pattern has been completed, the team moves through a group of approximately four milling people in a loose pattern that must include one right and one left turn through the group. The team halts once while in the group, and the dog should sit automatically. The dog should be aware of the people around it, but should remain undisturbed and attentive to its handler.

Heeling off Leash (twenty points)

As the handler moves with his dog out of the crowd, he removes the leash and puts it in his pocket or around his shoulder. He walks back into the milling group and repeats the heeling exercise. At the judge's command, the team heels away from the group. When the dog and handler have gone approximately fifteen paces, a gun is fired once and then again several seconds later. The dog should not react strongly to the shots. If the dog shies from its handler's side, showing fear or stress, it will be dismissed from the trial. The animal will lose some points if it shows aggression or seems gun-sensitive. If the judge is not sure of the dog's reaction, he may have additional shots fired. The rest of the heeling pattern is the same as the heel on leash.

Sit in Motion (ten points)

Beginning from a sit at heel, the dog moves forward briskly off leash with its handler. After the team has gone at least ten paces, the handler commands his dog to "Sit!" The dog should stop and sit immediately. Without looking back or hesitating, the handler continues at a normal rate for an additional thirty paces and then turns and faces his dog. After a few seconds, he returns to his dog and walks around it to its right side. If the dog stops, but stands or downs instead of sitting on command, it will lose half the points for the exercise.

Down with a Recall (ten points)

Beginning from a sit at heel, the team moves forward off leash. After they have gone at least ten paces, the handler commands his dog to "Down!" The dog should stop and lie down immediately on command. The handler continues moving thirty additional paces and then turns and faces his dog. At the judge's signal the handler recalls his dog. The dog should come rapidly and sit straight and close in front of its handler. Then, on the handler's command, the dog finishes to the heel position. It is considered a double command if the handler uses the dog's name on the recall. The dog will lose half of the possible points if it stops on the "Down!" command but fails to lie down.

Retrieve on the Flat (ten points)

With his dog sitting at the heel position, the handler throws a dumbbell or a personal article approximately ten paces in front of the dog. He may not signal his dog to stay, as in the AKC regulations for this exercise. When commanded to do so, the dog immediately fetches the dumbbell and returns with it to its handler. Once the dog sits straight in front and presents the dumbbell, the handler removes it and commands the dog to finish to the heel position. The dog will lose points if it drops or plays with the dumbbell, or if the handler moves from his original position during the retrieve. The dog will also lose 20 percent of the exercise if its handler must give it additional commands.

Retrieve over the Meter Jump (fifteen points)

The handler, with his dog sitting at his side, stands an appropriate distance from the jump. He throws either a dumbbell or a personal article over the jump. He then commands his dog to "Hup!" As the dog clears the jump in midair, the handler may give it an additional command to take the dumbbell. The dog should retrieve the dumbbell, come back over the jump and then sit directly in front of the handler and present the dumbbell. After the handler has taken it, he commands his dog to "Heel!" and the animal finishes to heel position. Points are deducted for the following:

2 points—lightly touching the hurdle
3 points—stepping on the hurdle
4 points—dropping, mouthing or playing with the dumbbell
10 points—refusing the return jump, article retrieved
10 points—refusing the jump going out, remainder correct
10 points—jumping correctly, article not retrieved

Send Away and Down (ten points)

The dog and handler move forward briskly off leash. After a few paces, the handler signals straight ahead with his right arm and commands the dog to "Go out!" The dog should move out quickly in a straight path for at least twenty-five paces. When commanded "Down!" it should turn toward the handler and drop immediately to the ground. The handler pauses a few seconds, then walks out to the dog and steps around to the animal's right side. The exercise is complete when he commands his dog to "Sit!" Deductions will be made if the dog does not go out the proper distance or does not go straight. The dog will also lose points for dropping slowly or before the command is given.

Long Down under Distraction (ten points)

In this exercise a dog performing obedience exercises is used as a distraction for another obedience competitor. At the beginning of one dog's obedience exercise, the other dog is placed on a down stay. The handler heels the dog to the place indicated by the judge, removes the leash and downs the dog. He walks away approximately forty paces and then stands with his back to the dog. The dog must remain in the same position throughout the other dog's first six obedience exercises. It receives a fraction of its points if it remains in the down position for the first three exercises. If the dog moves approximately three yards from its original position (regardless of when), no points will be awarded for the entire exercise.

While heeling through the group, the dog should be aware of people nearby, but should remain undisturbed and attentive to its handler. (Officer Kyle Howard and "Zorro.")

Retrieve over the meter jump. (Officer P. J. Walk and "Derry.")

SCHUTZHUND II OBEDIENCE TEST

Heeling on Leash (ten points)

The dog begins the pattern sitting at the heel position. With the command "Heel!" the handler and dog move forward approximately fifty paces and then turn around and come back. The dog walks at its handler's left side, working with its shoulder approximately even with the handler's knee. The animal will be penalized for forging ahead, crowding, lagging behind or going wide. The judge may direct the exercise but more often the handler executes his own heeling pattern. Each pattern must contain movement at a normal, slow and rapid pace (the handler may command the dog to "Heel!" at each change of pace), and each pattern must contain a right and left turn, an about-turn and a halt. The about turn is made to the left, moving directly into the dog. When the handler halts, the dog should automatically sit straight and square. After the structured heeling pattern has been completed, the team moves through a group of approximately four milling people in a loose pattern that must include one right and one left turn through the group. The team halts once while in the group and the dog should sit automatically. The dog should be aware of the people around it, but should remain undisturbed and attentive to its handler.

Heeling off Leash (fifteen points)

As the handler moves with his dog out of the crowd, he removes the leash and places it around his shoulders or in his pocket. He walks back into the milling group and repeats the heeling exercise. At the judge's command, the team heels away from the group. When the dog and handler have gone approximately fifteen paces, a gun is fired once and then again a few seconds later. The dog should not react strongly to the shots. If the dog shies from its handler's side, showing fear or stress, it will be dismissed from the trial. The animal will lose some points if it shows aggression or seems gun-sensitive. If the judge is not sure of the dog's reaction, he may have additional shots fired. The rest of the heeling pattern is the same as the heel on leash.

Sit in Motion (five points)

Beginning from a sit at heel, the dog moves forward briskly off leash with its handler. After the team has gone at least ten paces, the handler commands his dog to "Sit!" The dog should stop and sit immediately. Without looking back or hesitating, the handler continues at a normal rate for an additional thirty paces and then turns and faces his dog. After a few seconds, he returns to his dog and walks around it to its right side. If the dog stops, but stands or downs instead of sitting on command, it will lose three points for the exercise.

Heeling off leash. The dog moves forward at the handler's left side, working with the dog's shoulder approximately even with the handler's knee. The dog should exhibit willingness and enthusiasm. (Dr. Gerry Pasek with Schutzhund III Labrador Retriever "Shadow.")

Down with Recall (ten points)

Beginning from a sit at heel, the dog moves forward briskly off leash with its handler. After the team has gone at least ten paces, the handler commands his dog to "Down!" The dog should stop and lie down immediately on command. The handler continues moving thirty additional paces and then turns and faces his dog. At the judge's signal the handler recalls his dog. The dog should come rapidly and sit straight and close in front of its handler. Then, on the handler's command, the dog finishes to the heel position. It is considered a double command if the handler uses the dog's name on the recall. The dog will lose half of the possible points if it stops on the "Down!" command but fails to lie down.

Retrieve a Two-pound (1,000 g.) Dumbbell on the Flat (ten points)

With his dog sitting at the heel position, the handler throws the dumbbell approximately ten paces out in front of the dog. He may not signal his dog to stay, as in the AKC regulations for this exercise. When commanded to do so, the dog immediately fetches the dumbbell and returns with it to its handler. Once the dog sits straight in front of its handler and presents the dumbbell, the handler removes it and commands the dog to finish to the heel position. The dog will lose points if it drops or plays with the dumbbell, or if the handler moves from his original position during the retrieve.

Retrieve a One-and-one-half-pound Dumbbell (650 g.) over the Meter Jump (fifteen points)

The handler, with his dog sitting at his side, stands an appropriate distance from the jump. The handler throws the smaller dumbbell over the jump. He then commands his dog to "Hup!" As the dog clears the jump in midair, the handler may give it an additional command to take the dumbbell. The dog should retrieve the dumbbell, come back over the jump and then sit directly in front of its handler with the dumbbell in its mouth. After the handler has taken it, he commands the dog to "Heel!" and the dog finishes to the heel position. Points are deducted according to the schedule for Schutzhund I. The dog will also lose 20 percent of the exercise if its handler must give it additional commands.

Retrieve over the Climbing Wall with the Dumbbell (fifteen points)

The handler, with his dog sitting at his side, stands an appropriate distance from the wall. He throws the dumbbell over the jump and then commands his dog to "Hup!" As the dog is scaling the wall, the handler may give it an additional command to take the dumbbell. The animal should scale the wall, retrieve the dumbbell, come back over the wall and sit directly in front of its handler with the dumbbell in its mouth. After the handler has taken the dumbbell, he commands the dog to "Heel!" and the dog will finish to the heel position. Points may be deducted at judge's discretion.

Send Away and Down (ten points)

The dog and handler move forward briskly off leash. After a few paces, the handler signals straight ahead with his right arm and commands the dog to "Go out!" The dog should move out quickly in a straight path for at least thirty paces. When commanded "Down!" it should turn toward the handler and drop immediately to the ground. The handler pauses a few seconds, then walks out to the dog and steps to the animal's right side. The exercise is complete when he commands his dog to "Sit!" Deductions will be made if the dog does not go out the proper distance or does not go straight and rapidly. The animal will also lose points for dropping slowly or before the command is given.

Long Down under Distraction (ten points)

In this exercise a dog performing obedience exercises is used as a distraction for another obedience competitor. At the beginning of one dog's obedience exercise, the other dog is placed on a down stay. The handler heels the dog to the place indicated by the judge, removes the leash and downs the dog. He walks approximately fifty paces away and then stands with his back to the dog. The dog must remain in the same position throughout the other dog's first six obedience exercises. The animal receives a fraction of the points if it remains in the down position for only the first three exercises. If the dog moves approximately three yards from its original position, no points will be awarded for the entire exercise.

SCHUTZHUND III OBEDIENCE TEST

Heel off Leash (ten points)

The dog begins the pattern sitting at the heel position. With the command to "Heel!" the handler and dog move forward approximately fifty paces and then turn around and come back. The dog remains at its handler's left side, working with its shoulder approximately even with its master's knee. The dog will be penalized for forging ahead, crowding, lagging behind or going wide. Each pattern must contain movement at a normal, slow and rapid pace (the handler may command the dog to "Heel!" at each change of pace), and each pattern must contain a right and a left turn, an about-turn and a halt. The about-turn is made to the left, moving directly into the dog. When the handler halts, the dog should automatically sit straight and square. After the structured heeling pattern has been completed, the team moves through a group of approximately four milling people in a loose pattern that must include one right and one left turn through the group. The team halts twice while in the group and the dog should sit automatically. The dog should be aware of the people around it, but should remain undisturbed and attentive to its handler. At the judge's command, the team moves away from the group off leash. When the dog and handler have walked approximately fifteen paces, a gun will be fired once and then again a few

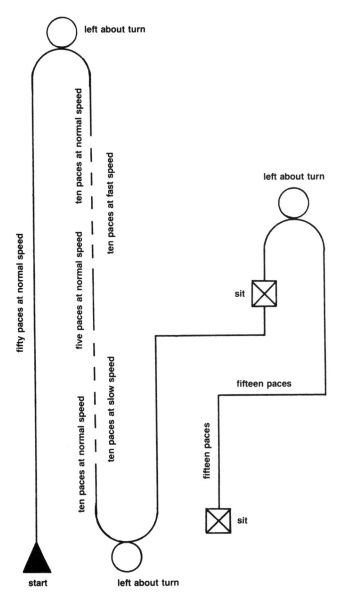

left about turn

ten paces at normal speed

ten paces at fast speed

five paces at normal speed

fifty paces at normal speed

ten paces at normal speed

ten paces at slow speed

left about turn

left about turn

sit

fifteen paces

fifteen paces

sit

start

A commonly used heeling pattern. Schutzhund I and II dogs perform the pattern twice in competition (first on leash and then off) while Schutzhund III dogs perform it only once.

seconds later. The dog should not react strongly to the shots. If the animal shies from its handler's side, showing fear or stress, it will be dismissed from the trial. The dog will lose some points if it shows aggression or seems gun-sensitive. If the judge is not sure of the dog's reaction, he may have additional shots fired. Throughout the entire Schutzhund III obedience routine the leash is left off the field.

Sit in Motion (five points)

Beginning from a sit at heel, the dog moves briskly forward off leash with its handler. After the team has gone at least ten paces, the handler commands his dog to "Sit!" The dog should stop and sit immediately. Without looking back or hesitating, the handler continues at a normal rate for an additional thirty paces and then turns and faces his dog. After a few seconds, he returns to his dog and walks around it to its right side. If the dog stops, but stands or drops instead of sitting on command, it will lose three points for the exercise.

Down with Recall (ten points)

Beginning from a sit at heel, the dog moves forward briskly off leash with its handler. After the team has gone at least ten paces, they begin to run. After an additional ten paces the dog must, upon command, lie down quickly. The handler continues without changing his pace for approximately forty paces, stops and immediately turns and faces his dog. At the judge's signal the dog is recalled to the come-fore position, then finished to the heel position.

Stand while Walking (five points)

Beginning from a sit at heel, the dog moves forward briskly off leash with its handler. After the team has gone at least ten paces, the handler commands his dog to "Stand!" The dog should stop, stand and remain in this position while the handler continues walking. The handler continues at a normal rate for an additional thirty paces and then turns and faces his dog. After a few seconds, he returns to his dog and walks around it to its right side.

Stand from a Run (ten points)

Immediately from the finish position after the walking stand, the handler and dog begin running. After at least ten paces, the handler commands his dog to "Stand!" and continues running for thirty more paces, stops and then turns and faces his dog. At the judge's signal, he recalls his dog. The dog should come in quickly and sit close and straight in front of its handler. When commanded to "Heel!" the dog finishes to the heel position.

The walking stand out of motion. (Charley Bartholomew and her "Gilly," Schutzhund III, Ring I.)

Retrieve over the climbing wall. (Photo by George Smith.)

Retrieve a Four-pound (2,000 g.) Dumbbell on the Flat (ten points)

With the dog sitting at the heel position, the handler throws the dumbbell approximately ten paces out in front of the dog. He may not signal the dog to stay, as in the AKC regulations for this exercise. When commanded to do so, the dog immediately fetches the dumbbell and returns with it to the handler. Once the dog sits straight in front of its handler and presents the dumbbell, the handler takes it and commands the dog to finish to the heel position. The dog will lose points if it drops or plays with the dumbbell, or if the handler moves from his original position during the retrieve.

Retrieve a One-and-one-half-pound (650 g.) Dumbbell over the Meter Jump (fifteen points)

The handler, with the dog sitting at his side, stands an appropriate distance from the jump. The handler throws the smaller dumbbell over the jump. He then commands his dog to "Hup!" As the dog clears the jump in midair, the handler may give it an additional command to take the dumbbell. The dog should retrieve the dumbbell and with the dumbbell in its mouth come back over the jump, and sit directly in front of the handler. After the handler has taken it, he commands the dog to "Heel!" and the dog finishes to the heel position.

Retrieve over the Climbing Wall for the Dumbbell (fifteen points)

The handler, with the dog sitting at his side, stands an appropriate distance from the wall. He throws the dumbbell over the jump and then commands his dog to "Hup!" As the dog is scaling the wall, the handler may give it an additional command to take the dumbbell. The dog should retrieve the dumbbell, come back over the wall and sit directly in front of its handler with the dumbbell in its mouth. After the handler has taken the dumbbell, he commands the dog to "Heel!" and the animal finishes to the heel position.

Send Away and Down (ten points)

The dog and handler move forward briskly. After a few paces, the handler signals straight ahead with his right arm and commands the dog to "Go out!" The dog should move out quickly in a straight path for at least forty paces. When commanded "Down!" the dog should immediately turn toward its handler and drop immediately to the ground. The handler pauses a few seconds, then walks out to his dog and steps to the animal's right side. The exercise is complete when he commands his dog to "Sit!" Deductions will be made if the dog does not go out the proper distance or does not go straight and rapidly. It will also lose points for dropping slowly or before the command is given.

Long Down under Distraction (ten points)

In this exercise a dog performing obedience exercises is used as a distraction for another obedience competitor. At the beginning of one dog's obedience exercise, the other dog is placed on a down stay. The handler heels the dog to the place indicated by the judge, commands it to "Down!" and then walks to the designated hiding place at least forty paces away. The dog must remain down through the other dog's first seven exercises to receive full points. If the dog moves approximately three yards from its original position, no points will be awarded for the entire exercise.

SCORING

To pass the obedience phase of a trial the dog must earn a minimum of seventy points out of 100. The point-total ratings are as follows:

96 to 100 points	Excellent (*Vorzüglich*)
90 to 95 points	Very Good (*Sehr Gut*)
80 to 89 points	Good (*Gut*)
70 to 79 points	Satisfactory (*Befriedigend*)
36 to 69 points	Faulty (*Mangelhaft*)
0 to 35 points	Insufficient (*Ungenügend*)

The Schutzhund dog must make an impression in obedience. It should show in every line of its body its delight in being at work with its master. (Lou Woolridge on trial day with Belgian Groenandael "Brio," Schutzhund II.)

9

An Overview of
the Obedience Phase

THE SCHUTZHUND obedience phase is continually compared to the American Kennel Club obedience competition. The reason is perhaps that many American trainers view Schutzhund from a perspective developed during many years in the AKC obedience ring. Unfortunately, this perspective sometimes leads to less than insightful comparisons between Schutzhund dogs and AKC dogs.

Viewed from the diehard AKC enthusiast's standpoint, Schutzhund dogs often lack precision, and some of them are too lighthearted and boisterous about their work. Superficial comparisons of this sort overlook the fundamental differences between the two sports.

The most obvious is the difference in scale. The Schutzhund dog does not traverse a twenty-by-forty-foot ring during the obedience routine. It traverses an entire playing field. It has far more ground to cover, and the routine is more flowing and faster paced.

More important, the Schutzhund dog is a working dog, not just an obedience dog. It is not a specialist but a generalist that is expected to display all-around talent and utility. On the same day that it competes in obedience it has two other phases in which to perform that involve many hours of training, a great number of skills to learn and some rare qualities of character.

The most important distinction between Schutzhund and AKC trials is that Schutzhund is not only a training test but also a breed test. The obedience phase is used not just to examine the dog's schooling, but its character as well. For this reason, the Schutzhund's obedience program includes two tests of nervous stability that do not appear in AKC competition: response to gunshots and heeling in a group of people.

Because the trial is a breed test, the Schutzhund judge looks as much to the dog's attitude about working as he does to the animal's precision during the exercises. The Schutzhund dog must make an impression in obedience. It should show in every line of its body its delight in being at work with its master.

According to the old German saying about obedience, "The fast dog loses points slowly, while the slow dog loses points fast." We wholeheartedly endorse this ideal. From our perspective as breeders of working dogs, the obedience phase is primarily a character test for willingness. Some of the old-time German breeders and trainers knew willingness by the term *pack drive*. They saw eager obedience as the product of the dog's intense need to belong to and associate with other social beings. We believe that all the useful work that dogs perform all over the world—from search and rescue to narcotics detection, from herding to guiding the blind—is founded upon the dog's bond to its people and its willingness to subordinate its own desires to theirs.

Furthermore, willingness is a genetic trait that is by no means automatically bestowed upon a dog when it is born. Willingness, like other character traits, is variable. Some dogs have a great deal, other dogs little or none. And it is a sad fact that, no matter how brave or beautiful or clever, a dog that is unwilling is useless to us. It is without value because we are of little value to it.

Precision is also required in the obedience phase—but not to the extent seen in the AKC ring. In AKC obedience competition trophies are won and lost on the basis of minute differences in exactitude—on inches and fractions of inches. There exist countless ways to be suddenly disqualified from competition. For example, in AKC competition it is a serious fault for the dog to bump or rub against its handler while heeling. Bumping is also a fault in Schutzhund, but a much less serious one. Furthermore, if the dog bumps through eagerness, its spirit will delight the judge and move his pencil to leniency.

Precisely because of the spirit and energy demanded on the Schutzhund field, obedience is arguably the most difficult of the three phases of the sport. In addition, every season the obedience phase becomes increasingly important in deciding the outcome of competition. For the last few years, the major trials in both the United States and Germany have been won and lost in obedience. Because many of the dogs in the top ranks of competition are nearly perfect in tracking and protection—scoring 98s, 99s and 100s—and are therefore basically equal in these phases, now it is in heeling, retrieving or jumping that championships are decided.

Why? What is the difference?

Tracking and protection training are based upon the dog's powerful and instinctive urges to eat, to hunt and to fight. The trainer's role is merely to activate the animal's urges and shape its innate behavior.

Obedience, on the other hand, is primarily inhibitory in nature. Obedience is mainly concerned with *preventing* the animal from acting like a dog; it restrains its impulses to roam and explore, to hunt and to try its strength against other dogs. It is much more artificial than either tracking or protection, and for this reason it is difficult to train obedience really well.

Good obedience depends upon creating motivation in the dog. Therefore, the animal's willingness, its eagerness to please us, is absolutely essential. We cannot do without it. In addition to this basic requirement in the dog, the animal's handler must take care to:

- use, at the proper moments, a great deal of vigorous, sincere and unselfconscious praise
- practice emotional restraint and self-control
- be patient and meticulous
- have the sense and the skill to apply the least amount of force to the animal that will accomplish his purpose

Used together in a thoughtful way, these guidelines will help to produce a dog that is lively and free-moving in obedience—a pleasure to look at and a pleasure to work with.

The great challenge is to bring to obedience something more, something of the intensity that the dog carries in bite work. We do this by harnessing the animal's *prey drive*. Later in this book we will see that a great deal of Schutzhund bite work is founded upon prey drive—the dog's urge to chase, catch and kill prey. Retrieving a ball or toy is founded on precisely the same instinct. The strong retriever does not chase a ball simply because it pleases its master, or because it has been taught to retrieve. The animal does it because it is a hunter, and the act of chasing an erratically moving object and biting it is intensely satisfying to an impulse very deep within.

Actually, the term *play retrieve* is something of a misnomer. For many dogs, especially those bred for work, retrieving is a serious endeavor, much closer in nature to hunting or aggression than it is to play. These dogs pursue the ball with an awesome intensity of purpose. This is the sort of animal we need for Schutzhund obedience because, when it chases the ball, it experiences an intensely strong physiological rush of excitement. The dog comes alive with spirit.

We call this process *arousal*, and our basic method of motivating the dog for obedience is to associate arousal with the obedience exercises, so that they are infused with its energy. We make the association through extensive use of a prey object like a ball in training, using it to reward well-performed exercises and also to help establish eye contact between handler and dog.

INDUCIVE TRAINING VERSUS COMPULSIVE TRAINING

In the past it always was (and often still is) taken for granted that some sort of physical force is required in order to train a dog. Therefore, traditional dog training was almost wholly compulsive in nature.

It is in heeling or jumping that championships are often won or lost.

Our basic method of motivating the animal is to associate prey arousal with obedience, so that the exercises are infused with its energy. (Barbara Valente and "Mucke," Schutzhund I.)

The A-frame climbing wall seen in today's Schutzhund trials is a comparatively recent invention. In von Stephanitz's time, the obstacle was vertical. This dog scales the wall at seven feet, six inches. (From von Stephanitz, *The German Shepherd Dog,* 1923.)

Compulsive training punishes and rewards the animal through the use of unpleasant stimuli. The handler punishes the dog by presenting it with something unpleasant. For example, if the animal breaks a down stay, it is corrected with a slap of the leash on its withers. The handler rewards the dog by taking away or omitting something that is unpleasant for it. For example, he shows the dumbbell to the dog, begins pinching the animal's ear and stops pinching only when the animal takes the dumbbell into its mouth.

Traditional dog training depends upon physically manipulating the animal, and this is why traditional methods are inseparable from the use of a leash. Only comparatively recently have some trainers thrown away their leashes and discovered another way to train, an inducive way.

Inducive training punishes and rewards the animal through the use of pleasant stimuli. The handler rewards the dog by presenting it with something that is pleasant. For example, he praises the animal, gives it a piece of food, or even throws the ball for it when it performs a correct, fast finish. The handler punishes the dog by taking away or omitting something that is pleasant for it. For example, he punishes a crooked come-fore by refusing to praise or feed the dog, or throw the ball for it.

Of course, in actual practice, the distinction between compulsive and inducive methods is often blurred. For instance, the distinction is unclear when the "force" used to compel the dog is very gentle, as when a handler guides a puppy into a sit with his hands and the leash. This procedure is not easily construed as unpleasant. It is also unclear when, as is customary, the handler corrects or punishes his dog, and then immediately praises and pets it a moment later. In this case we would seem to combine the two different kinds of training.

We can make the distinction in another way by examining the issue of choice, or free will. In inducive training the animal is free to choose what it will do. When told to sit, it is at liberty to instead lie down, stand or run in circles. The only constraint on its behavior is that we will reward only a sit, and all other responses will be punished by omitting the reward. In compulsive training, the dog has no choice and no free will. There is only one response possible for it. All others will be corrected—forcibly stopped before they can be gotten underway. This is what the leash is all about, and why traditional training methods have for so many years been dependent upon it or some other method of restricting the animal's freedom of choice.

In the last ten years or so this country has seen a revolution of sorts, a movement toward inducive training. It is difficult to say why it occurred so recently, because the inducive aspect of animal training was already well understood by behavioral scientists in the 1960s and even earlier.

The inducive revolution was undoubtedly influenced by the appearance of academically educated dog trainers who make a profession of helping owners of pets with behavioral problems. These behavioral therapists, as they are called, primarily use inducive techniques and normally disapprove of compulsion.

Events far from the world of working dogs may have played a role in the inducive revolution as well. In the last two decades commercial marine mammal

Inducive techniques are used, above all, in training puppies. (Susan Barwig with "Quella.")

training facilities such as Sea World have gained tremendous prominence. The trainers at these facilities have mastered a very high form of the art of inducive training. In marine mammal training, inducive expertise is a necessity because a dolphin deep in its tank has nearly unlimited freedom of choice. It is impractical, and many people believe unethical, to try to compel it to do anything. All that remains is to reward it when the animal does as desired and omit reward when it does not. Some of these experts in inducive technique have crossed over to the world of dog training, most notably Karen Pryor.

Inducive technique came on the scene in the late 1970s and early 1980s. A small group of people immediately embraced it. Old-time "snatch-and-jerk" dog trainers scoffed, and became even more adamant in their insistence that reliable, competitive training could only be accomplished with compulsion.

The debate quickly became reactionary. Both sides entrenched, and there appeared two groups that vociferously espoused pure forms of each method. Thus, inducive trainers said that *they did not need force*, while compulsive trainers insisted that *they were not using force*.

Then, as so often happens, it became evident that the conflict in theory was not as insurmountable as we thought and that, all along, the most consistently successful dog trainers were using a combination of both methods.

Nowadays, a seemingly obvious conclusion has been reached. We do not see induction and compulsion as separate, distinct and incompatible systems of training, but instead as parts of the same system. Induction and compulsion serve different purposes. They are each used at different stages in the dog's development, and also at different stages in the teaching of any given exercise.

Inducive methods are used to introduce dogs to new skills and concepts (to *teach*). They are used to convey understanding to the animal. Furthermore, they produce better motivation for most tasks, and a better, more pleasing appearance in almost all tasks. They are used, above all, in training puppies, but they are also invaluable in dealing with sensitive adults.

Compulsion and force are used only when the dog has attained a precise understanding of the skill expected of it (to *train*), and only when it has established a habitual, lively pleasure in performing it. Compulsive methods are used to polish the dog's performance and make it absolutely reliable.

However, the conversion from an inducive to a compulsive method is by no means inevitable. It is instead a function of the animal's character. Some dogs are too soft and sensitive to support much force. Other dogs are so willing and talented that force is not really needed to polish the majority of their exercises. In the case of an animal like this, if it comprehends what it is that we want from it, then it happily and reliably does it. This dog therefore can and should be handled inducively all its life.

The proportions of compulsion versus induction in a training program are not solely a function of the dog's stage in training or its character; they are also a function of the handler's character. Some people are simply not comfortable using force in dog training, while others see it as the only way. It is perhaps best to view the inducive versus compulsive question as a continuum that runs from pure inducive to pure compulsive, with all trainers falling somewhere on that continuum according to their preferences. Quite simply, it is a question of temperament. For instance, of the two authors of this book, one regards the conversion to compulsion as a necessary and desirable development, while the other regards the conversion to compulsion as a last resort, the thing to be done when all inducive strategies have failed.

EQUIPMENT NEEDED FOR OBEDIENCE TRAINING

Leash

For convenience in making quick, precisely timed corrections, the obedience leash is much shorter (two to three feet long) and much lighter (½ inch) than the all-purpose six-foot lead.

Correction Collar

There are many different correction collars that can be used for obedience training, ranging in severity from a plain leather or nylon webbing choke collar to a tightly fitted pinch collar. The choice of collar depends upon the character of the dog and the temperament and ability of the trainer. It is interesting to note that, although it does not look harsh, the nylon cord choke collar—simply a thin cord connecting two steel rings—is, in our opinion, among the most punishing of collars and must be used with great care.

As a general rule, it is far better to have a powerful collar, and to use this collar precisely and with little physical effort, than it is to be ''undergunned'' and compelled to use a great portion of one's physical strength in order to dissuade the animal from some misguided intention.

Prey Object

To bring the dog into spirit, some sort of prey object like a ball or kong is indispensable. For the dog, chasing and retrieving a thrown toy is analogous to chasing fleeing prey. Retrieving, therefore, excites and arouses the animal and provides a ready source of energy for work.

Revolver

A .22 caliber starter pistol (firing either crimped blanks or the longer blanks packed with wadding) is the most common revolver used by American Schutzhund clubs. However, there is sometimes great variability in the types of gun used in trials, ranging up to .38 caliber and 9mm. Therefore, during training the handler should expose the dog to as many different types of gunshot as possible. Starter pistols are available from a number of the training equipment vendors.

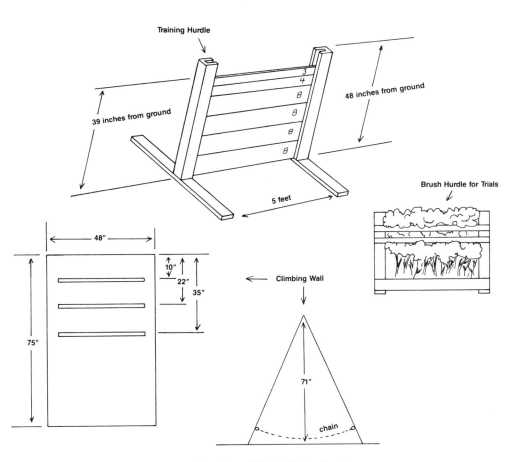

Training Hurdle

39 inches from ground

48 inches from ground

3/4

8

8

8

8

5 feet

Brush Hurdle for Trials

48″

10″

22″

35″

75″

Climbing Wall

71″

chain

One-Meter Hurdle and Scaling Wall (39 inches)

The hurdle and wall are normally built by Schutzhund club members. See the illustration above. Hurdles used in sanctioned Schutzhund trials are normally brush jumps and topped with either vegetation or broom bristles. Training hurdles, however, are made with wooden slats so as to be adjustable for height. The scaling wall is most commonly made of ⅝- or ¾-inch plywood and is adjustable for height.

Dumbbells

The dumbbells used in Schutzhund are made of hard woods and are specifically weighted. The best and more durable ones are made in one piece, lathed out of a solid block of wood. They are available from a number of vendors in the United States. The various sizes and their uses are:

14-ounce dumbbell—Schutzhund I retrieve and jump
1½-pound dumbbell—Schutzhund II and III jump
2-pound dumbbell—Schutzhund II retrieve
4-pound dumbbell—Schutzhund III retrieve

We begin teaching puppies their obedience exercises as early as eight or nine weeks. With a handful of food and a steadying hand on the loin, the pup can quickly be induced to stand and stay. (Officer Jack Lennig with "Seth.")

The net effect of vigorous prey-oriented play on the obedience field will be to teach the dog an intense arousal response. (Stewart Hilliard with cross-bred Laekenois "Ufo," Schutzhund I.)

10

Obedience:
Basic Training

THE TRADITIONAL WISDOM handed down from Germany is that one should never begin obedience training a Schutzhund dog before the animal is at least one year old and both biting hard and tracking confidently.

Protection and tracking are—in contrast to obedience—somewhat independent activities. In a sense, the dog tracks on its own and bites on its own. In both these phases we are forced to rely upon the animal's initiative to carry it through a task that we have prepared it for but in which we cannot help.

According to tradition, early obedience training kills the dog's initiative, and should therefore be avoided. Some trainers, both German and American, carry this idea to an extreme. They neither obedience-train their young dogs nor give them any commands that might inhibit them, not even "No!" They forbid their puppies nothing, and basically the animals run wild, free of any obligation, during their first year of life. These trainers believe that the dog must first develop adult strength and resiliency before it can withstand the stress of obedience training.

Their assumption is that obedience training is a demoralizing experience and, in the context of traditional German training methods, this was often the case. If we think about it for a moment, we realize that a young adult dog that has never been forbidden anything in its life, and is completely new to the idea that anyone might place restraints upon its behavior, is hardly likely to enjoy obedience. Not only has this animal never learned to take pleasure in doing for its handler but also, because it has now grown tough and headstrong, a great deal of force will be required to obtain its "cooperation." German training techniques are therefore traditionally very forceful, and only the most willing dogs retain their spirit and liveliness when suddenly encountering these methods after a puppyhood spent in freedom.

The drawback in waiting until the dogs are one year of age before beginning obedience is that this practice virtually wastes the entirety of the animals' young lives, when they are at their most impressionable. When they could be learning to be willing and eager, they are instead learning to be willful and independent. When they could be learning how to learn from us, how to quickly grasp what we teach them, they are instead learning to be headstrong and inflexible.

At the same time, it is sheer folly to begin obedience training a young puppy using conventional compulsive techniques. However, the inducive training revolution provided knowledge and techniques that enable us to begin meaningful work on obedience early in the dog's life, with absolutely no fear that we will damage the animal's ultimate potential for character.

We therefore begin teaching puppies their obedience exercises as early as eight or nine weeks of age. At this time we also begin rudimentary tracking and the rag play that will eventually lead to formal agitation. All the obedience training is inducive. The pups are rewarded by being patted, played with and fed tidbits, and they are punished by *not* being patted, played with and fed.

This does not mean that the youngsters are not disciplined in everyday life. In order to not resent and fear discipline, the pups must experience it as a normal, consistent and predictable part of their lives from the very beginning. They are housetrained, physically punished for mouthing and physically punished for indiscriminate chewing. All punishment is impartial—that is to say it does not take the form of vengeance or arise from anger. In addition, it is consistent and predictable so that the puppies know when they are in trouble and why, and it is always appropriate in severity to very young dogs.

Unfortunately, this book does not allow the space for a treatment of puppy training. But we do describe in some detail how we introduce older dogs to obedience training. Because we perform the teaching phase of any dog's training entirely inducively—no matter what its age—the reader should be able to get an idea of how we perform the same work with puppies.

GOAL 1: The dog will learn to play before it learns to work.

Our discussion of obedience training is based on the assumption that we are working with a naive adult—an animal that knows nothing of obedience, but is crazy about its handler and plays intensely and joyfully. This animal, no different than a puppy, should be worked inducively in the beginning—while it is learning to understand the concepts and skills involved in training—and then more and more compulsively, if necessary, in order to hone its performance and make it absolutely reliable.

Important Concept for Meeting the Goal

Conditioning arousal to the context of obedience

When we acquire a new adult dog, or when our puppy grows to an age when we will begin training it formally in obedience on the practice field, our first task is to train the dog to become aroused in response to the context of the training field. Quite simply, before we ever teach the dog to work on the field, we teach it to play.

The handler arrives at the field and, rather than bringing the animal out on leash and then standing around with it so that they both gradually become bored, he leaves the dog in a crate or in the car until it is time to work. Always be aware that dogs need adequate shade and water and should not be put in cars where ventilation is limited.

When ready, the handler goes to the dog, excitedly brings it out of the car, runs onto the training field and then plays with it vigorously for three or four minutes. The two can wrestle and run, or play tug-of-war with a sack, but most of all their play centers around some kind of prey object that will be included in all further obedience training. The authors prefer to use large rubber balls or kong toys.

All retrieving is entirely in play, meaning there is no control of the dog by command. The animal is not heeled onto the field or off, it is not made to stay while the ball is thrown and then sent to get it and it is never told "No!" If the animal must be restrained, this is done by physically taking its collar.

After a few minutes of vigorous play, the handler returns the dog, on the run, to the crate or car. In a while he will return and repeat the whole process. A visit to the Schutzhund club thus involves for the animal a period of waiting punctuated by brief, extremely arousing and gratifying trips onto the field.

After a few days or weeks, the net effect will be to teach the dog an intense arousal response in association with the context of the obedience field. When it comes out of the car or crate at the Schutzhund club, the dog will automatically be in tremendous spirit. This spirit will be our main fuel, our primary source of energy for work.

GOAL 2: The dog will sit on command.

In obedience training, we make use of four major classes of stimuli in order to reward and punish the animal's behavior:

1. Praise and petting
2. Food
3. Prey objects
4. Physical punishment (correction)

Praise and petting are always used in conjunction with three other classes of stimuli. Taking this into account, we present the schooling of each of the basic obedience skills in three stages:

1. Work for food
2. Work for the prey object
3. Pairing of the prey object with compulsion

The work for food stage is part of the pure inducive phase of training—the teaching phase—in which we bring the animal to understand a command and the skill associated with it. This work is normally performed at home, away from the excitement and distractions of the training field. Food produces a moderate level of arousal and the dog, although excited, is easily managed and manipulated.

The work for the prey object stage begins after we have taught the animal a number of skills, and also after we have conditioned it to become aroused in response to the context of the obedience field. We are still in the teaching phase (the work is still almost entirely inducive), but in place of the desire for food we have substituted the prey motivation associated with retrieving the ball. The dog's level of arousal is much higher, providing abundant energy for work, but also making the animal harder to manage and manipulate.

Pairing is the stage at which we bring compulsion into the picture—the training phase. In pairing we begin for the first time to use force to correct errors, enforce immediate responses to commands and increase precision. However, the force is paired or coupled with the use of a ball. For example, we might correct the dog sharply three times in a row for slow sits; if, on the fourth attempt, the animal sits quickly and there is no need for a correction, we throw the ball for it. The advantage is that prey arousal desensitizes the animal, making it hard and resilient. As a result the corrections, while retaining their power to alter the dog's behavior, do not depress its spirit.

Again, in all three stages of training the reward properties of the food or ball are enhanced through being accompanied by a great deal of verbal praise, encouragement and petting.

As we train them, the obedience exercises progress independently of each other—they are taught separately. But there is no need to perfect one before progressing to another. For instance, we may be teaching a particular animal to heel at home for food while we are working it on the finish at the training field and perfecting the sit, down and stand by pairing leash corrections with the ball.

Important Concepts for Meeting the Goal

1. Sitting for food
2. Sitting for the ball
3. Pairing compulsion with the ball

110

1. Sitting for food

It is a comparatively simple matter to sit the dog by making use of its orientation toward food. The handler lets the dog smell a very small piece of food in his hand, and then lifts the hand up and over the animal's head toward its rear, at the same time commanding the dog to "Sit!" The dog will strive for the food, jumping up at it and perhaps pawing or barking. The handler ignores all undesired behaviors (remember, the dog must have free choice in the teaching phase of obedience!) and waits, signaling with his hand and occasionally repeating the "Sit!" command. Eventually—out of puzzlement if for no other reason—the animal will sit and the handler immediately feeds it, at the same time praising and petting it.

It is a relatively simple matter to teach the stay by feeding the dog several times in succession, pausing a moment or two between each reward. Once the animal is sitting the handler commands "Stay!" He holds the food high over the dog's head to provide a focus for the animal and keep it still. Then, after perhaps three or four seconds, he bends down, feeds the dog and again commands it to "Stay!" The handler performs several of these brief stays and then releases the dog with the command "OK!" and praises it.

As training progresses we can easily prolong the stay to thirty seconds or a minute by waiting a little longer each time before feeding the animal.

2. Sitting for the ball

Once the dog sits instantly on command and stays put, waiting for the release, we can begin working the sit with the prey object.

Just as he did before in order to condition arousal to the context of training, the handler runs his dog excitedly out onto the field and begins to play with the dog using the ball. At some point when the animal is very stimulated, the handler holds the ball up out of reach and commands the dog to "Sit!" Because the context is different, and because the animal is so much more aroused now than it was in the work for food, it may not do so immediately. The dog will probably leap and bark and strive for the prey object for a while, but eventually it will sit. The instant that it does so, the handler throws the ball for it.

When the dog returns with the ball, the handler plays with it a while more, perhaps sitting the dog two or three more times before taking it back to the car. The animal will gradually become quicker and quicker to sit when it hears the command, and also its sits will be energized by the arousal of prey motivation.

It is here that we begin the important work of coupling retrieving, and the intense excitement that it brings, with obedience.

3. Pairing compulsion with the ball

As training progresses the dog will learn to switch from a frenzy of leaping and barking in one instant to a tightly coiled and energized sit in the next. The animal will begin gaining the ability to hold its energy in check, guiding it into the behaviors its handler indicates in order to obtain the object of its desire—the ball in its master's hand.

However, the dog's excitement will interfere with precision. It will frequently make errors, such as jumping at the ball after the command has been given instead of sitting immediately, or breaking the sit on those occasions when it is carried away by its enthusiasm.

We clean up these errors and polish the sit and the stay by pairing compulsion with the ball. The handler uses a leash in one hand to correct the dog into a quick, clean sit and then make it stay perfectly in place. At the same time, he shows the dog the ball with the other hand in order to preoccupy it so that it is not upset or inhibited by the corrections. As soon as he has what he wants from the animal, the handler releases it with an "OK!" while simultaneously dropping the leash and throwing the ball for the dog.

GOAL 3: The dog will down on command.

Along with the recall, the down is one of the most important commands in obedience. Through the course of training, the down takes on a very powerful character. It is the command we use as the last resort to control the animal. If it wants to fight another dog, we down it. If it refuses to let one of our guests into the house, we down it. If the dog habitually rebites after the out, we teach it to release the sleeve and then automatically lie down at the agitator's feet.

Although it is to become a very compelling command, we must introduce the down inducively, rather than with force.

Important Concepts for Meeting the Goal

1. Downing for food
2. Downing for the ball
3. Pairing compulsion with the ball

1. Downing for food

In the beginning, we always down the dog from a sit, never from a standing position. Once the dog is sitting, the handler does not feed it but instead encloses a few tidbits in his hand so that the animal cannot take the food but only smell it, and then places his hand on the end of the dog's nose to call its attention to it. A hungry dog will "glue" itself to the hand, snuffling and licking at the food. The handler then lowers his hand very slowly to a spot on the ground about six inches in front of the dog's forefeet. The animal will follow with its head and, in the effort to get the food, crouch so that its elbows touch the ground. If it stands instead, the handler merely lifts his hand up high so that the dog sits again, and then he tries again to get the animal to lie down by lowering his hand to the ground. When, eventually, the dog downs, the handler feeds it several pieces of food in a row and then releases it with the "OK!" command.

The handler begins by stimulating the dog with the ball.

Suddenly the handler commands "Sit" and corrects the animal sharply, if necessary. The dog's excitement and preoccupation with the ball will prevent any inhibition or upset as a result of the correction.

The instant the dog sits, the handler throws the ball.

In order to get a stay the handler, rather than trying to stand up, which will almost certainly attract the dog up out of its down, instead remains kneeling. He downs the animal and feeds it one piece of food and then, with the command "Stay!" he very quickly shifts his hand and the food it contains away from the dog. Keeping the hand near the ground, he holds it at arm's length out in front of the dog in order to provide a focal point and keep the animal still. He pauses for one instant and then, before the dog breaks the down and moves toward the food, he quickly shifts his hand back to the animal's head and feeds it.

The dog will soon learn that the down, like the sit, must be held until its handler releases it.

2. Downing for the ball

Now we are ready to add the down to our play sessions on the field. In the midst of retrieving, the handler occasionally asks the dog to first sit and then lie down in order to get the ball. The animal will initially be reluctant to drop when it is so excited, but it will soon learn that the faster it hits the ground the quicker its handler will throw the ball.

The handler can then begin shuttling the dog from sit to down and back to sit again, and also downing it from a standing position without first sitting it.

3. Pairing compulsion with the ball

Just as with the sit, after a while the handler begins to insist on near-perfect work, so that the dog downs on precisely the spot where it heard the command and in exactly the same orientation, so that there is no delay before it lies down and no skewing of its body as it does so.

The handler can experiment with various forms of compulsion in order to bring this about. A leash correction down at the ground and back toward the dog's rear end can work well; with some dogs a quick slap on the skull between the ears is effective. However, the handler should absolutely avoid trying to push, crush or wrestle the dog to the ground because, unless this is done with overwhelming force, it just breeds resistance.

As always, when the dog does as we require, the handler releases it with "OK!" and throws the ball for it.

GOAL 4: The dog will hold the long down.

So far, we have worked the down as a spirit exercise. The handler used the ball to teach the dog to lie down as dynamically as possible, and to remain energized in the down, like a coiled spring.

Now, however, we have the long down to worry about. During the dog's obedience performance it will be required to lie down on a spot indicated by the judge and remain there for approximately ten minutes, despite the presence of another dog–handler team working the field, and despite two gunshots. Rather than aroused, for the long down we need the dog calm and rock-steady.

Important Concepts for Meeting the Goal

1. Forcing the stay
2. Habituating the dog to gunshots
3. Combining gunshots with the down stay

1. Forcing the stay

We begin to work seriously on the down stay only after the dog lies down quickly and eagerly on command. Teaching the down stay involves physical punishment. We will be obliged to make use of compulsion in order to make the ''Stay!'' command a strong and vivid one for the dog.

We begin by concentrating on the ''break'' itself, the act of rising from the down without permission. By standing near the dog on the correction leash the handler can punish the animal as soon as it stirs with a quick jerk on the leash and a ''No!''—making crystal clear to it that it must not move from the down.

We proof the stay by putting the dog down in very distracting or stimulating circumstances (among a group of other dogs running free, for example). The handler remains near the dog and watches it closely, ready to correct it in the act of getting up.

Sooner or later the handler will have to walk away from his dog and out of sight. With the dog all alone on the field like this and off leash, the context of the exercise will be completely different. Provided with some enticing distraction, like a ball thrown for another dog, the animal will be sure to break the stay at least once. Of course, when it does, it is impossible to catch it in the act. We will instead be forced to punish it after the fact.

The handler does so calmly and quietly. He does not scream with anger and run at the dog to take vengeance upon it. This is neither necessary nor advantageous. By charging at the animal we risk frightening it and making it shy away from us. Above all, we risk teaching it to run away in order to avoid correction. If the dog learns to wait until its handler leaves it and then breaks the down stay and runs about the field, avoiding anyone who might catch and correct it, then we will have created a serious training problem for ourselves.

Instead the handler sharply tells the dog ''No!'' at the instant that it gets up from the down, in order to mark for the animal the exact moment where it went wrong. Then he strides calmly over to the dog and lays hold of it by the scruff of the neck forcefully but not violently, drags it bodily all the way back to the spot it was left to stay and mashes it back into the down, taking little care for the dog's comfort or dignity in the process. He then lets go of the animal, turns on his heel and walks away again. During the entire procedure, he says only two words: ''No!'' when the dog gets up, and ''Stay!'' as he turns the animal loose after the correction.

The correction itself, while unpleasant for the animal, is not violent or

For the long down the dog must be calm and rock-steady (and sound under gunfire). (Howard Glicksman's V Igor von Noebachtal, Schutzhund III, FH.)

The handler uses a piece of food in the right hand to lead the animal into a stand.

vengeful. The handler depends upon persistence rather than retribution to convince the dog that it is in its best interests to stay where it is left. As many times as the dog breaks, the handler calmly and forcefully drags it back and mashes it down, a little more harshly each time. Eventually the animal will give up and hold the down stay in spite of the distractions we offer it, and then the handler goes to it and praises it.

2. Habituating the dog to gunshots

For a steady dog with good character, gunshots are not frightening or in any way a problem—certainly nothing it must be trained to withstand. However, in dog training it always pays to be careful. Once created, problems with sound sensitivity can be maddeningly persistent and even insurmountable.

Therefore, we take some trouble introducing a dog with even a very sound character to the gun, and definitely not in the context of a down stay where it has nothing to think about but the gunfire. Instead, we introduce the gun during play.

The handler brings his dog onto the field and begins to arouse it and play with it using a ball. When the animal is very excited, an assistant fires the gun several times from a distance of seventy-five to 100 yards. The handler watches his dog closely, and if the animal shows any sign of a startled response, he waves the assistant even farther away. Only when the dog shows absolutely no sensitivity to the sound of the gun will the assistant begin to advance, coming progressively closer to the dog as he shoots the gun. After just a few training sessions, he should be able to fire the shots just fifteen or twenty feet away while the handler keeps the animal preoccupied with vigorous play.

3. Combining gunshots with the down stay

Once the dog appears to be totally oblivious of the sound of the gun during play, we are ready to fire the gun over it during a down stay. However, to avoid any potential problem, in the beginning we take two precautions. First, the handler remains close to his dog and watches it for any sign of anxiety in response to the shots. Second, the assistant goes back out to 100 yards to fire the first few shots, advancing toward the dog only when the handler tells him to.

GOAL 5: The dog will stand on command.

It is important to teach the stand right from the beginning, rather than wait until the animal is two years old and ready to advance from Schutzhund II to Schutzhund III. Too often, we delay introducing the stand until the last few weeks before the dog's first Schutzhund III appearance.

The choice of command is also a consideration. The two most obvious choices—"Stand!" or "Stay!"—are not ideal because they begin with the same sibilant consonant as "Sit!" and are therefore likely to be confused with it. Consequently, we use the command "Back!" for the stand.

Important Concepts for Meeting the Goal

1. Standing for food
2. Standing for the ball
3. Forcing the stand

1. Standing for food

At first we bring the dog to a stand only from the sit. The handler sits the animal and then, with a piece of food, he leads the dog forward one step from the sit, at the same time commanding "Back!" Once the dog is standing, he feeds it, steadying the animal if necessary with a hand on its loin and against its stifle.

Soon all that will be necessary to bring the dog to a stand will be a small gesture that leads the animal out of the sit or down. Over time, we then progressively "fade" the hand signal out, so that the animal stands in response to the voice command alone.

2. Standing for the ball

Of all the obedience skills, we make little use of prey motivation for rewarding the stand. This is because the stand is inherently less stable than either the sit or the down. All the dog needs to do to break the stand is to take a tiny step with one foot. Once it takes this step it is then natural for it to take another. In short, the stand easily turns into a walk!

Therefore, we try to keep the animal's response to this command very calm and quiet. We do not incorporate prey arousal into the stand because any excitement or strong attraction toward the handler will pull at the dog irresistibly, making it take that first tiny step.

Therefore, we reward the dog for stands only with food, praise and petting, not the ball.

3. Forcing the stand

Polishing the dog's stand with force is a ticklish proposition. Because of the animal's previous schooling on the sit and down, it will tend to quickly do one or the other any time we "get after it" and the dog becomes confused. We must find a way to use force in such a way that it teaches the dog to freeze, to lock its feet into their tracks when it hears the "Back!" command.

We concentrate particularly on stopping forward motion—getting the animal to halt and stand instantly. For this purpose a slap of the handler's foot broadside against the animal's forechest works quite well. Leash corrections, on the other hand, usually do not work because the dog strongly associates them with the sit and the down.

During training for the stand exercise, the handler can use a flank strap in order to prevent the dog from sitting or lying down in response to a correction.

The handler runs the dog onto the field, plays with it a little and executes a sit or down or two. Then, with the ball in hand, he turns slowly in place or walks backward so that the dog, whose attention is riveted upon the ball, follows him. Abruptly the handler commands "Back!" and taps the animal gently on the chest with his foot in order to stop its forward progress. Any movement of the paws, fidgeting or creeping forward will be corrected with this same soft but smart rap of the foot.

If reflexive downing or sitting in response to the correction is a persistent problem, the handler can try using a *flank strap,* a cord tied snugly around the animal's loin. The handler can prevent the animal from dropping its hindquarters when it is corrected by applying a gentle tug on the flank strap.

GOAL 6: The dog will finish quickly and precisely.

There are two possible types of finish. In the traditional Schutzhund finish the dog goes around its handler to the heel position. In recent years more and more Schutzhund dogs have been taught the military finish, in which the dog flips to its handler's left side directly from the come-fore position.

The military finish is much more difficult to teach because the dog must learn exactly where heel is and then it must also learn the totally unnatural crabbing movement required to get it there. In the traditional finish the dog, by virtue of the fact that it goes around, winds up at heel basically parallel to its handler. All that is needed is to stop its forward progress and get it to sit. In contrast, a dog that does a military finish must turn its body 180 degrees and then line itself up as exactly as possible with its handler.

Despite the added difficulty, we invariably teach our dogs the military finish because it teaches the animals such a complete understanding of where the heel position is.

Important Concepts for Meeting the Goal

1. Finishing for food
2. Finishing for the ball
3. Pairing compulsion with the ball

1. Finishing for food

The handler begins by sitting his dog and then stepping around in front of it so that the dog is in the come-fore position. He interests the animal in the food enclosed in his right hand, and then abruptly steps backward with the command "Heel!" In the same motion he turns at the waist and draws his hand, and the dog with it, off to his left and as far back behind him as possible. Then he steps forward again to his original spot, looping his hand in toward his hip so that the dog turns toward him and steps forward to the heel position.

The instant the dog is precisely at heel, exactly parallel with the handler and even with his knee, the handler stops the dog and sits it by lifting his hand abruptly straight up, so that the dog's eyes and head lift and its hindquarters drop; the handler simultaneously commands it to "Sit!"

2. Finishing for the ball

The hardest thing about the military finish is inducing the dog to get its body turned all the way around, so that it is parallel with its handler. In the beginning we do this by getting the animal to spring well back past its master in order to give itself room to turn. Later, when the animal is a polished obedience dog, we will expect it to do it by "flipping" to heel—jumping into the air toward its handler's left shoulder, flipping its hindquarters around under it and landing like a cat at the master's left knee.

Both of these methods of returning to the heel position depend upon one thing, energy, and that is where the ball comes in. Once the dog is finishing well with little help from the handler and shows a good understanding of exactly where the heel position is, we begin to work with the ball.

The handler plays with the dog, gets it very excited and wound up and then abruptly sits it. Before the dog's excitement wanes the handler steps quickly in front of the animal to the come-fore position, shows it the ball in his right hand and commands it to "Heel!" while simultaneously sweeping the hand up and off to his left. The dog will leap after it, its momentum carrying it well behind its handler, and then turn around and jump forward to the heel position. The handler sits the dog precisely on the right spot by raising the ball up high near his left shoulder, lifting the dog's eyes and head and dropping its hindquarters.

3. Pairing compulsion with the ball

Despite the precision the dog learned while finishing for food, the pull of the ball will be too strong and will tend always to draw the dog's head in toward the handler and make the hindquarters swing wide, so that rather than being precisely straight at heel the animal is instead crooked.

We cure this problem, and put the finishing touches on the finish, with force. Just as before, the handler finishes the dog with the ball but, when the animal reaches the heel position and before it sits, the handler strikes it sharply and quickly with the flat of his left hand on the left hip. The animal will flinch away from the slap, draw its hindquarters in toward the handler's feet and sit tight and straight. The handler then rewards it with a quick toss of the ball.

GOAL 7: The dog will heel precisely and with spirit.

For the average dog owner the "Heel!" command is of little importance. He makes far more use of "Come!" and "Down!" and some sort of loose walk

The military finish for the ball. The handler teaches the dog to spring into the air by snapping the ball up toward his left shoulder and giving the "Heel" command.

on leash command. The fact is that heeling is not a terribly practical skill, as we teach it for competition. The proof of this is that a competitive dog trainer avoids using his dog's heeling in everyday life if at all possible, for fear of wearing the polish off it.

Heeling is, pure and simple, an attention exercise. We use it to create attentiveness and absolute obedience in the dog, and in trial we use it to exhibit to the judge how we have been able to create this attentiveness and obedience without killing the animal's liveliness.

Important Concepts for Meeting the Goal

1. Heeling for food
2. Heeling for the ball
3. Pairing compulsion with the ball
4. Teaching the Schutzhund about-turn
5. Heeling in the group
6. Heeling under gunfire

1. Heeling for food

In order to teach the dog to walk at heel, we must be able to attract it and draw it along with us as we move. We accomplish the attraction by using food.

The handler begins with his dog sitting at heel. Holding the food enclosed in his right hand, he reaches the hand across his body and touches it to the animal's nose so that the dog can smell the food but not take it. Then with a bright, encouraging "Heel!" command he steps smartly off into a tight turn to his right.

As he goes, he holds his hand and the food it contains down low and just ahead of his left hip so that, as the dog pursues it, the animal will move perfectly along at heel. The handler continues around in a small circle, ruffling the dog's head and neck with his left hand and praising it extravagantly with, "Good! Heel! Good dog!"

When he reaches his starting point, the handler stops abruptly, commands "Sit!" and lifts the hand with food in it sharply up, so that the dog quickly sits straight at heel without forging or swinging in toward the handler. If necessary, the handler can give a little tap with his left hand on the dog's left flank to gather the animal in tight as it sits. The handler then feeds the dog, pats it and sets off quickly into another right-handed circle, perhaps feeding the dog a tidbit or two as they move along.

For the first few training sessions, the handler practices only small, right-handed circles while heeling. Later he begins walking a straight line with a right about-turn at each end (like the path that a sentry walks). Eventually, he will expand the heeling patterns into rectangles and figure eights, taking care to move quickly and talk excitedly to the dog to keep it moving along tightly at heel.

2. Heeling for the ball

When the dog is heeling precisely and well for short periods of time, we begin to increase its animation and the intensity of its focus on its master by going to the ball, which the handler holds in his hand in place of the food. Instead of feeding the dog as the reward for good work, the handler gives it the ball every now and then, throwing it quickly against the ground so that it bounces a short distance ahead with the animal in hot pursuit.

The result will actually be less accurate work. The dog, aroused by the sight of the ball, will probably "mob" its handler somewhat during heeling, leaping against him and bumping in its eagerness to get the prey object.

This unruliness is fine. If the animal heels happily, with intense concentration upon its handler and approximately at heel, we can at any time easily get it down on the ground and teach it to be more precise. If, on the other hand, the dog learns to heel precisely but with that hangdog look, we will be put to endless trouble in the effort to bring it back into spirit. At this stage in training, the only real concession that the handler makes for the sake of accuracy is that he makes a point of never throwing the ball for the dog unless it is on the ground with all four feet and heeling reasonably precisely.

3. Pairing compulsion with the ball

We can sometimes obtain extremely good results in heeling using entirely inducive methods. However, with the vast majority of dogs we must eventually resort to using the leash to polish this skill.

The handler corrects his dog for inattentiveness of any kind with instantaneous right turns or right about-turns accompanied by sharp jerks on the collar. He corrects going wide with right-handed turns and circles and gentle corrections, combined with encouragement and praise when the dog closes up to heel. He corrects crooked or slow sits with abrupt halts and instantaneous corrections upward and back for the sit. He corrects forging with tight, somewhat punishing left-handed circles in which he presses in on top of the dog, banging into it with knees and feet until the animal comes back into station.

The trick is to make the dog precise, but without losing the delightful spirit it showed when its work was unruly. Therefore, the harder the handler must be on the dog in order to polish the heeling, the more frequently he brings the ball out and plays with the animal. Still using the leash, the handler keeps the dog perfectly in station while the animal learns the changes of pace—from normal to slow to normal to fast and back to normal.

We prefer sudden changes of pace to the slow, gradual transitions that many trainers use to make the changes easy for the dog and keep it in station. Fast transitions are difficult, and we use them because they keep the dog's interest and require it to watch its handler closely. In addition, fast transitions show the judge that the dog is really working instead of just daydreaming at heel.

Heeling is, pure and simple, an attention exercise. (Janet Birk and "Jason," Schutzhund III.)

Once the dog is heeling well for food, we begin to increase animation and intensity of focus by introducing the ball.

In the Schutzhund about-turn the handler turns to the left while the dog turns to the right.

4. Teaching the Schutzhund about-turn

The Schutzhund about-turn is utterly different from the AKC about-turn. In Schutzhund the handler turns to the left into his dog, while the dog turns to the right, going entirely around its handler and back to heel.

The most straightforward way to introduce the about-turn is to simply guide the dog around with the leash, changing it from one hand to the other behind one's back. The handler can also use the ball to lead the animal around the turn, switching the toy from one hand to the other. If the handler makes his turn smoothly and decisively, the dog will quite naturally go around.

It is common to see dogs in competition that run wide on their about-turns or come around slowly. In training, their handlers often accentuate the problem by slowing down and pausing a beat in the middle of the turn in order to give the dog time to catch up.

Instead of pausing a beat, the handler should actually speed up in order to teach his dog to hurry. He should snap a fast about-turn and then sprint forward five or six steps. The dog will be left behind and will hurry to catch up. When the animal comes perfectly into station, the handler throws the ball for it. The animal will soon pick up the habit of hurrying through the about-turns.

5. Heeling in the group

The group poses difficulties only for dogs of unsound character. These animals are nervous in the group because they are afraid of the people who comprise it. For dogs of sound character, the group is merely another distraction.

In either case, whether we are preparing a fine young dog for competition or trying to compensate for the deficiencies of a mediocre animal, we train for heeling in the group about the same way. The main focus is to have the handler move very briskly and make many abrupt turns in the group. He simply keeps the dog too busy to look about and become either distracted or afraid, as the case may be. The handler corrects any momentary inattentiveness or break in eye contact with a quick right turn and a sharp pop on the leash.

6. Heeling under gunfire

Heeling under the gun is normally less demanding for the dog than holding a down stay while shots are fired, because during the heel the animal is preoccupied with the work and close to its handler. Therefore, since we have already finished work on the dog's down stay under the gun, we should expect no problems with heeling under gunfire.

The running stand out of motion. The dog must come to a clean stand from a fast trotting pace.

The down out of motion is the easiest of the three exercises out of motion to teach. However, great care must be taken to ensure that it does not interfere with the sit and the stand out of motion.

11

Obedience:
The Exercises
out of Motion

AFTER THE HEELING PATTERN in a Schutzhund III obedience routine comes a series of four closely related exercises that account for thirty of the 100 points available in the obedience phase. We call them the *exercises out of motion,* and they consist of (1) the walking sit, (2) the running down, (3) the walking stand and (4) the running stand.

We use the phrase *exercises out of motion* to refer not only to the skills listed above, but also to the recalls and finishes that the dog must perform after the down and the running stand.

GOAL 1: The dog will stand out of motion instantly on command.

Schutzhund obedience requires a number of difficult skills, and one of them is the stand out of motion. The average dog has little trouble learning the sit and down out of motion. But with the introduction of the stand things can go mysteriously wrong. The animal may simply seem unable to comprehend the stand, or may catch on to the stand just fine but in the process lose either the sit or the down—or both!

It sometimes appears as though the dog can only handle two possibilities in the exercises out of motion. Because it is called upon to react so quickly and decisively when it hears a command—and has so little time to decide which command it is that it is hearing—the stand often becomes the straw that breaks the camel's back.

To prevent this problem, we introduced the stand itself very early on in training, and for the same reason we will now begin teaching the stand out of motion *before* introducing either the sit or the down out of motion.

Important Concepts for Meeting the Goal

1. Standing from a walk
2. Standing from a run

1. Standing from a walk

The handler begins with the dog on leash and wearing a flank strap. He heels the animal very slowly along and then abruptly commands "Back!" and corrects somewhat sharply with the leash, at the same time stepping away from the dog. If the animal tries to follow him or take a step in any direction, the handler corrects it again and repeats "Back!" If, on the other hand, the dog becomes confused and attempts to lie down or sit, the handler prevents this with a tug on the flank strap.

As soon as the dog stands still, the handler steps back to it and praises it quietly. He then commands the dog to "Heel!" and walks a few feet before immediately doing another stand out of motion.

After a few sessions the animal will have the idea, and the handler can begin to stand the dog and then drop the leash and continue walking away. He walks out about thirty yards, turns to face the dog, pauses five to ten seconds and then walks back and praises the animal.

2. Standing from a run

Once the dog has learned to freeze instantly into a stand from a slow walk, the handler can begin to dispense with both leash and flank strap so that the dog is completely off leash. He will also begin moving more quickly. He walks at an increasingly faster pace as he gives the "Back!" command, until eventually he begins running. The dog must now come to a clean stand out of a fast trot.

We must not allow the dog to take even one step after hearing the command. If it takes a step or two, then we are just teaching a bad habit that will be very persistent and cause both handler and dog a lot of headaches.

GOAL 2: The dog will sit out of motion instantly on command.

Only after the dog is doing a perfect, clean running stand do we begin to teach the sit out of motion.

Sitting from a walk

The handler heels his dog on leash at a slow walk. When he is ready, he commands "Sit!" and corrects the animal into a sit with the leash. As he does so he stops walking, pausing just long enough to bring the dog fully into the sit, and then continues on past to the end of the leash. He stops, turns and faces the dog for a moment, then returns to it and praises it. Then he heels forward again and repeats the exercise.

As training progresses, the handler makes less and less of a complete stop while the dog sits down. Eventually he heels along at a fast walk, commands the dog to "Sit!" and continues without breaking stride. If the dog's sit is still crisp and fast, he can begin dropping the leash on the ground and walking out an additional thirty or forty paces. As the dog progresses, the handler can finally omit the leash altogether.

GOAL 3: The dog will down out of motion instantly on command.

Only when the dog sits cleanly out of motion and still has a perfect stand do we introduce the down out of motion.

During basic training, the dog has already learned a strong "Down!" command. By strong we mean that the command has weight and power and that, if the handler raises his voice a little and glares at the dog as he utters it, it virtually crushes the animal to the ground.

For this reason, it is extremely easy to teach the down out of motion. In fact, it is by far the easiest of the three exercises out of motion and that is precisely why we teach it last—in order to *avoid* the straw-that-broke-the-camel's-back syndrome. Our main concern is to keep it from interfering with the sit and stand out of motion exercises.

Important Concepts for Meeting the Goal

1. Down from a walk
2. Down from a run

1. Down from a walk

The handler heels the dog slowly along and, with a sharp command and a somewhat threatening lunge toward it, he downs the animal. He pauses in his walk just long enough for the dog to hit the ground, and then he continues a pace or two to the end of the leash and turns to face the dog. He pauses, returns to the dog and praises it and then heels forward and repeats the exercise.

After just a few practice sessions the dog will begin to drop out of motion as if shot, and then the handler can begin

- pausing less and less as he says "Down!" so that soon he gives the command without breaking stride
- downing the dog from a faster and faster pace
- dropping the leash as he gives the command, and continuing up the field thirty or forty paces before stopping and turning to face his dog

2. Down from a run

If the handler increases his pace gradually enough, while always taking care that the dog's down is quick and clean, the down from a run should be no problem. However, if the dog tends to lie down slowly or take a step or two after the command, this error is easily corrected with the leash. The handler uses it somewhat like a flail. As he heels the dog on the run he holds the loose end in his right hand, with about two feet hanging free. At the moment that he gives the command he swings the leash over and across to his left and slaps the dog very sharply on the withers with it.

We must be careful not to make the dog's response to the down too strong, or overdo it with the leash correction, because then the sit and stand out of motion exercises would suffer. In addition, each training session begins and ends with a little practice of both the sit and the stand.

GOAL 4: The dog will run at top speed to the handler when recalled, sit close and perfectly straight in front and then finish quickly and precisely when commanded.

In the case of a willing dog that has been well reared and adores its handler, there should be no question of having to force it to come. Left behind by its master on the field in a down or a stand, the animal should be positively quivering to rejoin him. For the willing dog, the command "Come" is a release rather than an obligation. It means "You *may* come to me now," not "You *must* come to me now."

Precisely because the dog's desire to recall is so strong (and we will make it even stronger with the ball), the main difficulty in this exercise is *anticipation*.

If we make a practice of recalling the dog frequently from the down out of motion and the running stand, we will cause the animal to be quite preoccupied with the recall even as it is performing its exercises out of motion. This anticipation of the recall, an exercise it enjoys a great deal, will "drag" it down the field after its handler, making the dog creep when it should be stopping instantly on command.

In precisely the same way, if we habitually recall the dog and then always finish it from the come-fore position, we will also find the animal's anticipation of the finish interfering with a good, straight sit in front. The dog may sit crooked, leaning toward its handler's left, or it may even omit the come-fore position altogether and instead recall straight to heel.

We can prevent these problems of anticipation by *compartmentalizing* the

For a willing dog, the command "Come" is a release rather than an obligation. It means "You *may* come to me now," not "You *must* come to me now."

In order to keep the dog's stand rock-solid, we recall it from the stand out of motion only infrequently. This precaution prevents anticipation of the "Come" command and keeps the dog from creeping downfield.

recall from the exercises out of motion, and the finish from the recall. In other words, we teach and practice all these skills separately.

Important Concepts for Meeting the Goal

1. Motivating the dog for the recall and separating it from the sit, down and stand stays
2. Teaching a close, straight come-fore position
3. Separating the finish from the recall

1. Motivating the dog for the recall and separating it from the sit, down and stand stays

The first step is to give the dog speed—to make it come as fast as its legs will carry it when called. For this we use the ball and a great deal of repetition. We prevent this repetition from ruining the down and stand stays by the simple expedient of *not using them to practice the recall.* Instead of leaving the dog on a stay we give the animal to an assistant, who keeps it from following the handler by holding the dog's collar.

The handler leaves his dog with the assistant and runs away across the field. The dog is under no command at all. It is free to bark and lunge and surge into the collar, and its handler encourages it to do so by calling to it excitedly and throwing the ball up in the air. The handler runs perhaps sixty or seventy yards, until the dog's frustration at watching him go drives the animal into a perfect frenzy of excitement. The handler then turns to face the dog, pauses and, in very formal posture and voice, calls ''Come!'' The assistant releases the animal, which vents its frustration by sprinting into a dead run toward its master.

When the animal draws near, within twenty or thirty feet of its handler and coming in fast, the handler suddenly throws the ball. The direction of the throw is important: The handler always throws the ball behind him, over his shoulder or between his legs, in order to bring the dog in straight. The animal will spring closely past him, grab the ball and then the handler praises it exuberantly.

Quite naturally and properly, coming to its master will soon be the dog's favorite obedience exercise.

2. Teaching a close, straight come-fore position

The next step is to teach the dog to sit close and straight in front when it comes to its handler. We cannot accomplish this by running long recalls across the field, because a well-motivated dog will come scorching in and undoubtedly bounce off the handler (being knocked down is not uncommon) and then sit crookedly. So, we teach the dog to come-fore perfectly from a short distance before we ever ask it to do so from all the way across the field.

The handler begins by repeatedly calling the dog from a sit stay, but no farther than one leash length, so that the animal stays calm and moves slowly. By using his hands and the ball to attract the dog to the middle of his body, the handler can center the animal perfectly. Each time the dog starts to sit crookedly, the handler steps back a pace, repeating the ''Come! Sit!'' commands, and again attempts to guide the dog into a straight come-fore position. Only when the dog is sitting straight and close does the handler throw the ball.

3. Separating the finish from the recall

When the handler wishes to practice his dog's finish, there is no need to run repeated recalls. Instead, he merely sits his dog, steps in front of the animal to the come-fore position and then gives the ''Heel!'' command. Once the dog reaches his left side and sits, the handler can reward it with the ball or step in front of the animal and finish it again.

In this way, we can school the finish as much as we wish while still keeping it compartmentalized from the recall and come-fore.

GOAL 5: The dog will not confuse the different exercises out of motion and will keep all the parts of the exercises clean and distinct.

At this point, we have taught all of the constituent parts of the exercises out of motion:

1. The sit, down and stand in motion
2. The recall and come-fore
3. The finish

We have also been careful to keep them separate and distinct from each other in the dog's mind. Now we must gather them all together so that they mesh into polished and impressively executed exercises.

Important Concepts for Meeting the Goal

1. Differentiating the commands
2. Randomizing the recall and finish exercises

1. Differentiating the commands

When the dog has good exercises in motion it reacts very quickly— meaning that it stops as though it had hit a wall. The animal has just a fraction of a second in which to discriminate which command it is hearing and decide what to do—sit, lie down or stand. It is therefore vital that the handler take pains to differentiate the commands, making them sound as different from each other as possible: The ''Sit!'' command is upwardly inflected. It is a gentle, high-pitched command beginning with a distinct hiss. The ''Down!'' is guttural,

The handler teaches the dog a close, straight come-fore position, separate from the recall itself and also separate from the finish.

compelling and authoritative in tone. It comes from the belly. The "Back!" is staccato and clipped-off ("Bek!").

2. Randomizing the recall and the finish exercises

We *never* recall the dog from the down and the running stand until it has perfectly mastered all four of the exercises in motion, and the come-fore position as well. Even once we do begin recalling the animal from the down and the stand, we do not make a constant habit of it, because anticipation can still be a problem for us. If we are not careful, we will inadvertently untrain the exercises we have worked so hard to teach.

Instead, the dog is seldom recalled from the exercises in motion, and this is done completely randomly, so that the dog has no idea when it will be recalled and when not. Although the handler runs thirty or forty paces up the field, stops, turns and faces his dog as he would in a trial before giving the "Come!" command, most of the time he just returns to the dog and praises it.

Likewise, most of the time when we recall the dog formally (across a long distance and complete with a come-fore) we do *not* finish the animal. Instead, we do most of our practice on the finish isolated from the recall.

All the pieces of the exercises in motion and the recalls are kept separate from each other and well polished in training; they are fitted together only during trials and during a few practice sessions leading up to the trials.

12

Obedience:
Retrieves, Obstacles
and Send Away

$\mathbf{W}$E LEAVE the two most difficult obedience exercises, the retrieves and the send away, for last.

GOAL 1: The dog will retrieve the dumbbell quickly and reliably and without tossing or chewing it.

It seems ironic that the retrieves are difficult, because we have insisted throughout this book that, for Schutzhund competition, one must have a dog that is a strong natural retriever. A dog like this will happily retrieve a heavy balk of timber, and certainly a light wooden dumbbell. It seems a simple thing to interest this dog in the dumbbell, and throw it and then send the animal after it while it is still rolling. A good retriever will certainly go and bring it back. The problem is the *way* the dog brings it back. Because the animal is motivated by prey drive and play, and because it is terribly happy and pleased with itself, the dog chews the dumbbell, rolls or tosses it in its mouth and maybe even drops it on the ground, the way it habitually does with its ball.

If, in trial, the dog plays like this with the dumbbell on each retrieve, it will lose twelve points in all. Assuming that the animal performed perfectly in all the other obedience exercises and did not lose another point (an unlikely prospect), it would still be down to an obedience score of eighty-eight—far below the ninety-six points required for an Excellent rating, and low enough to cost its handler a lot of trophies.

Therefore, most Schutzhund trainers teach their dogs a *forced retrieve* because, by making the retrieve an obligation instead of a game, it cures the dog of playing with the dumbbell.

Important Concepts for Meeting the Goal

1. Taking the dumbbell from the hand
2. Taking the dumbbell from the ground
3. Retrieving the dumbbell on the back tie
4. Retrieving the dumbbell free

1. Taking the dumbbell from the hand

The first prerequisite for teaching the forced retrieve with our method is to establish a mechanical advantage over the dog so that it cannot physically resist us. We must be able to control the dog, and control it very easily, so that we can be precise in everything that we do with it.

Just as we do for training the out in bite work, we use a *back tie* to secure a mechanical advantage. The dog is tied to a post or tree on about eight feet of line leading to a leather collar buckled snugly around its neck. The animal also wears a correction collar that is reversed so that the live ring hangs in front, underneath the jaw. The handler stands in front of the dog with a leash that is attached to the correction collar. Most often we use a pinch collar rather than a simple choker.

The purpose of this exercise will be, quite simply, to compel the animal to take the dumbbell in its mouth and hold it. With the leash in his left hand and the dumbbell in his right, the handler begins to pull on the leash strongly enough to cause the dog some discomfort. At the same time he says, "Take it! Take it!" At one point or another the dog will open its mouth, either in the process of resisting the collar or in order to give a yip of distress—or, in the case of a tough customer, to try to bite. At that instant the handler inserts the dumbbell in the dog's mouth and, just as soon as he has it between the dog's jaws, he relaxes the tension on the leash and praises the animal softly and quietly.

The dog will immediately spit the dumbbell out. The handler begins to pull on the correction collar again the instant he sees the dumbbell come loose, and catches it as it drops from the dog's mouth. Very quickly he presents the dumbbell to the dog again, urging it to "Take it! Take it!" He keeps after the dog until, in response to the discomfort, the dog opens its mouth again and then the handler quickly reinserts the dumbbell. As always, as soon as the dumbbell is actually in the dog's mouth, he relaxes tension on the leash.

The proposition for the animal is a simple one. Taking the dumbbell in its mouth after hearing the command "Take it!" will turn off the discomfort caused by the correction collar. Dropping it or refusing it will turn the discomfort on again.

The forced retrieve. This dog shows, by the way that it reaches for the dumbbell, that it is beginning to understand what is expected.

The dog will quickly see where the advantage lies, and someone who is really good at teaching the forced retrieve with this method can have a dog taking the dumbbell and holding it after about fifteen minutes of careful work.

Once he has compelled the animal to take the dumbbell, the handler praises it quietly and calmly while the dog holds the dumbbell, petting it gently if he can do so without disturbing the dog's grip on the dumbbell.

After a few seconds of holding the dumbbell, the handler commands "Give!" and tries to get the dumbbell back. At this point many dogs have their jaws set stubbornly and somewhat resentfully on the dumbbell, and will require a mild correction in order to get them to give it up. The correction is not given with the leash, because we have just finished teaching the dog that tension on the leash and the discomfort that it causes mean to take and hold the dumbbell, not drop it. Therefore, we correct it another way. A very light bump on the chin or the end of the dog's nose should "unclinch" the animal from the dumbbell.

The handler works with his dog once or twice a day on the back tie until the animal will quickly take the dumbbell on the command "Take it!" and hold it calmly, and then give it up readily on the "Give!" command—without the necessity for any corrections.

2. Taking the dumbbell from the ground

Once the dog takes the dumbbell from its master's hand, it is time to teach it to pick the dumbbell up off the ground.

With the dog kept on the back tie, the handler gradually presents the dumbbell to the dog from farther and farther away, so that at first the animal must reach six inches for it, then eight, then ten and so on. If the dog refuses at any point to take the dumbbell, the handler causes it discomfort with the collar, and keeps on causing discomfort until the animal reaches out and takes the dumbbell in its mouth. Once the dog has learned to reach and even take one step forward in order to take the dumbbell, the handler begins to hold it lower and lower until finally he holds it against the ground.

3. Retrieving the dumbbell on the back tie

So far, the dog has remained stationary. Now the handler must teach his dog not just to reach for the dumbbell, but to run to it. The dog must also learn to carry it back without chewing or dropping it. This does not follow naturally once the dog has learned to take the dumbbell. The typical dog must be carefully taught to carry, because it tends to remain clamped like a vise onto the dumbbell until we ask it to take a step, and then the dog spits it out on the ground.

The handler works the retrieve along the arc of the back tie. He thereby retains the ability to perfectly control the animal, but at the same time he can create the room to move the dog as much as a dozen feet to the dumbbell and a dozen feet back.

He stands close to the limit of the back tie tether with his dog at heel. He gives the command "Take it!" and, rather than simply placing the dumbbell on the ground, he steps forward quickly and throws it four or five feet along the arc of the back tie. In the same motion the dog goes with him and takes the dumbbell. As soon as the dog has it, the handler steps back a pace toward his starting spot, calling the animal so that it turns around and brings the dumbbell back. The handler helps it with voice and gestures to do a perfect come-fore, and then commands the dog to "Give!" and takes the dumbbell from it.

If at any point the dog drops the dumbbell, the handler instantly begins to correct it and keeps correcting it until he can find some way of finagling it back into the dog's mouth. After a certain point, it will do no good to simply pick the dumbbell up for the dog and place it back between its jaws. The animal must instead be made to understand that before the discomfort will cease it must actively seek the dumbbell, go to it and take it in its mouth.

4. Retrieving the dumbbell free

The first few times that the handler takes his dog off the back tie for retrieving practice, he proceeds very cautiously. Using just a leash and correction collar, he has the dog take the dumbbell first from his hand and then from the ground. Only if everything goes without difficulty does he pitch the dumbbell out a few feet in front of him and let the dog go after it.

Initially he walks the animal through each retrieve, stepping out toward the dumbbell with the dog and then walking backward a few feet so that the dog can come-fore and deliver the dumbbell. He stays alert and remains close to the dog, ready to correct at any moment if the dog refuses.

If the dog proves absolutely reliable on these walk-throughs, the handler then throws the dumbbell and sends the animal out alone to retrieve it for the first time. Initially he makes the throw no longer than the length of the leash. As training progresses he throws farther so that, eventually, he must drop the leash and let the dog run out by itself.

GOAL 2: The dog will retrieve over both the hurdle and the climbing wall cleanly and with confidence.

The obstacles in Schutzhund are not particularly demanding. Any reasonably athletic dog can easily negotiate them. However, in order to do so the animal must be a little "in spirit." If it feels inhibited or nervous, the dog will jump badly. If it jumps badly it will continually hurt itself. As a result the dog will hate and fear the obstacles and possibly the retrieve as well.

Therefore, the obstacles are taught in fun and play, and absolutely separately from the forced retrieve. Only when the dog is easily and joyfully negotiating the full height on both obstacles *and* retrieving reliably do we bring the forced retrieve and the obstacles together.

Important Concepts for Meeting the Goal

1. Jumping the hurdle
2. Scaling the climbing wall
3. Retrieving over the hurdle
4. Retrieving over the climbing wall

1. Jumping the hurdle

The training hurdle must be a board jump made with planks, so that it is possible to raise the height gradually from a point very close to the ground.

The handler begins by setting the hurdle up with just one slat of perhaps twenty centimeters (7.8 inches) in height. He starts the dog on leash from one side of the jump with the command "Hup!" and excitedly runs the dog over it and back, jumping with it each way, and then praises the animal and plays with it with the ball.

The animal will think that this is a wonderful game, and we will stay at the lowest height of the hurdle for a while until the habit begins to sink in that the dog will always go between the standards of the jump (that is, over the hurdle) and never around them, and that when it jumps out it always jumps back. Then the handler begins to gradually raise the height of the jump in five centimeter increments until it reaches the full height of one meter (39 inches). When it becomes too high for him to jump with the dog, the handler runs alongside instead.

2. Scaling the climbing wall

Technically, the wall is not a jump, because it is not desirable that the dog jump it. If the animal bounds to the top and then sails off the other side its shoulders will take a completely unnecessary pounding.

Instead, we teach the animal to *scale* the wall, to climb up one side and then climb down the other. We do this by opening the wall up so that it is only about four feet high. Because the sides of the wall then ramp very gently, the dog begins by simply trotting up one side and then down the other.

Just as he did with the hurdle, and with the same "Hup!" command, the handler runs the dog on leash over the wall and back, lavishing it with praise and playing with it with the ball after the return. Of course, he cannot run over the wall with the dog, so he just runs alongside. As training progresses, we gradually creep the feet of the wall together, so that it grows higher and the sides grow steeper.

As the wall nears full height, the handler takes particular care to slow the dog down as it tops the wall, so that the animal will keep the habit of climbing down the far side of the wall instead of simply jumping off.

A dog that leaps from the top of the wall to the ground instead of climbing down shows good spirit but also takes an unnecessary pounding. ("Derry.")

The handler teaches the dog to scale the wall rather than jump it by opening up the wall so that it is only about four feet high. Then the handler walks the dog over it on leash.

TEACHING THE RETRIEVE OVER THE CLIMBING WALL

After the handler sends the dog, and while the dog is making the retrieve, the handler scuttles forward, jumps to the top of the wall and then calls the dog and slaps the obstacle with her hands. As the dog heads for the wall, the handler jumps back down off it, steps backward a meter or two and . . .

. . . waits for the dog to deliver the dumbbell.

In our opinion, a strong, driving send away is the most difficult skill to teach in Schutzhund obedience.

3. Retrieving over the hurdle

Once the animal easily negotiates the hurdle at full height, we can combine the retrieve with the hurdle. However, rather than just setting the jump up at full height, flinging the dumbbell over it and waiting to see what happens, we instead repeat our careful progression.

We return to the lowest possible height and practice the retrieve for a while with the dog just hopping over the twenty-centimeter board. If there are absolutely no problems, then we gradually begin to raise the height of the jump to the maximum, just as we did before.

4. Retrieving over the climbing wall

Because of the size and dimensions of the climbing wall, it is a little more difficult to ensure that all goes well on the first few retrieves. This is one reason that we come to the retrieve over the wall last.

We prefer not to put the wall down at a low height and then walk the dog through the exercise with the leash the first few times (as is the most common practice). In our experience the handler causes more problems doing this than he prevents, simply because he gets in his dog's way.

Instead, the handler puts the wall at a medium height, throws the dumbbell out over it and then sends his dog free. But while the animal is running the retrieve the handler scuttles forward and jumps to the top of the wall. When the dog picks up the dumbbell and turns, the first thing it sees is its handler at the top of the wall. The handler calls to it and slaps the wall with his hand. When he sees the animal start for the obstacle, the handler jumps off and runs backward. The dog follows him up and over the wall, and then comes-fore and delivers the dumbbell to him.

GOAL 3: The dog will run away from its handler as fast as it can and in a straight line until it is commanded to lie down.

In our opinion, the send away is the most difficult of the Schutzhund obedience exercises to teach. In all the other exercises, the dog orients toward its master, looking to him, listening to him, moving with him or moving at him. In the send away the animal must do something entirely different. It must orient completely away from its handler and run out fast and straight until it hears the "Down!" command. Experienced trainers know how hard this is to teach to the average dog.

Of course, here we are not talking about what we call "home-field" send aways. Like all other Schutzhund competitors, we have shown our dogs often on their home field where we trained them. When time was short before a home-field trial we have, like everyone else, faked the send away. This is easily done by simply teaching the dog to go to a place, usually at one end of the field by the fence, where it will always find food or the ball. The only day on which it does not find the reward is on trial day.

A fake send away is extremely easy to teach. But, of course, the dog will only do it on its home field, and only toward the spot by the fence where it is accustomed to finding the reward. Both of the authors have experienced the consternation of putting together a fake send away during the week before our dog's first Schutzhund I appearance, using a spot at the east end of the field, and then having the judge decide that the send aways would instead be run west on trial day!

A true send away is another matter entirely. The trainer can take his dog to any field, point it in a direction, send it, and the dog will go out fast and straight. The animal is not going *to* anything. Rather, it is going *away* from its handler.

After a lifetime of being taught to look to the handler and move toward him always, this concept can be very difficult for the dog to learn.

Our method of teaching the send away depends upon the animal's desire to retrieve, and it is based upon the techniques that field-trial and bird-dog trainers use to train their hunting dogs. In retriever training, the send away is the fundamental skill upon which a great deal of the other work is based, and field-trial trainers routinely teach fast and straight send aways of up to 300 yards over broken ground.

In Schutzhund, we are doing wonderfully if our dog goes out sixty-five or seventy paces on a flat, level field. (The rules for Schutzhund III require only forty paces, but if our dog has a good send away we will let it go much farther before giving the "Down!" command. Always give the judge a good look at anything that the dog does well!)

Success in the send away depends upon patience, good methods and plenty of time. We allow at least several months of work to teach this exercise.

Important Concepts for Meeting the Goal

1. Placed retrieves
2. Multiple placed retrieves
3. Generalizing the placed retrieve to other locations
4. Teaching the dog to lie down instantly at the end of the send away

1. Placed retrieves

The first task in training the send away is to teach the dog to run out at a target on command. If the animal is "ball-crazy," it is quite easy to get the dog to do this by placing a ball on the ground where the dog can see it and then sending it to retrieve. This is called a placed retrieve.

The handler begins by leaving his dog on a sit stay and walking out just a few feet in front of it. He shows the ball to the animal, tossing it up in the air and catching it a time or two, and then places it on the ground.

The place on the field where the handler puts the ball is the *target spot* and, for the time being, we will not move it. The dog will always be sent to exactly this spot.

The handler returns to his dog, steps to heel position and gives the dog the "line"—meaning that he points with his left hand at the ball. Then, with the command "Go out!" and a sweeping arm gesture toward the target, he sends the animal.

The dog bounds across the fifteen or so feet that separate it from the ball and grabs it. Meanwhile, the handler takes several steps backward, so that he is now perhaps twenty-five feet from the target spot. When the dog happily retrieves the ball to him, the handler pats and praises it lavishly and then takes the ball and puts the dog on another sit stay. He takes the ball back over to the target spot, leaves it there, and again sends the dog to retrieve it.

Over several training sessions, the handler repeats the placed retrieve again and again, each time retreating a little father from the target spot while the dog is making the retrieve. Soon, he is sending the animal from 100 feet or more. This is far enough so that, with any ground cover at all, the dog is not able to actually see the ball during much of its run. The animal will go perhaps fifty feet "blind" before it can even see the target. But, because it has learned where the target spot is, and knows that it will always find the ball at that exact spot, the dog goes there straight and goes as fast as it can.

What we are doing, of course, is setting the dog up to believe that, if it takes the line its handler gives it and goes, it will find the ball. In order to accomplish this, we need the dog to:

- go out hard and fast and "true to the line"—meaning that it does not weave or curve or wander, but runs a beeline between its handler and the target spot
- go out a long distance, during much of which it cannot actually see the ball

The traditional way of increasing the distance so that the dog would practice running blind was by changing the location of the target. The handler sent the animal always from the same place on the field, making him travel farther each time by gradually moving the ball away.

This meant that each time the handler moved the target spot, the dog did not know exactly where it would find the ball. Hopefully the animal found it the way we wanted it to, by running as fast as it could in a straight line until it saw the ball. However, unless the handler was extremely careful and meticulous, a lot of other things could happen. The dog could begin weaving as it ran, searching for the ball. The animal could even miss the line or run a curve and go right past the ball, and then wind up finding it by quartering randomly about the field. However, more commonly the dog would run out to the certain distance from the handler at which it was accustomed to find the ball, and then it would slow down to a canter or a trot and put its head to the ground and continue slowly up the field, searching for the ball with its eyes and nose.

The dog's stable strategy for finding the ball in the send away could thus easily become a tentative, head-down gallop in which it weaved as it went out, turning back and quartering the instant it thought it might have gone too far.

In our method, the dog always finds the ball in the same spot, the target spot, and the handler gradually increases the length of the send away *by moving back away from the target spot*. The animal knows exactly where it is going. The animal travels blind farther and farther, but it never weaves, drops its head, runs past the ball or finds it by casting about. The dog goes right to it and it goes at a dead run.

2. Multiple placed retrieves

We are making progress with the dog, but we are still a long way from having a formal send away. The dog goes out only because it knows there is a ball waiting and it knows there is a ball waiting because, before each send, it sees its handler go out to the target spot and put the ball there. Obviously, if the dog does not first see its handler go out into the field, it will not go either.

There is a simple, elegant way to "fog" the relationship between the handler's doings and the presence or the absence of a ball at the target spot. When the handler goes out to the spot that first time, he does not leave just one ball, but three or four.

The first send away is a "hot" one. The dog has just watched its handler walk out to the target spot a few seconds before, and it therefore has every reason to believe that a ball awaits it there. But the second send is a little "colder." The memory trace of seeing its handler out there is fading, and the third and fourth sends are strictly on faith. The animal goes to the spot out of habit and each time finds a ball. Soon it begins to have the blind conviction that, even if it can't see a ball out in the field, and even if it hasn't seen its handler put a ball on the target spot, if it goes out it will still find one.

The handler can strengthen this conviction in two ways:

1. By concealing the cluster of balls a little bit more all the time so that, eventually, the dog cannot see them until coming within twenty or twenty-five feet of the target spot. As a result, the dog makes by far the greater part of its run blind.
2. By placing the balls on the target spot without letting the dog see him do it. (He leaves the animal in the car.) In this way the first send is also a "cold" one.

3. Generalizing the placed retrieve to other locations

Of course, if we took the dog to another training field and tried to run a cold-placed retrieve, it wouldn't go out. The dog's understanding of the send away (and its conviction that it will find a ball out in the field) is specific to a certain location. The dog is still running *to* something—a spot on a particular field with which it is acquainted. In order to get the dog to take a line and run *away* from its handler (and go even though it has never found a ball out where we are sending it), we must generalize the exercise to other fields.

The handler begins almost at square one in another location. He establishes a target spot there by doing quite a few short placed retrieves until he is absolutely sure that the dog knows exactly where it is going. Then he works his way back until the animal is running multiple placed retrieves at long distance in this new location.

Then the handler takes his dog to a third field and starts again. This time, however, he can work through the progression a little more quickly because the dog is becoming more sure of its work and more bound by habit.

By the time the handler has taught his dog four or five target spots in four or five different locations (parks and empty lots will do just fine, there is no need for five dog training fields), it will take him just one session to show the animal another target spot in a new location and get it running full-length multiple placed retrieves to it.

At this point, the handler tries something new. He goes back to a location where the dog has already learned the send away, to a target spot that the animal knows but has not visited in a while. He places several balls, but without letting the dog see him do it, and then sends it (completely ''cold,'' right out of the car) a rather long distance to the target spot. If the animal runs hard and true on the first retrieve (the first one is the hard one), then we are ready for the most difficult step yet.

The handler now takes his dog to a field where the animal has never worked before. He places several balls in a spot, but does not let the dog see him do it. He brings the animal out, gives it the line to the target spot with his hand, and sends it.

The handler can take two precautions in order to make sure that the dog will run straight and true to the line, and come down right on top of the target spot:

1. He runs a heeling pattern up and down the field on the same axis as the send away. Later this practice will stand him in good stead, because in a trial the send aways always run along the same axis as the heeling patterns. The dog will soon make this association and, in competition, the direction of the heeling pattern will help to give it the line.
2. He selects a perfectly flat, level and relatively narrow field, with parallel, fenced sides that will help to establish the line and guide the dog straight down to the target spot.

4. Teaching the dog to lie down instantly at the end of the send away

Now the dog goes any place that we send it, but we still do not have a complete send away exercise.

On trial day, there will be no balls lying on the field for the dog to find. We will send it out and then down it at sixty or seventy yards. At this distance, as excited as the animal is, and as accustomed as it is to running until it finds a ball, downing it is not simply a matter of giving it the command.

If our control of the dog is tremendous, we can undoubtedly get it to lie down by screaming the command repeatedly, but probably not before it has searched about the field enough to be convinced that there is no ball to be found. This is, of course, not acceptable. We need it to drop instantly on the run as though shot. If we try to use sheer force and muscle to do the trick, running up the field at the dog in order to give it "what for" when it downs slowly, we will soon create some major training problems. Instead, in another beautifully elegant solution (taught to the authors by Janet Birk), we manipulate the dog's expectations in order to make it eager to down for us.

The handler takes the dog to an old target spot that the animal knows well, and runs a series of multiple placed retrieves at very short distance—say forty feet or so. The target spot should have sufficient ground cover that the dog can only see the balls—or, conversely, can only tell that there are no balls on the target spot—when it is very close to it.

The handler runs a number of retrieves so that, every once in a while, he sends the dog to the target spot when it is empty. (All the balls have already been retrieved and are in the handler's pockets.) When the dog gets to the spot, the handler shouts "Down!" If his control of his animal is good, at such a short distance the command will drive the dog quickly to the ground. The instant that the dog downs, his handler throws the ball to it, slinging it over the dog's head and past it up the field.

As time passes, and this sequence occurs more frequently, the animal will make a discrimination:

- If the handler does not give the "Down!" command, then there is a ball out in the field waiting for the dog to run down on top of it. All that it must do in order to have the prey object is to keep going in a straight line.
- If, on the other hand, the handler says "Down!" *then there is no ball out in the field for the dog.* The ball will come instead from the handler and in order to have it the animal must turn toward him and drop to the ground.

Great care must be taken to balance the dog's anticipation of finding the ball out in the field against its anticipation of having it thrown by its handler. If the ball comes too many times from the handler, the dog's preoccupation with thinking about and looking for the throw will interfere with the send away. The animal will tend to look back over its shoulder, curve or even stop and turn and lie down prematurely. If, on the other hand, the dog finds the ball on the target spot too often, it will be slow to lie down when commanded, because it is certain that the ball awaits it out in the field, and it wants to keep on going until the ball is found.

The balance is a delicate one, and difficult to maintain. Sooner or later with most dogs we must use some compulsion to polish the send away and make it absolutely reliable.

13

Protection:
Requirements
of the Trial

SCHUTZHUND I PROTECTION

Hold and Bark (five points)

Before the dog–handler team walks onto the field, the helper hides behind one of the blinds. On the judge's command, the team heels to the midline between two blinds. On the judge's signal, the handler removes the leash from the dog's collar and then sends it to the blind. When the dog reaches the helper, it must harass him by staying close and barking powerfully and aggressively. The helper does not move or show aggression toward the dog in any way, and therefore it must not bite him. The dog will lose points for bumping or biting, not barking forcefully enough or being less than completely vigilant.

Attack on Handler (thirty-five points)

At the conclusion of the hold-and-bark exercise, the judge instructs the handler to go to his dog and, taking the animal's collar, pull it away from the helper. The helper leaves the blind and, once he has vacated it, the handler and dog step into it. Meanwhile, with the dog's vision of him obscured by the blind, the helper moves to a new blind. At the judge's signal, the team heels on leash

"The protection dog must be sharp, but sharpness must be disciplined by training turned in the right direction and conditioned by the most perfect obedience."—Max von Stephanitz

in the direction of the new hiding place. Still in motion, the handler removes the leash and continues heeling toward the blind. Suddenly the helper charges out of the blind, simulating an attack on the handler. Without command, the dog should immediately attack the helper and bite hard and full on the sleeve. During the fight the helper drives the dog and strikes the animal twice with a flexible reed stick. At the judge's command the helper stops fighting and "freezes." The handler commands his dog to "Out!" and the animal must release its bite. The dog will not be granted a Schutzhund degree if it does not out properly at least once during the routine. After the "Out!" command the dog should remain near the helper and guard him closely. The dog may bark or not, and it may sit, stand or lie down but must remain vigilant and concentrated upon the helper. At the judge's signal, the handler advances and again takes his dog by the collar so that the helper can step away.

Pursuit and Courage Test (sixty points)

The helper runs away down the field, making threatening gestures at the dog–handler team as he goes. On the judge's command, the handler sends his dog to pursue the helper, who is now approximately fifty paces downfield. When the dog is about thirty paces away from him the helper turns around and runs directly toward the dog while at the same time making threatening motions (yelling and waving the stick menacingly). The dog should not hesitate: it should charge straight into the helper and bite. The helper fights the dog for five or six seconds, but without striking it with the stick, and he then freezes. The handler, who has remained in the spot from which he sent the dog, then commands the dog to "Out!" The handler should wait for the judge's signal before going to his dog (approximately thirty seconds). At this point, he approaches the dog, searches the helper and confiscates the stick. The handler and dog then escort the helper to the judge. The handler walks on the helper's right with the dog, on leash, walking between them. The dog should remain vigilant during the escort, but nicely at heel and under control. This exercise is called the *side transport*.

The judge evaluates the fighting instincts of the dog throughout the entire performance. The animal must show strong spirit and an intense desire to fight, and display a firm, full grip on the sleeve in order to receive maximum points. If, during any of the guarding phases (during the hold and bark or after the outs), the dog returns to its handler or is inattentive to the helper it may receive no more than a *sufficient* fighting drive evaluation from the judge (rather than *pronounced*). A dog that is not under the control of its handler, that does not release its grip when commanded to "Out!" or that refuses to bite during the courage test or the attack on handler will not pass the protection phase.

SCHUTZHUND II PROTECTION

Revier, or Search for the Helper (five points)

Before the dog–handler team arrives on the field, the helper hides behind one of the blinds. On the judge's command, the team walks to the midline between the first two blinds. The dog is off leash. The handler sends the animal to search either the first blind on the right or on the left, according to the judge's instructions. He then walks up the midline of the field, using hand and voice signals to call his dog back and forth across the field in a zigzag pattern, making the animal search all six blinds in order. The overall appearance of the exercise should be one of fluidity and intensity of desire on the part of the dog. In order to control the animal and direct its search, the handler can use the command "Come!" as well as the dog's name.

Hold and Bark (ten points)

The helper is hiding in the sixth blind, and when the dog finds him he remains still. The dog must harass the helper by barking aggressively at him but without touching or biting him. On the judge's signal, the handler proceeds to the designated spot, usually about four paces behind the dog, and upon another signal from the judge he recalls his dog to heel. The handler then orders the helper out of the blind, tells him "Hands up!" and commands the dog to lie down in front of him. The handler searches the helper and then moves back into the blind. Meanwhile, the dog should guard the helper vigilantly.

Escape (ten points) and Defense (forty points)

At the judge's instruction, the helper attempts to escape by running from the dog. The dog should stop him immediately by biting hard on the sleeve. When the helper stops fighting, the dog should out from the sleeve on command and guard him vigilantly. Upon a signal from the judge, the helper reattacks the dog, threatening it with the stick and driving it. Once the dog is firmly on the sleeve, the helper strikes it twice on the back or withers with the stick. The helper freezes and the handler commands the dog to "Out!" He then commands the helper with "Hands up!" and downs his dog. He then searches the helper. Because the helper will need the stick in the following exercises, the handler does not take it from him during the search. The handler then instructs the helper to move forward and the team transports him, following at a distance of five paces.

Transport (five points)

Handler and dog transport the helper approximately fifty paces through a series of turns specified by the judge. During the transport, the dog should remain responsive to its handler and also alert to the helper.

In the Schutzhund I attack on handler, the helper hides behind a blind and then, on the judge's command, charges out and attacks handler and dog. (Charley Bartholomew and Gillian de Loup Noir, Schutzhund III, Ring I.)

After the hold and bark in Schutzhund II and III, the handler recalls the dog to heel and then commands the helper to step out of the blind. (Officer Chris Worsham and "Beny," Schutzhund I, PD II.)

The escape. The dog guards the decoy vigilantly while the handler searches the blind. When the decoy attempts to escape, the dog pursues and stops the decoy without being commanded. ("Beny.")

Attack (ten points) and Courage Test (twenty points)

While the helper is being transported, he turns on the judge's command and simulates an attack on the handler. The dog should attack him immediately and bite hard and full. The dog may cease its attack either when the helper stops fighting and freezes or when it is commanded to "Out!" The helper now moves off approximately 100 paces and begins making threatening motions. The handler, holding his dog by the collar, verbally challenges the helper, who runs away. The handler sends his dog. When the dog is within forty paces of him, the helper turns and runs directly at the animal. The dog should not hesitate and should bite him hard and full. When agitation ceases, the dog should again release the sleeve and then stay in close to the helper and harass him. The handler picks up his dog, searches the helper, removes his weapon and then escorts him in a side transport to the judge.

SCHUTZHUND III PROTECTION

Revier, or Search for the Helper (five points)

Before the dog–handler team arrives on the field, the helper hides behind one of the blinds. On the judge's command, the team walks to the midline between the first two blinds. The dog is off leash. The handler sends the animal to search either the first blind on the right or on the left, according to the judge's instruction. He then walks up the midline of the field, using hand and voice signals to call the dog back and forth across the field in a zigzag pattern, making the animal search all six blinds in order. The overall appearance of the exercise should be one of fluidity and intensity of desire on the part of the dog. In order to control the animal and direct its search, the handler may use the command "Come!" as well as the dog's name.

Hold and bark (ten points)

The helper is hiding in the sixth blind, and when the dog finds him he remains still. The dog must harass the helper by barking aggressively at him but without touching him. The dog will lose points both for biting and also for being inattentive or not barking. On the judge's signal, the handler proceeds to the designated spot, usually about four paces behind the dog, and upon another signal from the judge he recalls his dog to heel. The handler then orders the helper out of the blind, tells him "Hands up!" and commands his dog to lie down in front of him. The handler searches the helper and then moves back into the blind. Meanwhile, the dog should guard the helper vigilantly.

Escape (ten points) and Defense (twenty-five points)

At the judge's instruction, the helper attempts to escape by running from the dog. The dog should stop him immediately by biting hard on the sleeve. When the helper stops fighting, the dog should out from the sleeve (on command or automatically) and guard the man vigilantly. Upon a signal from the judge, the helper reattacks the dog, threatening it with the stick and driving it. Once the dog is firmly on the sleeve, the helper strikes it twice on the back or withers with the stick. The helper freezes and the handler commands his dog to "Out!" He then commands the helper with "Hands up!" and downs the dog. He then searches the helper. Because the helper will need the stick in the following exercises, the handler does not take it from him during the search. The handler then instructs the helper to move forward and the team transports him, following at a distance of five paces.

Back Transport (five points)

The handler and dog transport the helper approximately fifty paces through a series of turns specified by the judge. During the transport, the dog should remain responsive to its handler and also alert to the helper.

Attack (ten points), Pursuit (ten points) and Courage Test (twenty-five points)

While the helper is being transported, he turns on the judge's command and simulates an attack on the handler. The dog should attack him immediately and bite hard and full. The dog may cease its attack either when the helper stops fighting and freezes or when it is commanded to "Out!" The handler picks his dog up, searches the helper and disarms him and then side-transports him to the judge. The judge sends the first helper off the field and out of sight. The dog–handler team heels to the opposite end of the field and steps behind a blind momentarily. Meanwhile a second helper hides in a blind at the far end of the field. At the judge's signal the handler and dog move out of the blind to a point midway between the last two blinds, and the handler takes hold of his dog's collar. On the judge's signal the helper emerges from his blind at the opposite end of the field and challenges the handler and dog, yelling and brandishing the stick. The handler yells at him to stop. The helper ignores the handler's command to stop and instead flees. At the judge's signal the handler releases his dog to pursue the fleeing helper. When the dog is within approximately forty paces of him, the helper turns and runs straight toward the dog, yelling and threatening with the stick. The dog should not hesitate. It should charge straight into the helper and bite hard and full on the sleeve. The helper fights it for five or six seconds, and then freezes. The dog should again out from the sleeve, remain near the helper and guard him vigilantly. After just a moment, the helper again attacks the dog. He drives the animal before him and strikes it sharply twice on the back or withers with the stick and then freezes. The dog yet again outs from the sleeve and guards the helper. Upon a signal from the judge the handler walks all the way down the field to his dog. He tells the helper to "Step back!" and then "Hands up!" He downs his dog and searches the helper, takes the stick from him and then side-transports him back to the judge, who waits approximately fifty paces

When a dog's heart is brave, the courage test can produce some spectacular moments. (Susan Barwig's "Derry.")

away. He presents the stick to the judge, announces his name and the dog's and informs the judge that he has just completed the Schutzhund III protection routine.

SCORING

To pass the protection phase of a trial, the dog must earn a minimum of eighty points out of 100. The dog's numerical score is based on its total performance throughout the protection phase and assigned a rating on the following scale:

96 to 100 points	Excellent (*Vorzüglich*)
90 to 95 points	Very Good (*Sehr Gut*)
80 to 89 points	Good (*Gut*)
0 to 79 points	Insufficient (*Ungenügend*)

The judge also evaluates the dog's courage and fighting instincts and marks them down in the animal's scorebook as one of the following:

Pronounced (P), or in German *Ausgeprägt* (A)
Sufficient (S), or in German *Vorhanden* (VH)
Insufficient (I), or in German *Nicht Genügend* (NG)

Only a dog that displays pronounced courage and fighting instincts, a hard and full-mouthed bite on the sleeve and "clean" outs can receive full points in the protection phase. Dogs that are not under their handler's control, that do not out or that refuse to bite at any point during the protection exercises cannot pass the trial.

After the judge has critiqued the dog's performance in protection and announced its score, he will also add the dog's tracking and obedience scores to the protection score in order to obtain the animal's point total for the day. This point total is assigned a rating on the following scale:

286 to 300 points	Excellent (*Vorzüglich*)
270 to 285 points	Very Good (*Sehr Gut*)
240 to 269 points	Good (*Gut*)
220 to 239 points	Satisfactory (*Befriedigend*)
110 to 219 points	Faulty (*Mangelhaft*)
0 to 109 points	Insufficient (*Ungenügend*)

14

An Overview of
the Protection Phase

THE PROTECTION PHASE of Schutzhund work has raised more eyebrows than any other aspect of the sport. Some people consider it cruel and savage. Others say that it is too dangerous. Still others believe that protection training somehow returns the dog to a wild state. Despite these misapprehensions and the criticism that arises from them, we consider protection to be the most exciting of the three phases of training. It is also at the core of the purpose of Schutzhund sport—to test, select and promote dogs of character and working ability.

These myths and misconceptions surrounding Schutzhund bite work still persist and must be refuted. One frequently voiced concern regarding protection is that the training will alter the dog's temperament. However, experience has shown that a dog that is confident and friendly before protection training will remain confident and friendly after protection training. We do not brainwash the animal in any way. We merely strengthen and mold a perfectly natural facet of its behavior that we can already see in some form or degree in the dog before it is ever exposed to agitation.

Another myth surrounding Schutzhund bite work is that the training involves cruelty to the dog. Nothing could be further from the truth. After all, the primary objective in bite work is to build and maintain confidence, and this state of being cannot be evoked by cruelty or by force. Confidence and self-assurance evolve instead as a result of a carefully designed series of exercises that teach the dog, first, to display aggression in appropriate circumstances and, second, that it

The protection phase of Schutzhund has raised more eyebrows and more controversy than any other aspect of the sport. (Stewart Hilliard and Chuck Cadillac's "Gitte.")

can always expect success in so doing. The dog must develop the self-assurance necessary to oppose a human willingly, with conviction and with force. This it will not do if abused or mishandled.

The use of the reed stick during Schutzhund protection routines caused much criticism and concern during the early years of Schutzhund in the United States. However, for a number of reasons, the stick hits are not dangerous for the dogs nor even particularly unpleasant. Stick hits are carefully and precisely administered by an agitator who is expert at his craft, and the blows fall to one side or the other of the dog's spine, on the thick dorsal muscles of the back. Because the stick is very light and flexible, the dog is covered with fur and the agitator is skilled and experienced, no harm comes to the animal. Although the stick hits, characterized by sharp, menacing gestures, reflect a threat to the dog that it must withstand in order to pass a Schutzhund examination, they inflict at most a brief sting.

Indeed, the animal shows us clearly whether this pain is important to it, for it has the choice to undergo the stick hits or not. If the dog finds the blows truly unpleasant, if it is frightened by them, then it will bite badly or not at all while under the stick. Consequently, because it does its trainer no credit, the dog will be retired from Schutzhund and it will never see the stick again. If, on the other hand (like a football player who repeatedly endures far worse than a brief sting for his love of the game), the dog is so transported by the passion and excitement of bite work that it is oblivious of the blows, then we can unmistakably see that the dog has made its choice to go eagerly under the stick. We therefore admire the dog and use it for precisely this quality in it. The issue of the stick hits illustrates most clearly the central dynamic of Schutzhund sport: The Schutzhund dog loves the game.

A final misconception involves the common conviction held by many dog owners that their dogs will, without benefit of training or experience, protect them in a dangerous, real-life situation. This is extremely unlikely. Most family dogs are systematically discouraged from behaving aggressively under any circumstances. In addition, the majority of dogs simply do not possess the necessary courage to bite when suddenly threatened. Their immediate and quite reasonable response is to retreat from an ominous situation with which they have not had any previous experience. The fact that a dog barks aggressively from behind the safety of a fence or a door is no indication that it will protect its owner when push comes to shove. Even in the case of a dog of unusual quality, a great deal of schooling is necessary to overcome the dog's ultimate inhibition against biting and to develop its confidence and expertise in protection.

In fact, it is extraordinarily difficult to induce a dog to bite a human for real, and as trainers we spend an inordinate amount of time and energy striving to overcome this problem. Many dogs are willing to threaten, harass and even nip when they have someone on the run or when they confront a person who is not particularly dangerous. However, this is not the sort of person against whom we need protection. For a dog to enter into close combat with a person who is unafraid and genuinely means to hurt somebody is a different matter altogether.

Remember, *biting is an extreme act*. The animal in question must be either extremely frightened or extremely brave.

In an emergency, it is best if the dog is not only brave but also well trained, and a dog that has proven its courage and steadiness on the Schutzhund field and that is then schooled in personal protection can provide many years of service as a reliable family guardian.

Despite the advantages of owning and training a well-schooled Schutzhund protection dog, there can also be decided disadvantages. Training a dog to a high level of competence in bite work is a long and arduous process. To begin training and then not follow through to this level of competence is to invite problems. A dog that is not fully trained has neither the control nor the judgment necessary to make a good decision, and a mistake of judgment with such a powerful animal can result in injury to an innocent party and a possible law suit.

In perfect truth, whether well trained or not, dogs simply do not possess the capacity to safely and reliably judge when and whom they should bite, and when not. Therefore, the responsibility for this judgment rests entirely in the hands of the owner. It is up to him to constantly and accurately predict his dog's reactions in daily situations and to restrain the animal if there is a possibility that the animal will behave aggressively when in reality there is no danger.

For this reason, the person who is considering Schutzhund must be reflective regarding his own needs and competencies. His attitude toward the dog must be one of respect for a powerful weapon. The owner must have the determination and the ability to make good decisions regarding the safety of his dog and of other people.

It should be evident that, contrary to the lurid image bite work conjures up in the imaginations of the uninformed, training is carried out gradually and in a humane manner.

The process of building the dog's confidence and developing its instincts is called *agitation,* and it is an art. The person who performs this work is called the *decoy,* the *agitator* or the *helper,* and his function is to serve as the dog's adversary in order to progressively develop the animal's desire to bite and to increase its courage. The agitator must be an athlete, physically strong and agile, but more importantly he must also be a person with what we call "feeling"—an accurate intuition for what makes dogs behave the way they do. The agitator must have the ability to observe a dog for a moment and then know what is in its heart. An expert agitator makes a good dog better. A mediocre agitator can make even a good dog look mediocre. A poor agitator can ruin a dog.

Throughout the protection section of this book we use the terms *agitator, decoy* and *helper* interchangeably. We prefer the term *agitator* because it best describes what the person actually does. However, we also use *helper* because this has become, for the sake of public relations, the officially accepted title ("help" has a more innocuous connotation than "agitate"). We include *decoy* because this term is commonly used on the training field in many parts of the country.

Early German service dog trials. Two exercises that no longer play a part in Schutzhund: the attack under gunfire *(top)* and guarding an object *(bottom)*. (From von Stephanitz, *The German Shepherd Dog,* 1923.)

In addition to a competent handler and a gifted agitator, a Schutzhund team requires the right dog. The dog must have certain qualities of character. It is easy to imagine that the most aggressive, nasty, suspicious, hyperexcitable animal possible would be a good candidate, but this impression is totally incorrect. Rather than suspicious (a trait founded upon unsureness), the Schutzhund dog must be strong in character—steady, friendly, reliable and confident. The dog must be rational, in the sense that it must be capable of distinguishing between real threats and the normal, sometimes chaotic events that surround it. Thus, the single indispensable character trait of a working dog is stability. The animal must be steady, neither timid nor inappropriately aggressive. It may be friendly or it may not, but above all it must not be unreliable or dangerous.

The animal that snarls at a person approaching it, or tucks its tail and anxiously growls in a group of people, is not representative of the Schutzhund dog, both because it is not safe or reliable and also because it does not express the necessary power. It is from steadiness and neutrality—and the courage they bespeak—that the dog's ultimate power in bite work arises. Contrary to common belief, the Schutzhund dog is not filled with suspicion or hate for the agitator. It does not bite from rage, fear or malevolence. It does it because the activity fulfills a great number of its instinctual needs. Quite simply, the Schutzhund dog bites because it likes biting.

The animal's nature is that of a hunter, a predator, a fundamentally aggressive animal. Its urges to chase, bite and struggle are part and parcel of its *life instincts*. Just as it finds pleasure in eating and mating, so it also gains intense gratification from biting.

This point must be absolutely clear: We do not teach the Schutzhund dog to bite. Biting is not an artificial or contrived behavior, like wearing clothes or riding a bicycle are for a circus bear. As Schutzhund trainers we merely take a behavior that is already native to the dog and we channel it, strengthen it and mold it to suit our purposes. Therefore, it should be evident that we can only train the dog *if it wants to bite*. If it does not, then nothing remains but to find a new dog.

In Schutzhund protection the dog is a voluntary, even an intensely eager participant.

CANINE AGGRESSION

The basic requirement of Schutzhund protection is the bite itself—the dog's grip upon the sleeve. The power and quality of the bite are important not only from the standpoint of getting the job done (that is, stopping and disabling an aggressor). They are also important because how the dog bites provides an index to its quality as a working dog and as a prospect for breeding.

The ideal bite is what we call *full*, so that the dog grips the sleeve with its entire jaw, including the molar region. The dog need not fight this way in order to fight a human effectively. But working dog trainers have found over many years that dogs that bite full are normally the best and the bravest animals.

What makes the difference between the dog that bites full and the dog that does not is, to a great extent, their differing degrees of courage. But it is also a fact that the two animals are motivated to bite for different reasons, by different types of behavior. Their *characters* are different.

The dog that bites full displays at least a certain degree of *prey drive*. It pursues and bites the decoy for the same reason that it would chase and bite a rabbit. It is "hunting." The dog in prey mood is unafraid. It bites quietly, its eyes are tranquil and its expression, although intensely keen, is neutral. This dog does not snarl or grimace or flinch as it bites. It enjoys itself and, most important, it will pursue. For the opportunity to bite it will run hundreds of yards or even search for extended periods of time.

The animal that bites with only half of its mouth, or with just its canine teeth, shows a different kind of behavior, a different urge that we call *defense drive*. This dog bites not because it is fun for it, but because it feels it must. It is stressed. It feels endangered, and to at least some extent afraid, and it bites primarily to defend itself. It is therefore much less keen to pursue a person or search in order to find him and engage him in combat. In addition to biting with just the front of its mouth, the defense dog also tends to chew, or nervously shift his grip, especially when under pressure. This dog bites violently and with malevolence. The defense dog is also noisy while it bites, growling and snarling, and it often bristles, erecting the hair on the withers, back and rump.

Almost every animal has the capacity (to some extent) to express both prey- and defense-motivated aggression. Because each type of behavior has its advantages, during agitation we make use of them both.

Prey brings with it eagerness and pleasure in biting. But a "pure" prey dog lacks intensity. In addition, it is also woefully unprepared to bite in a real-life "street" situation in which it is called upon to protect itself and its owner from harm. *Remember, a Schutzhund dog should also be a civil protection dog.* During agitation, the prey dog is taught to regard the protective sleeve that the agitator wears as *prey,* like a rabbit or some other animal that the dog would naturally chase down and bite. It will happily bite anyone that wears the sleeve, even its handler. Consequently, when faced with a person who means to do it or its owner harm, and who wears no sleeve and does not follow the rules of agitation, it is very much at a loss.

The defense dog, on the other hand, is what we call *sharp*—it is always ready to fight, and fight in earnest, in threatening or disorienting circumstances. It is "strong-civil," meaning that it is less interested in the sleeve than the prey dog and more eager to close with the agitator himself. Defense brings with it intensity and violence, and the power to fight in a deadly situation.

However, defense also brings with it stress. The fact that the animal behaves defensively implies that it feels endangered, that fear is at the root of its actions. Consequently, the pure defense dog leaves many things to be desired. For example, it does not bite with a full mouth on the sleeve, and it is frequently too overstimulated during agitation to learn well.

In training, we strive to make the protection dog a balanced animal that

Prey behavior. As the helper reaches to steal the grounded sleeve—the dog's prey—the animal orients at the sleeve itself rather than at the person. The dog's facial expression is neutral, reflecting only keenness and strength of effort to reach the prey.

Defense behavior. Now the helper attacks the dog. The animal focuses on the attacker rather than the sleeve, and the change in the dog's expression is dramatic.

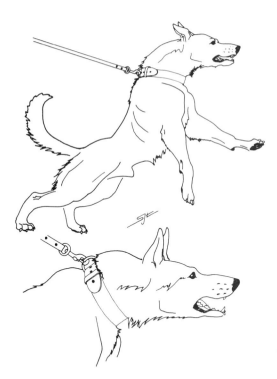

In prey mood the dog does not threaten, seeking only to reach the prey and bite.

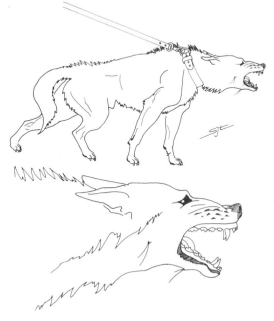

In defense mood, the dog threatens.

169

expresses both prey- and defense-motivated behavior. However, although with intelligent work we can change the dog's basic orientation to some extent, its basic prey-versus-defense characteristics are mainly a product of genetics. The animal comes to us primarily prey-oriented or primarily defense-oriented. Therefore, as trainers and sportspeople, it is important to choose the type of dog with advantages and disadvantages that suit us best.

The authors prefer an animal that is fundamentally a prey dog. It bites for fun, day after day, clearheaded and happy, but there is a deadly serious edge of defense to it that lends it intensity. Prey will give it pleasure in biting and durability over years of competition and training, while defense will give it the raw power and violence we can call on in time of need.

THE ART OF AGITATION

During basic agitation, the helper's function is to serve as the dog's adversary in order to intensify the animal's drives and desire to bite. It is the decoy's responsibility to increase the dog's courage and confidence, and also to modulate precisely and with split-second timing between the moods of defense and prey.

He modulates between prey and defense by changing his posture and his attitude so that the dog responds differently to him from one moment to the next. He causes the moods of prey and defense in the animal and then attracts the behaviors that they drive toward himself.

The attraction for prey drive is primarily movement. When the decoy moves laterally or away from the dog, especially in a jerky or erratic fashion, he excites the animal's predatory instincts, and the animal begins to hunt him. The dog pursues the decoy as though he were a big rabbit, and the desire to bite awakens.

The attraction for defense is threat. Dogs have many ways of conveying threat to each other, and the agitator must understand them all. Dogs communicate with gestures, postures and movements. Human beings also use this nonverbal or body language. A good decoy is in touch with body language. He grasps how people use movements and postures to communicate, and he understands how human body language must be subtly altered in order to convey his intent to the dog.

First and foremost, for a dog, and throughout much of the animal kingdom, threat is made through eye contact. For example, baboons have bright patches on their eyelids that emphasize their eyes and the threat that they represent; some butterflies have great dark spots on their wings that frighten predators because they mimic eyes; and human prizefighters stare impassively into each other's eyes before a bout.

Another canine threat is immobility, stillness. Who has not seen how slowly dogs move when they confront one another and how perfectly still they stand, staring fixedly at each other? Thus, the more still the decoy remains as he stares, the more threatening he will seem.

The agitator rewards defensive behavior with retreat. The animal is incited by threatening. When it "counters," defending itself and the prey powerfully, the agitator flees. Note the change in expression from defense to prey and the renewed interest in the sleeve after the agitator retreats.

Animals also threaten through inflation of body size. When they feel endangered, owls extend their wings and flare their feathers; some species of lizards gape their mouths and extend great shields of skin around their heads and shoulders; and cats and dogs *pilo erect* (raise the fur on their backs). A gifted decoy can achieve the same effect by expanding his chest and lungs, drawing himself erect and letting his elbows rotate out from his sides.

The decoy uses a combination of these elements of threat, as well as movement directly toward the animal, to alarm the dog and attract defensive behavior. A truly gifted decoy can sense just what combination to use with each dog at the right moment to make it "come out."

However, the helper does not merely pressure the dog. He must also encourage it. By rewarding the animal's efforts, he can intensify drive and induce the dog to become more and more confident about behaving aggressively.

The agitator rewards prey behavior with movement and by allowing the dog to bite. He starts the dog with a little motion, and then moves more and more quickly and erratically in response to the dog's pursuit. As the animal begins to become excited, the decoy feeds on this energy, becoming more and more frenetic and intensifying still further the animal's desire to catch him. At a peak moment, when the aroused dog is putting out an intense effort, the decoy rewards it by allowing a quick bite on a rag or sleeve.

The decoy rewards defensive behavior with retreat, by yielding to the dog's counterthreat. He first incites the animal by threatening it. Then the dog, alarmed, threatens back and the agitator rewards its attempt to defend itself by running away. The dog learns that it can shatter the decoy's threat by threatening back.

When the decoy returns, he threatens a little more strongly and the dog, emboldened by its recent success, will lash out at him more intensely. Progressively, we teach the animal to withstand a greater and greater threat.

EQUIPMENT NEEDED FOR PROTECTION

Six-Foot Leather Leash

The leash is perhaps the single weakest link in the system of safeguards that preserves the agitator's skin. In most training situations, the helper takes care of himself by staying alert and reacting quickly and effectively to emergencies that arise. Because he carries a rag or a sleeve much of the time, he is normally in little danger from a dog that breaks loose on the field. However, when he is working close to an animal, especially over a grounded rag or sleeve, only the reliability of the leash and snap protect him from a nasty bite wound.

A heavy-duty, one-inch-wide leash with stitching and riveting at both snap end and wrist loop is strongly recommended. The snap should be of a size, strength and quality corresponding to the leash. Brass snaps, although not as strong as steel, will not corrode and are often better made. Well-sewn nylon leashes are stronger than leather, but they tend to be very hard on the hands.

172

Long Line

Normally, the line used in tracking training is not strong enough to provide perfect safety in bite work, especially because we often use the long lines not just as corrective devices but also as tie-out lines to secure the dogs to posts or trees for agitation. The best lines are thirty feet in length, and made of one-inch tubular nylon webbing. The flat, nontubular webbing long lines sold by most vendors are more than strong enough, but they are extremely punishing to the hands. We often find it necessary to make our own lines, and we buy the nylon at a mountaineering shop.

Leather Collar

The first function of the agitation collar is to restrain the animal without any possibility of failure. The second function, just as important, is to allow the dog, even encourage it, to use itself physically as hard as it can against the collar.

The agitation collar should therefore be double layered, at least one inch wide so that it will not choke the dog, and fashioned of leather that is soft enough so that the edges of the collar will not bite into the animal's neck when it throws its weight into the collar. Hardware and rivets should be extremely strong.

Safety Collar

In the initial stages of training, the dog is taught spirit, not control. This means that, if it breaks loose suddenly during agitation, the handler may not be able to control it by voice, even if there is time to give commands before the dog reaches the decoy.

Agitation collars are seldom broken. However, among groups of novice trainers they are frequently slipped, meaning that the dogs spin and, in so doing, back their heads out of their heavy leather collars. This is especially a problem with smaller-headed breeds like Doberman Pinschers and Belgian Malinois. This cannot be prevented by tightening the agitation collar without defeating its purpose: With the collar cinched down tight upon its throat the dog cannot strain with all of its power against the leash without choking itself. Therefore, in normal practice the agitation collar should be left relatively loose so that it rides down around the massive muscles of the animal's neck. Insurance against the dog slipping the collar is provided by the trainer's skill in handling and also by a safety collar.

The best type of collar for this purpose is a thin nylon choker collar (really just a cord connecting two steel rings) sized much too large for the dog so that it encircles its neck leaving six or eight inches to spare. The safety collar is placed lower on the dog's neck than the agitation collar, and the live ring is snapped into the leash along with the D ring of the agitation collar. Very often, even if the animal manages to slip its leather collar, the safety collar will stay on and draw tight as it backs out of the leather one.

Correction Collar

In order to control the dog, to teach it when it should and should not bite and to pay attention to commands even when it is extremely aroused, a correction collar is needed. With many dogs, especially top-quality working-breed animals that are both physically and psychologically "hard," a normal chain choke collar will not be sufficient. Therefore, we use a pinch or prong collar.

Because fitting the prong collar to the dog is complicated, the reader should have an experienced trainer demonstrate how this is done. The most important consideration is that the collar be snug, so that the yoke does not hang loose. When fitted in this way the pinch collar is intentionally rather severe, and requires in its use not crude strength but sensitivity and good timing. This sensitive touch should also be demonstrated by an experienced handler.

Six Blinds

The blinds must be portable, yet very durable because they are subjected to tremendous amounts of abuse. They should be large enough to conceal a person, and there must also be a means of staking them to the ground so that the wind will not fell them (a constant nuisance otherwise). Several vendors in the United States sell ready-made, light and compact versions.

Bite Pants

In the case of well-trained dogs, there is little danger that they will bite the helper anyplace other than the arm. (It is the agitator's job to ensure that it is the sleeve arm!) The animals soon become attuned to the sleeve, and come to regard it as their prey, their goal. However, accidents do happen, especially in the blind, after the outs and when making the acquaintance of new dogs.

Accordingly, the agitator should make a habit of wearing bite pants, which are really a sort of overall. These pants will stop teeth, but they will not save one from the considerable pain of a bite and an appalling bruise. It is normally after his first bite in the legs that a brash young decoy learns respect for the dogs.

Even when the agitator estimates the chances of a leg bite at nil, he will still find the pants necessary because of the surprising amount of damage the dogs will do both to his clothes and his body with their claws.

Sacks or Rags

Burlap feed sacks work very well as a biting surface for puppies and novice dogs. They can be rolled and stitched to preserve their shape.

Tugs

A very good dog that is well prepared and bites the sack eagerly will also bite the sleeve without hesitation. However, for the majority of dogs of less than outstanding quality, it is often useful to have a puppy tug in order to prepare the animals to move to a harder, more unyielding and bulky biting surface.

Puppy Sleeves

The same goes for puppy sleeves (soft, pliable and easily bitten sleeves designed for young and novice dogs). Very good or well-trained dogs do not need puppy sleeves and can move directly from the rag to the hard sleeve. However, in training the typical dog a puppy sleeve is normally necessary, if only for a few transitional bites before the animal advances to the hard sleeve.

In addition, puppy sleeves have the advantage that, because they are relatively soft, they are easily bitten and present little hazard to the teeth, jaws or spine of a hot-blooded young dog that is perhaps on the sleeve early and working itself hard. The puppy may be quite willing and eager to bite the hard sleeve, but it is best to protect the novice dog from impacts and accidents until it is older and physically more rugged. Furthermore, it is nearly impossible, no matter what mistake is made, to break a dog's canine tooth with the soft sleeve. Accordingly, we restrict novice agitators almost exclusively to the use of soft sleeves until they have become competent.

Hard Sleeve

In competition, Schutzhund dogs are judged specifically on the quality—the fullness and the power—of their bite, and awarded point totals and courage ratings accordingly. In trial, the animals bite what is called a bite-bar sleeve. This sleeve is made of plastic or leather, has a blade or bar that provides a V-shaped biting surface, and, when uncovered, is nearly as hard as a piece of wood. To give the animal's teeth purchase and to protect the sleeve an expendable jute sleeve cover is used with it. This bite-bar sleeve allows the dog, if it has the desire, to bite with its entire jaw, all the way back to the molars. Thus, it allows the judge to evaluate the animal's quality of bite.

There are schools of training that employ a great number of techniques and devices in the effort to teach the dogs to bite full. Accordingly, these trainers use several different types of progressively harder sleeves, often concluding with an enormous hard barrel sleeve which theoretically gets the dog in the habit of using a huge, mauling mouth to bite.

This approach views the bite as a fundamentally mechanical event, a skill or habit that must be meticulously taught. We disagree. To us the bite is an emotional event. The basis of a crushing, full-mouth bite is in spirit, not in mechanics, and a correct bite is not a function of how the dog is "taught" to bite and what sort of sleeve is used in order to involve the maximum number of its teeth. The bite is a function of the dog's basic motivation for biting, whether defense or prey, and of how badly it wants to bite in the first place.

If the animal only half wants to bite, then we can expect it to bite with a half mouth. If, on the other hand, it is consumed by its desire, so that neither hesitation nor prudence exist for it, then it will engulf the sleeve (no matter what its form, shape or hardness) and no one will have cause to doubt its courage.

We urge the prospective Schutzhund enthusiast to see to the dog and its spirit, not some arsenal of sleeves, devices and techniques.

The ideal bite: full-mouthed and hard. (Brandon Mathias' "Nico," Schutzhund I, on Kirk Maze.)

Sticks

The stick is a section of reed. It is light, flexible and approximately thirty inches in length. In training we also use other sorts of sticks in order to harden the dogs. Rattly split-bamboo batons, riding crops, whiffle-ball bats filled with handfuls of noisy gravel and other devices can all be used to inure the animals to challenges and intimidation of any sort.

15

Protection:
Drive Work

In SOME WAYS bite work is the least artificial and most interesting of the three phases of Schutzhund training, because it is here that we see raw dog behavior at its purest. In protection we observe the dog doing what comes naturally to it. Obedience, by contrast, is primarily inhibitory in nature. Obedience is mainly concerned with teaching the animal to restrain impulses to roam, explore, hunt animals and try its strength against other dogs. Tracking is certainly founded on the animal's natural behavior, but Schutzhund tracking is so stylized by the necessity to determine a winner that it little resembles a hunter searching out prey.

To our mind, nothing distills the essence of what a dog is, nothing smacks so much of the predator, as the sight of a dog coursing in full stride downfield after a person, heading for a collision that it wants with every fiber of its being. The animal is momentarily unfettered, free and impelled solely by its own desire.

In bite work we see the character of the individual dog most clearly. Good trainers can and do "fake" dogs of deficient character through obedience and tracking. It is much more difficult to counterfeit a dog in bite work. On the protection field, as the dog copes simultaneously with the challenge posed by the agitator (whose job it is to test its nerve) and pressure from its handler (who demands that it obey), we can steal a quick look into the dog's heart and see what is there.

We look for courage, because without courage the animal is empty, hollow. We also look for a dog that is "in hand," that obeys the handler utterly, in spite of an urge to bite and forget all else.

But what we look for first in the dog is raw power. Power arises from desire, and we look for a dog with a desire that drives it to use its body to the utmost—an animal that hurls itself with a crash into the agitator. This kind of desire arises first from genetics (the dog must be born with a full complement of vigorous drives) and second from the first few months of its training. We call this initial stage of schooling *drive work.*

Drive work has three basic objectives:

1. To establish in the animal boldness, commitment and power by creating an intense desire for combat with the agitator
2. To strike in the dog the best possible balance between defense- and prey-motivated aggression
3. To teach the dog to bite with a full, hard mouth

During the second phase of training, *field work,* we teach the dog control, harnessing its power to the exercises of the Schutzhund I, II and III protection routine. We cannot proceed to field work until we have fully accomplished the three basic objectives.

In drive work we lay the dog's foundation. If the dog is not solid, steady of nerve and passionate in desire, then it will not weather the inevitable discouragements of field work. Each correction that the dog receives will diminish its quality and, in the end, we will all wonder why such a good-looking young dog did not turn out as well as we thought it would.

A fundamental difference between the two phases of protection training is that in drive work we physically restrain the animal, while in field work we begin to teach it to restrain itself.

In drive work all control of the dog is physical. We don't command it—we hold it back. There is no obedience in drive work, because obedience kills drive. There is no punishment, no correction. The dog is manhandled from one place to another, free to strain and fight the collar to its heart's content. Not only do we allow the animal to struggle against its handler in order to get at the helper, we encourage it. Being physically held back creates the frustration that builds drive.

It is extremely important to understand that protection training is utterly different from obedience. This applies especially to those who, although novices in Schutzhund, are experienced in obedience training and already have their own way of doing things. We do not compel or command the dog to bite, we allow it to. The dog does it on its own and there is little that we can do to help if its nerve fails, especially when it is defending us from someone *we* are afraid of. It is entirely the dog's endeavor, and it needs both spirit and a sense of independence to accomplish it. The animal must develop an initiative and a will apart from ours, and obedience training (especially heavy-handed obedience) has just the opposite effect. Slaves make poor bodyguards.

To put it another way: We don't need brakes until we have some horsepower.

GOAL 1: The puppy will bite the sack.

Important Concepts for Meeting the Goal

1. Playing with the sack
2. Working on the agitator
3. Making prey over the sack
4. Beginning runaway bites

1. Playing with the sack

Ideally, drive work begins in puppyhood. But, because puppies are neither physically nor psychologically fully developed and are consequently more fragile than adults, the vast majority of puppy work is based on prey.

The first step is simply to play with the puppy and establish a biting response to the burlap sack. This response will be automatic and very strong in some puppies. With others the desire must be awakened and the mechanics of the bite itself worked upon (puppies are clumsy!).

It is not necessary to use an agitator in this initial stage. The handler can accomplish a great deal by playing with the puppy himself. There are two important points to remember. First, the puppy must always be the victor and win the rag from its handler, so that it does not learn the habit of giving up. Second, we must never play the game until the puppy grows tired or bored with it. In fact, throughout training, no matter what the age or level of the dog, the fundamental rule of agitation is: Never allow the animal as many bites as it wants.

2. Working on the agitator

Once the puppy displays a strong biting response to the burlap rag, and once it is accustomed to the leash and collar, it is ready for formal agitation. This may be as early as ten or twelve weeks of age.

Very confident, driven puppies can work all by themselves, one on one with the training decoy. Less confident puppies will profit from being agitated in groups that include older, more experienced animals that pursue the helper hotly, so that the youngsters can learn by watching them. If a puppy is too interested in pursuing the other dogs instead, and ignores the decoy, then wait a few sessions to see if it begins to transfer its interest to the decoy. If not, begin agitating the puppy by itself.

The best group agitation method is line agitation. The dogs and handlers are arrayed in a line at evenly spaced intervals. The decoys run up and down the line, zigzagging, jinking and waving sacks, and hiding in blinds when they need rest. Movement is continuous, fast and very exciting, and the decoys take care never to run directly *at* any of the younger puppies. For the first few sessions, the completely naive animals are placed at the ends of the line and ignored by the

"Zorro" in flight downfield after the agitator.

Ideally, drive work begins in puppyhood. (Birke v. Haus Barwig.)

The first step in protection training is establishing a strong prey-biting response to the burlap rag. The handler can accomplish this simply by playing tug-of-war with the puppy. (Ann Weickert and Blitzkrieg v. Haus Barwig.)

helpers until they are accustomed to the situation. If they show no fear of the decoys or the other dogs, and if they pursue the sack, then they are gradually included in the activities of line agitation.

Once the puppy is comfortable in the line, and once its desire for the sack is intense, the helper begins allowing it bites. At first, he just lets the pup snatch the rag out of his hand as he passes by. Later, he keeps hold of the rag for a moment or two after the puppy seizes it, and tugs lightly. If the youngster bites impetuously and with a big mouth on the sack, and holds fast to it, the helper begins progressively to make it fight harder and harder in order to win the prey.

While struggling over the rag, the agitator must be active and vigorous with the puppy without either intimidating it or being physically punishing with the youngster. The trick is to *appear* violent but to be gentle.

3. Making prey over the sack

Once the decoy allows the puppy to take the rag away from him, he waits quietly while the handler praises the animal and then gently forces the puppy to give it up and drop it on the ground. Then the decoy moves in toward the grounded sack—the puppy's prey. The decoy should act submissive and fearful as he approaches. He directs his attention always toward the rag, not the puppy, reaching tentatively for the burlap and then skittering back. Furthermore, he makes no attempt to threaten or stimulate defensive behavior. However, if the pup suddenly becomes a little aggressive toward him, he must react, retreating in order to reward the animal's attempts to guard its prey.

As the helper reaches for the sack, the puppy will normally strive to repossess it, straining toward it and trying to bite it. The helper should encourage this prey-guarding impulse by grabbing the sack as if to steal it and then flicking it, in the same motion, up into the youngster's jaws.

Eventually, the agitator steals the prey, snatching it away with a motion that causes it to flare out, bringing it alive again so that the pup is stimulated to pursue it once more.

4. Beginning runaway bites

When the young dog bites with energy and also some force, and shows an intense prey urge to possess and guard the sack (sometimes as early as twelve to fourteen weeks of age), it is time to begin teaching it to pursue the decoy.

At a moment during agitation when the puppy is especially aroused, the helper passes by the puppy quickly, letting it try for but not reach the rag, and keeps going a few steps. The handler lets the puppy run a short way against the resistance of the collar (running with it but holding it back in order to inspire it) and carefully allows the puppy to overtake the decoy and bite the sack. Gradually, these *pursuits* become longer and longer until finally the handler just drops the leash and allows the puppy to run free.

These fledgling runaways are the young working dog's first taste of the

The handler lets the puppy run a short way against the resistance of the collar, and then carefully allows the dog to overtake the agitator and bite the sack. (Charley Bartholomew handling Ann Weickert's "Blitz.")

heady excitement of the chase. If its heart is brave, runaway bites will begin to build in it a warlike passion for the driving sprint and crashing impact of the courage test.

GOAL 2: The puppy will bite the sleeve.

When the puppy begins to teethe at around four months of age, do not discontinue agitation. Simply allow it very few bites, and be sure to be very gentle with its mouth. If the desire to bite has already been well awakened, then several weeks of vigorous, frustrating agitation with very few bites will do the young dog nothing but good.

In general, it is best to wait until the dog is ten to twelve months old before introducing it to the sleeve, even if it has a great deal of quality and is more than willing to bite the sleeve at five to six months, as some puppies are.

Important Concepts for Meeting the Goal

1. Using drive to bring the puppy onto the sleeve
2. Repeating the progression

1. Using drive to bring the puppy onto the sleeve

Do not introduce the youngster to the sleeve carefully, by agitating slowly and then gently offering it to the dog. This method gives the dog too much time to recognize that the sleeve is something different, something it hasn't seen before, and to hesitate. It is virtually the worst possible way to approach the animal. Always remember that it is the puppy's drive that gives it power, and that drive arises from intense agitation. We must use the animal's drive to make it impetuous, so that it dives into new situations without hesitating.

In order to prepare the puppy for its first sleeve bite, it is best to run it through several frustration sessions in which it is agitated but not allowed to bite, so that it is aroused and completely in spirit.

We always "fool" the puppy into biting the sleeve the first few times. The agitator wears a sleeve on his left arm and carries a rag in his right hand. He agitates very energetically for a few moments, running past the puppy and letting it try for the sack, and then, when the animal is quite beside itself with excitement, he steps away. Very quickly, before the moment passes, he wraps the sack loosely about the sleeve and, giving the puppy no time to reconsider, steps in and lets it bite the sack and the sleeve under it.

It is important to drop the sleeve the instant the youngster grabs it. Let the animal win the sleeve before its new weight and texture cause the puppy to have second thoughts. The handler should allow it to maul the sleeve for a moment and then break the puppy loose from it and move the animal back, so that the decoy can snatch the sleeve away and begin to agitate again.

After the decoy allows the dog to take the sleeve, the handler praises the animal, and then forces it to give up its prey by lifting up on the collar, holding the forequarters suspended in the air until the sleeve is released. (Chuck Cadillac and "Gitte," Schutzhund III.)

The agitator "fools" the puppy into biting the sleeve for the first time by stimulating the animal with a sack, and then wrapping the sack around the sleeve. ("Blitz.")

2. Repeating the progression

As training progresses, the sleeve bites become progressively longer in duration and more challenging. However, we proceed very cautiously. Because the sleeve seems at first to be part of the helper's body (while the rag is obviously not), biting the sleeve is much more demanding of the puppy's nerve. For example, we do not assume that just because the young dog does a good, fast runaway bite on the sack that it will automatically do the same on the sleeve. Instead, we repeat the same careful progression we employed on the sack:

- obtain a good, hard bite on the sleeve
- introduce short pursuits on leash
- progress to long pursuits on leash
- introduce short runaways off leash
- progress to long runaways off leash

GOAL 3: The dog will perform committed runaway bites.

By the time that the dog is one year of age it should be biting *hard* with a crushing, full-mouth grip on the sleeve. If it does not shift its grip while biting, show any sensitivity to the agitator or growl on the sleeve (growling is profoundly defensive, and thus the product of unsureness), then we can begin letting it run free to the bite. The quality of the bite (and of the dog) is seen not only in what the dog does while on the sleeve, but also in how it gets to it. The bite is not just a grip, it is also a strike. When the dog is powerful, when its desire is so overwhelming that it leaves no room in its heart for fear or hesitation, then the dog *hurls* itself at the agitator.

We first look for commitment in the young or novice dog during the runaway bites. This will be the first time we will have the chance to see the dog bite without the support of a tight leash connecting it closely to its handler.

Important Concept for Meeting the Goal

Catching the dog correctly

Once the young dog drives hard into the collar and chases spiritedly in the on-leash pursuits (see Goal 1, Concept 4), it is ready to go off leash. The first runaways should be very short, perhaps ten to thirty feet. If the dog throws itself into the sleeve and bites convincingly, we can gradually make the runaways longer and longer.

Runaway bites are the decoy's job. How well he catches will determine how hard the dog hits. He must be smooth and well timed so that the young dog does not pay a price in pain for a good, hard impact.

First, he must not run too fast, as a fast pace demands too much calculation

186

on the dog's part and will slow it as it tries to match its stride to the decoy's. The trick is to run quite slowly while still giving the impression that one is desperately fleeing. The dog should overtake the agitator like a bolt of lightning!

The decoy must not be unsteady or unpredictable. He must not swerve! He should make a good, reliable target for the animal. There will be plenty of time later on to teach the dog to catch people that try not to be caught. For now, the person should be a sitting duck.

Last, and most important, the agitator must absorb the dog's momentum effectively. The agitator must pivot smoothly with the animal as it enters the bite, minimizing the impact on neck and jaws. We must not make a good young dog suffer for its courage.

The courageous, spirited animal will thrive on runaway bites, and we will soon begin to use them to reward it when it has done fine work.

GOAL 4: The dog will withstand the stick and drive without anxiety or disturbance of its bite.

In Schutzhund protection, there are two main phases during which the judge gauges a dog's courage and spirit: the courage test and what we will refer to as the stick and drive. In Schutzhund I the stick and drive takes place in the attack on handler, in Schutzhund II during the reattack after the helper's attempt to escape and in Schutzhund III during both the reattack and after the courage test.

The stick and drive poses two main difficulties, two stressors for the dog: It is struck with a reed stick and is driven before the decoy. Fighting a person who rushes forward, driving the dog backward, is a far different matter for the animal than fighting one who pulls away, struggling to escape.

In training the Schutzhund, it is always useful to subdivide exercises and isolate the sources of stress or confusion for the animal. We therefore compartmentalize the stick and drive, and teach the dog first to withstand the stick hits alone and then the drive alone. Only then will the helper stick-hit the dog and drive it at the same time.

Important Concepts for Meeting the Goal

1. Accustoming the dog to the stick
2. Introducing the drive
3. Combining the stick hits with the drive

1. Accustoming the dog to the stick

We further divide the threat represented by the stick into two different stressors: the actual contact with the stick (the blows themselves) and the very powerful and menacing gestures that the agitator makes in wielding the stick.

(Stick-shy dogs almost invariably seem to have as much fear of the gestures as they do of the stick hits.)

Early in agitation, the decoy takes great pains to accustom the puppy or novice adult dog to his hands, to direct contact with them and also to the sight of them moving past or toward its head and eyes while it is biting. If the dog shows no fear of these gestures or soft blows of the open hand, then the agitator begins to carry a stick.

At first he uses the stick very little, and his gestures are mild. With time, as the animal becomes more powerful, the agitator uses the stick more and more menacingly. He begins to lash out, making the stick hum through the air about the dog as it bites. Although he never strikes the dog, the helper frequently and gently touches the animal with the stick, to show the dog that it will not hurt. The objective is to accustom the dog to progressively more and more intense threats without ever actually awakening fear. If the dog blinks or winces at the stick, seeks to pull away from it while it bites or growls, then the decoy is progressing too quickly. Remember, growling on the sleeve is not a sign of strength but of weakness. Ideally, the dog should seem oblivious of the stick.

If the animal shows no anxiety in response to very strong gestures, the decoy begins striking objects around it with the stick. He hits the ground, the handler, a fence, but never the dog. Eventually, he hits the dog's leash where it runs taut from the collar to the handler, so that the dog can for the first time see the gesture directed at itself and feel the shock of the blow through its collar.

Only after the dog has enough experience to be fully accustomed to the stick whistling all about it will the agitator actually strike the animal. At first, although the gestures are very strong, the blows themselves are very light. Gradually, the intensity of the blows increases to match that of the gestures, so that the dog both sees and feels the stick used on it. However, the stick is never, under any circumstances, used full force. A good helper never hits a dog harder than he himself would be willing to be struck in the pursuit of a rough game. In addition, the dog is struck only in a very specified manner, on the upper sides of its rib cage and never on the head, neck, legs, pelvis or tail.

All initial stick work should be performed on leash, and the decoy never uses the stick on a runaway bite until he is certain that the animal has no anxiety about the stick hits or the runaway itself.

2. Introducing the drive

Once the dog "stays" under the stick without difficulty, we begin introducing it to the drive. First, the agitator drives the dog laterally around the circle formed by the leash, with the handler at its center. In this way, the dog is driven laterally or sideways rather than straight backward, and also the handler can easily reassure the animal by maintaining tension on the leash.

Later, he drives the dog straight backward toward its handler, who maintains leash tension by backing up. Only if the dog accepts being driven on a tight leash without "backing-off" its bite (taking a smaller mouth on the sleeve), growling or changing its grip will the agitator drive it after a runaway bite, when it is far from its handler and there is no tight leash to encourage it.

3. Combining the stick hits with the drive

The decoy never combines both stick hits and the drive until the dog is absolutely comfortable with these two stressors individually. Furthermore, the first few times that he hits the dog while driving it, this will be done with the animal on a tight leash and with the handler close by to reassure the dog.

A very good dog will not require all this careful schooling on the stick and drive. However, in dog training, as in all else, caution almost always pays. If we proceed without caution and suddenly discover that our dog is not completely stick-sure—when it loosens or releases its bite under a rash stick hit—then, unfortunately, much of the damage has already been done.

GOAL 5: The dog will enter its bite at full speed in the courage test.

The courage test is the culmination of the Schutzhund protection routine. It is primarily here that the dog shows its quality or lack of it

The courage test is difficult for two reasons. First, this exercise carries the dog far away from its handler to where it feels itself to be alone. Second, in the courage test the agitator runs directly *at* the dog rather than away from it.

Our goal in training is to teach the dog to hit just as hard and enter its bite every bit as fast on a charging agitator as it does on a runaway. We prepare the dog to bite a charging agitator by breaking the exercise down into a progression, a carefully designed series of steps in training.

Important Concepts for Meeting the Goal

1. Biting a charging agitator on leash
2. Biting a charging agitator off leash but at short distance
3. Biting a retreating agitator at long distance
4. Biting a charging agitator at long distance
5. Catching the dog correctly

1. Biting a charging agitator on leash

The handler holds the dog at the full length of a six-foot leash attached to the animal's leather agitation collar. The agitator begins at a distance of about seventy-five feet, and charges straight at the dog. He rushes, at first somewhat cautiously, all the way to within six or eight feet of the dog, stops and runs back out to his starting point. Twice he rushes in and stops short like this, so that the dog undergoes the experience of being charged at without enduring the stress of actually having to bite in these new and challenging circumstances. Then, the

Fighting an assailant who drives forward, threatening and striking the dog with a stick, is a far different matter than biting an attacker who pulls away, striving to escape. (Susan Barwig's "Natz," Schutzhund III, FH, on Chuck Cozine.)

Here, where the dog is held on a tight leash and closely supported by its handler, we show the animal the most difficult courage tests it will ever experience. (Officer Russ Slade and "Amigo.")

third time, the agitator charges all the way in and lets the animal bite the sleeve.

In the beginning, the decoy keeps his distance from the dog on the two false starts; he stops well short to avoid intimidating the animal. And when he does close with the dog for the bite, he is not terribly forceful.

Later in training, he becomes progressively more unyielding and aggressive. He stops his charge only inches short on the false starts, and when he comes to the dog for the bite he will give the impression, until the last instant, that he is going to crash head-on into the animal. Here, where conditions are ideal for the dog because it is held on a tight leash and closely supported by its handler, we show the animal the hardest, most intimidating courage tests that it will ever experience, so that it will be absolutely accustomed to the worst a decoy can ever do. The helper must show no give to the dog. He must charge down at the animal as though he had no intention of slowing down. However, he must also be extremely adept at braking himself at the last instant and then slipping to the side so that the dog experiences only the very slightest collision as it bites.

Any satisfactorily prepared dog of fair character can be made to bite like a lion in this *static courage test*. The problem will be to get it to bite just as powerfully at a distance and unrestrained by the leash. We accomplish this by performing a careful transition composed of several intermediate steps.

First, we set up the static courage test exercise again, with one difference. On the third pass, instead of remaining stationary and waiting for the decoy to arrive, the handler runs the dog forward to meet him. Now the dog actually has the experience of charging at an onrushing agitator, but it is supported and inspired by the leash that tightly restrains it to half speed.

2. Biting a charging agitator off leash but at short distance

Second, on the final pass of the static courage test the handler drops the leash, allowing the dog to rocket forward across the last few yards still separating it from the charging agitator and crash into the sleeve. The effect of releasing the pent-up, frustrated animal at such a moment is much like loosing an arrow from a tightly drawn bow.

Next, we forego the initial two passes. The dog is released on the helper's first charge, when the helper is still fifty or sixty feet out.

3. Biting a retreating agitator at long distance

Next, we send the dog at long distance, with the agitator seventy-five to 100 yards away. Agitator and dog rush toward each other at full speed. The decoy yells and brandishes the stick menacingly. When they are still forty or fifty feet apart, he suddenly stops short and reverses direction. At the moment when the dog arrives, the decoy is in retreat, backpedaling as fast as he can.

It is the helper's job to protect the dog from injury during the courage test. The braver the dog, the more difficult this is to do. The helper avoids a direct impact by, at the last instant, stepping a little to the side, which moves the center of gravity out from behind the sleeve. This way the "catch" is not a collision but a smooth pivot. (Officer Chris Worsham's "Beny.")

4. Biting a charging agitator at long distance

Finally, we perform a full courage test at seventy-five to 100 yards. The decoy does not reverse, but instead bores all the way in. The dog is so inspired that neither fear nor hesitation exist for it, and it goes into the decoy with all its strength and spirit.

Thus, by approximating the courage test in several different ways and depending upon the animal's blind eagerness to carry it into the sleeve, we bring the dog to the point that it will perform a brilliant, spectacular courage test the first time that we give it the opportunity.

5. Catching the dog correctly

At this point, everything depends upon the helper. He must rush the dog in such a fashion that the dog is fairly challenged, but he must also, at all costs, avoid a head-on collision with the animal. A good decoy does this by, at the last instant, slipping his body mass—his center of gravity—out from behind the sleeve and allowing the dog's inertia to pivot him. The maneuver requires considerable experience and athletic ability and, if badly done, it can be dangerous for the animal. Therefore, with a good dog that bites bravely, one must be extremely cautious about sending it on courage tests.

However, at the same time, there is no need to practice the courage test frequently. Quite to the contrary, the fewer the full courage tests the dog performs, and the fewer impacts it experiences, the more impressive it will be on trial day.

The only problem we have encountered in using this method is that sometimes the dogs become *too* brave, too committed to the bite. In the case of a dog that is too fast in the courage test for its own safety (or the agitator's, for that matter) we simply practice the courage test repetitively. We use an expert helper, keep the distances short in order to keep the dog safe, and after repeated impacts the animal normally becomes more prudent.

SUMMARY

Depending upon the dog and the trainers, the drive-work phase of protection training may last anywhere from two to eighteen months. The time interval is not important. The task is accomplished and the dog is ready to progress only when it bites with a reasonably full mouth and great power, is reasonably well-balanced between prey and defense, has absolutely no fear of being driven and stick-hit and performs the most impressive courage test of which it is capable.

However, do not think that drive work is ever entirely finished. Throughout the dog's working career, we will concern ourselves constantly with maintaining (and intensifying, if possible) our dog's desire to bite. This task was vital early in its training, as we sought to establish its power. It may be even more important in field work, when we will begin, for the first time, to harness and control that power.

16

Protection:

The Hold and Bark

and the Out

A FEW YEARS AGO, while discussing the nature of control with a fellow trainer, we heard a story that illustrates the central problem of field work.

"I once had a wonderful young dog that bit like a lion. One day, very proudly, I showed him to an old-time German dog trainer, and asked this man if my youngster was not truly a good dog. The old man said, 'Show him to me again when he has three years and a clean bark and a clean out and still he bites like that, and then I will say that he is a good dog.' "

What the old man meant was simply this: A dog that bites with fire and bravery is not so rare. What is rare is an animal that has the strength to be strongly controlled by its handler, and *still* bite with fire and bravery.

Our German friend put his finger on an idea that we have since learned to be indisputably true. The acid test of a biting dog's quality comes when, for the first time, it is forced to restrain itself during agitation. Many animals simply cannot support being controlled and corrected in bite work instead of being constantly encouraged. When the only load on their nerves comes from the person in front of them, they shine. But when pressure comes from behind, from their handlers (and some very hard-looking dogs can be extraordinarily sensitive to pressure from this direction), they crumble. Where before they were sure under the stick, now they flinch. Where before they invariably bit with full mouths, now they chew and back off, rolling their eyes behind them and worrying about the out that they know is coming.

It seems that every generation of working dog trainers has an older generation behind it that is fond of telling how much harder the dogs of the old days were. We have heard these stories again and again. However, we are inclined to believe them, because we have seen how dogs were trained in the old days. They had to be hard.

For example, the old-time method of teaching the hold and bark involved standing a decoy thirty-one feet away, sending the dog at him and then correcting the animal very sharply with a long line when it hit thirty feet, six inches. This procedure is roughly analogous to knocking down in one instant a house that has been painstakingly constructed over a period of many months. All the dog's life up to this moment, its trainers have urged it on in bite work, stoked the flames of its desire, never asking it to hold one bit of itself back. Now, in one instant, they change the rules, with rather unpleasant consequences for the animal.

However, this crude sort of method does work, if only in the sense that we can use it to easily teach the typical dog not to bite a person who is standing still. The shock and confusion produced by the unprecedented correction inhibit the animal, damping its excitement. The dog's desire to bite brings it pain, so it powers down, resorting to other behavior. Because it feels unsure, it begins to bark, and the decoy rewards it for barking by moving and inducing the animal to bite. The lesson for the dog is clear: Cope with control and corrections by calming down, by stopping the flow of energy. Wait until conditions change, until control lifts, and then come into drive again.

We call this *training for control by inhibition.* It yields dogs that are one kind of animal when they are free to bite, and another, much lesser animal when they are restrained by control.

It is not difficult to train a dog this way. One needs only persistence and a heavy hand—and a hard dog. We can even produce a good dog by training with inhibition. But the difference between a good dog and a great dog is that a great dog is as calm, confident, aggressive and powerful when under control as when actually biting.

When a great dog is forbidden to bite, when commanded to ''Out!'' its drive does not diminish. It does not suddenly become less dog than it was a moment before. Instead, it energizes a new behavior, carrying all its energy intact as it outs and begins to bark powerfully.

We call this *training for control by activation,* and it depends upon making the animal understand perfectly what it is that it must do in order to get what it wants from us.

Nothing weakens the spirit like confusion, uncertainty and passive obedience to compulsion. The method of training for control by activation that we present here is designed to prevent both confusion and stress for the dog. By offering it clear, comprehensible alternatives that are both gratifying for it and also the result we desire, we avoid the necessity of using harsh compulsion to control the dog in bite work.

196

By training for control through activation rather than inhibition we can teach the dog to hold and bark powerfully and with spirit. ("Gitte.")

GOAL 1: The dog will hold and bark in front of a motionless agitator.

In Schutzhund bite work, there are really only four major skills that the dog must master: the hold and bark, the out, obedience on the protection field and the blind search. Of these four, the hold and bark and the out are by far the most important. Furthermore, the out is no more than an elaboration on the hold and bark—it follows quite naturally.

Therefore, we believe that the hold and bark is the fundamental concept of control in Schutzhund protection, and we teach it thoroughly before introducing any of the other skills.

How we teach the hold and bark is absolutely vital, because this exercise will constitute the dog's first encounter with the issue of control. If the dog learns to *channel* its energy, *to switch gears instantly from one behavior to another, carrying its drive intact,* then it will gain the primary ability needed for championship-level protection. If, on the other hand, we inhibit the animal in order to control it, then we will sacrifice something in it that we may never regain.

In drive work, we have already taught the dog that it must bark in order to bite and that its bark has the power to move the decoy, to animate him so that he becomes prey. However, during drive work the animal was always restrained from biting by the leather collar, and barking was inseparably coupled to lunging and fighting the leash. Our problem now is how to uncouple barking from lunging, so that the dog chooses to hold and bark instead of biting when there is no leather collar holding it back.

For this we need a third person. In bite work there is so much to be done all at once and so quickly that the handler needs an assistant who handles the lines for him. The assistant makes corrections, and does much of the physical work of restraining the animal, leaving the handler free to give commands and to praise and support his dog. From now on, when we refer to an *assistant*, we speak of someone who helps the handler by taking over some of the duties of controlling the dog.

Important Concepts for Meeting the Goal

1. Uncoupling barking from lunging
2. Correcting ''dirty'' bites
3. Keeping the dog ''clean'' when sending it from a distance
4. Keeping the dog ''clean'' when rounding the blind
5. Keeping the dog ''clean'' off leash
6. Proofing the hold and bark

1. Uncoupling barking from lunging

The assistant holds the dog on two leashes—one connected to an agitation collar, the other running to a correction collar.

198

As in all bite work up to this point, the dog is not under any obedience command and it is wild with excitement. The handler stands near and encourages the dog to bite the decoy, commanding "Get him!" The assistant restrains the animal with the wide leather agitation collar, letting the correction leash hang loose.

The exercise begins, as do all control exercises, with an excitation phase. Rather than soothe or calm the dog, we stimulate it. As if it were a turbine, we try to give the animal momentum by running it up as high as it will go. The helper therefore agitates the dog vigorously, moving in close to it and letting it try for the sleeve several times. After five or ten seconds of excitation, the agitator steps back a pace and "freezes." An instant later, two things happen simultaneously.

- the handler commands his dog to "Search!"
- the assistant drops slack into the agitation collar leash and, before the dog can lunge forward and bite, checks it sharply with the correction collar

Each time the animal surges forward it is met with a jerk just strong enough to stop it. The assistant's objective is to get the dog to stop lunging, stand back off the collar so that the leashes hang slack and bark. Furthermore, he must do this while inhibiting the dog as little as possible.

The dog is often very persistent about lunging and attempting to bite. As the animal fights the collar and the agitator stands still and the seconds tick by, the turbine winds down. As the animal calms, it gradually ceases lunging. Unfortunately, it often ceases barking as well, and only stares fixedly at the decoy.

It is the agitator's job, when he sees this happening, to jump away (the dog *loses* its quarry when it does not bark!) and restimulate the dog. As he does so, two more events occur simultaneously:

- the handler exhorts the dog excitedly, commanding it again to "Get him!"
- the assistant snaps the slack out of the agitation collar leash, bringing it tight, and drops slack into the correction collar leash, so that the dog is free to lunge into the leather collar in pursuit of the helper

After five to ten more seconds of excitation, the decoy freezes again, the handler commands the restimulated dog to "Search!" and the assistant changes over once more to the correction collar.

The perceptive reader will see that there are two phases to the procedure: a *drive phase,* in which the dog is free to strive against the collar, to bite the agitator if it can; and a *control phase,* in which the dog cannot strive, and must restrain itself instead.

We cycle repeatedly from one to the other, using the drive phase to stimulate the animal and then dropping it unexpectedly into the control phase, where it has nothing to do with its energy but bark. The more suddenly we make this

Above: The handler restrains the dog with the leather collar while the agitator stimulates the dog (drive phase).

The agitator freezes, and the handler prevents the dog from biting with the correction collar (control phase).

At right: After several repetitions, the dog barks without attempting to bite, and . . .

. . . the agitator rewards it by moving (return to drive phase) and . . .

. . . then immediately slips the sleeve.

200

conversion, the more drive the dog will carry into the control phase and express by barking.

If, after two or three cycles, we are not successful in uncoupling barking from lunging at the agitator—so that the dog does not do the former without the latter, but simply wears itself down into panting silence instead—then the decoy runs away, agitating furiously, and hides. Loss of the opportunity to bite will frustrate the animal and make it more likely to hold and bark next time.

Eventually when, due to chance or to frustration and perplexity on the dog's part, it finds the solution to the puzzle by rocking back off the collar and ripping out a bark or two, we reward it instantly. The agitator leaps backward, yelling, and the assistant drops the leashes so that the dog can surge forward and bite. The handler comes up and praises his dog extravagantly, patting and encouraging it while it bites.

Then, before the dog has enough of biting, the agitator slips the sleeve, the handler breaks the dog loose from it, the assistant takes up his lines and the cycle is quickly repeated while the memory of what it did to achieve gratification is still fresh in the dog's mind.

With this system we present to the dog some basic rules that will hold true throughout training. We also present it with a problem and let it learn actively and powerfully by waiting until it stumbles onto the solution itself. The sequence goes like this:

if we physically hold you back . . .

if the decoy is in motion . . .

if we command you ''Get him!'' . . .

. . . then go for broke, strive, get him if you can!

However:

if we stop restraining you physically . . .

if the decoy is motionless . . .

if we command you ''Search!'' . . .

. . . then you are responsible for holding yourself back.

But what do you do with your energy?

Channel it to another behavior . . .

BARK!

. . . and you will be rewarded!

2. Correcting "dirty" bites

If the procedure is executed perfectly, the dog will never have the chance to take a dirty bite when the agitator is standing still. The animal will attain its goal and relieve its frustration only by channeling to barking and thereby winning the opportunity to bite. As a result, it will soon lock in to the hold and bark. This is the way that dogs become clean for life in the blind.

However, in dog training very little works perfectly, and when we least expect it, an aroused dog will steal six extra inches of slack from us and grab the sleeve. What do we do?

The traditional method is to punish, to take vengeance, to physically correct so severely that the animal never forgets the retribution and pain associated with a dirty bite. The problem is that this treatment will inhibit the low- to medium-powerful dog, and it will enrage the very powerful dog, so that it bites twice as hard next time around.

There is another way. The object is not to take vengeance upon the animal when it makes a mistake; the object is to cheat it of its aim unless it does the job our way. What is the dog's aim? Not just to bite, but to spend drive, to make combat. That takes two. In order for a bite to be gratifying, the decoy has to fight back.

Accordingly, if the dog takes a dirty bite, the decoy simply stands absolutely still. The handler steps up, tells the dog quietly "No!" and breaks it off the sleeve very quickly. The exercise is immediately repeated. There is no yelling, no emotion, no excitement. The error is "glossed over" as though it never happened. The excitement and emotion will come next time when the dog does a fine hold and bark. The decoy will give it a wonderful, vigorous fight for the sleeve, and the handler will exclaim his pleasure and praise of the dog.

3. Keeping the dog "clean" when sending it from a distance

Thus far, the dog has remained stationary and the decoy has come to it for the hold and bark. Now we are ready for the animal to advance and the agitator to stand still. We must be prudent because, when the dog takes a run at a person, it has not only physical momentum but psychological momentum as well, and is very likely to forget itself and bite.

Therefore, in the beginning, the assistant carefully walks the dog up to the decoy on the leather collar, and then checks the animal with the correction command if necessary. As the dog becomes more and more reliable, the assistant will move it faster and faster and over progressively longer distances in order to reach the agitator, until he is finally running as fast as he can in his efforts to keep up with the dog.

During this procedure, the handler should vary his position about the field, giving his commands from different distances and directions. If the dog is absolutely clean, so that it stops short and begins to bark all on its own with no correction or cue necessary, then we are ready for the next step.

When the dog takes a dirty bite, the agitator should stand absolutely still. The handler tells the dog sharply "No!," steps up closely and breaks it quickly off the sleeve. The correction is made calmly and without anger, and then the exercise is immediately repeated.

We must now let the dog run free to the decoy—without the assistant at its heels. We keep the animal clean by sending it on a long line.

Beforehand, the assistant measures the line out on the ground and marks the spots where he will stand and where the decoy will stand. This way he knows just how much line he has to work with, and he can check the animal at exactly the right moment, if necessary. However, if its schooling is proceeding correctly, the dog is already much bound by habit, and the line should be almost superfluous.

If it *is* necessary to correct the animal again and again with the line, then the dog is not yet ready to progress to this stage of training.

4. Keeping the dog "clean" when rounding the blind

So far, we have performed all our work on the hold and bark in the open field. We have not yet tried the exercise in a blind. The blinds can present us with two difficulties:

- Some animals are a little shy of the blind, so that they are not quite as powerful when they are required to enter this more enclosed space in order to bark. This is normally easily remedied with just a bit of work in and around the blinds.
- In trial, the dog approaches the blind from behind. When it rounds the corner, it sometimes finds itself at a distance of less than two feet from a person that it has never seen before who is wearing a sleeve. The result of this sudden, almost startling encounter is often a dirty bite and the resulting penalty by the judge.

The solution is simple. Consider the blind to be the center of a clock face, with the opening directly at 12:00. On a long line, we send the dog for a series of holds and barks. The first is from 12:00, where the dog can clearly see the decoy. The next is from about 3:00, where the animal's vision of the decoy is partially obscured. The next is from 4:00, where it cannot see the decoy at all, and so on. However, the assistant never moves farther than 3:00. He always remains where he can see the opening of the blind and what happens there when the dog arrives, so that he is ready to correct with the long line if the animal nips or bites.

In this way we can gradually accustom the dog to staying clean during an increasingly sudden encounter with the decoy when it rounds the blind.

5. Keeping the dog "clean" off leash

The issue is not completely settled yet, because the dog is by now very conscious of the role the nearby assistant (and the correction collar, and the long line hanging from it) plays in controlling it. We cannot be sure that the dog is absolutely clean rounding the blind until we can send it fifty or seventy-five yards with nothing around its neck but a chain collar, and no one within 100 feet of the blind.

But this procedure could be very risky. If the animal bites, it will obtain a great deal of gratification before we can get to it and stop it. In addition, and far worse, the dog will learn something about the limitations of its trainers: *when we can control it and when we cannot.*

The first time that the animal runs free to a blind, we must be certain of two things: (1) that the dog is near certain to do just what we want it to, and (2) that, in the event it does not do so, we can surprise it with a totally unanticipated correction unrelated to the collar, long line or the assistant.

The solution is, again, simple, and one of the most elegant techniques that we have discovered in Schutzhund training, because it arises from such a sharp insight into what the dog can and cannot do with its mind.

The handler brings the dog onto the field wearing all the training paraphernalia—leather collar, correction collar and the long line—and then he makes a great show of removing all this equipment and throwing it aside, one piece at a time, as if to say to the dog, "Here, do what you want. Now I am helpless to stop you!"

The handler gives the dog, wearing only a chain collar, to the assistant. Suddenly the decoy appears and, from close range, begins to agitate the animal furiously, working it into a frenzy. Meanwhile, the handler sprints for the distant blind and hides in it. A moment later, the decoy follows him, still agitating, and piles into the blind on top of the handler, standing in front of him and hiding him from sight.

Because the dog is only a dog, and distinctly limited in terms of the kind of mental transformations it can make in space and time, it will always be surprised to find its handler in the blind with the decoy.

If the dog rounds the blind, beside itself with frustration, sees the agitator so temptingly close and bites, its handler will step out and grab it. The handler shouts "No!" while breaking the surprised animal off the sleeve and drags it back extremely brusquely, as though the dog were no more than a bag of cement, and gives it once more to the assistant. Note that there will be no abuse, anger or vengeance taken upon the dog. Then the exercise is immediately repeated.

About the time that we suspect that the dog has our stratagem figured out, we switch. This time the handler releases the dog, which, realizing that it is leaving its handler behind it in the open field, may be tempted to bite, only to find the assistant hiding in the blind and ready to correct it.

6. Proofing the hold and bark

The single most frequent complaint that we hear at Schutzhund trials is: "But my dog has never done that before!" And, invariably, it has never committed that particular error before. But it picked the day of competition to experiment for the first time with some utterly unexpected mistake, such as charging straight at the judge when commanded to "Search!" or some other appalling error.

These humbling occurrences are a reflection of the strange chemistry of the trial field. For, on trial day, something is different. Even though the exercises are the same—and the agitator, the blinds and even the field are often the same as in training—one thing is different: the handlers. We are so nervous that we are nauseated, with mouths so dry we can barely swallow. The animals reflect our anxiety in their behavior, and our seemingly stable, polished exercises disintegrate into vaudeville.

The effect is even worse when we "make the big time," when we travel out of our region or even to another country for a major championship. Here, the helpers are new, the field is totally different, the blinds may be constructed entirely differently and our nerves are raw.

A German friend told us once about the experience of competing in the German National Schutzhund III Championship, the largest working-dog event in the world. "You have no idea what it is like. You walk into the arena with your dog and there are twenty thousand people waiting to see you. Everyone is talking, cheering, so excited. You can cut the air with a knife! Your dog, it feels it, and it becomes so strong, crazy like you have never seen it. It won't listen. All it does is bite!" (This is the good kind of problem to have in these circumstances. The other kind is when your dog becomes weak like you have never seen it, and refuses to bite at all.)

The process of *overtraining* the animal so that this does not occur is called *proofing*. Some trainers approach proofing by relying upon routine. They run the whole series of exercises, in order and according to all the rules, so many times that for both the handler and the dog all commands and responses become automatic, mechanized. The problem is that this requires much useless rehearsing of exercises that are already nearly flawless and will only suffer by repetition. The process is boring, and will soon take the luster of power and energy off the animal.

We proof in a different way, by perfecting the dog's performance in bizarre situations that are far more demanding than the trial itself. We have no set progression of exercises. Instead, it is a matter of inspiration and improvisation. Here are some scenarios that we have used successfully for proofing the hold and bark:

- performing the exercise inside a building, or on a slick floor, in the near dark, or in the glare of headlights, among crowds of loud, jostling people, inside vans, or in the beds of pickup trucks, even on flights of stairs
- performing the hold and bark on seated agitators, costumed agitators or agitators equipped with bite suits or hidden sleeves instead of Schutzhund sleeves
- setting up foot races to the blind of thirty, forty or even seventy-five yards. The helper is given enough of a head start so that he can reach the blind and freeze just before the dog arrives. If the animal can control the white-hot desire produced by the pursuit—skidding into the blind,

bouncing off the agitator without biting him and settling into a hold and bark—then there is little that will disturb its performance on trial day. (This procedure is also excellent for lending power to its bark in the blind, because it will make the dog very "pushy.")

Our method of teaching the hold and bark produces dogs that are powerful and clean in the blind, not dogs that sit in front of the sleeve and yap politely for a bite, nor animals that bark helplessly from a distance. It produces animals that (for lack of another phrase) push in close to the agitator and "get in his face"— demanding that he move so that they can bite him.

GOAL 2: The dog will out cleanly on command.

Once the dog has a flawless hold and bark, the out is very simply taught. However, it must be well taught. If we school the out badly or incompletely, it will haunt us for the rest of the dog's working career.

Early on in training, when the animal is still comparatively naive, we have one chance to teach it that it must release its bite on command—one opportunity to convince it that we are omnipotent and that we can reach it anywhere on the field and correct it if it disobeys. If we squander this opportunity, if the dog learns that we are actually far from omnipotent, then we will create a very persistent training problem for ourselves.

The amount of force used is critical. Too much force will inhibit the dog, killing drive and disturbing its mouth so that it bites badly or uses only a half mouth when it senses an out coming. Too little force will give the animal the opportunity to resist us, to fight the out, and as the frustrated handler gradually increases the severity of his corrections, the animal's ability to endure them will increase as well. Soon the dog will burn as much energy fighting the out as it does fighting the decoy.

We differ from some other trainers in our desire to preserve, as much as possible, our dog's sensitivity to us and to the correction collar. (Intensely hard animals are prized usually only by those who have never attempted to control one in bite work.) We preserve sensitivity by giving the dog little experience with corrections, so that it never has the opportunity to get used to them. When we correct, we do so sharply and effectively, so that there is not even a question of the dog resisting us. The animal quickly does as we ask and therefore undergoes few corrections. This has the effect of saving both dog and trainer a great deal of grief.

Important Concepts for Meeting the Goal

1. Back tying the dog
2. Forcing the out
3. Preventing discrimination
4. Outing the dog at distance

The handler hides in the blind behind the decoy, ready to step out and correct the dog should it bite instead of hold and bark.

Our method produces dogs that are aggressive and bold in the blind, dogs that move in close to the decoy and demand their bite. (Janet Birk's "Jason," Schutzhund III, FH, IPO III, UDT, WDX. We believe that Jason is the most titled Chesapeake Bay Retriever in the history of the breed.)

1. Back tying the dog

The first step in teaching the out is to create for ourselves a great mechanical advantage over the dog. After all, we are preparing to take the sleeve from its mouth or, more correctly, to force the dog to relinquish it. We have already spent months teaching the animal to be extraordinarily passionate and stubborn about keeping its bite against all opposition. Now we will have to overcome this stubbornness, and it will have to be done smoothly and precisely and with as little fuss as possible.

If we attempt to wrestle the sleeve from the dog by simply pulling or prying or jerking it backward off the sleeve, we often just succeed in teaching the animal to hold on more tenaciously, because we inadvertently stimulate the same oppositional reflex in it that we exploited in order to fix its mouth on the sleeve during drive work.

The trick is to correct *into* the sleeve. We begin by tethering the animal to a post or a tree on its leather agitation collar with about ten feet of line. In addition to the agitation collar, the dog wears a correction collar, which is fitted so that the leash attaches to it under its jaw. In other words, the correction collar faces forward, not back.

The handler and his assistant (who controls the correction leash) both stand outside the dog's circle, facing it, and the decoy works in between them and the dog, being careful not to foul the correction line. If the agitator wears a left-handed sleeve, then the assistant stands to his left, or vice versa. Thus, when the dog is on the sleeve, the correction leash will run from the collar, under the decoy's elbow, and to the assistant. If the assistant cranes his neck a little, he can still see the dog's mouth on the sleeve—so that he does not inappropriately correct an animal that is already outing.

The tether line and the correction leash form a straight line running directly from the tree to the assistant's hands. With the tree to anchor it, all the force of any correction is transmitted directly to the dog's neck. Therefore, it is possible for the assistant to administer an effective correction with precisely the amount of force he intends, neither too harsh nor too light.

The traditional method, in which the handler corrected back and away from the helper with no anchoring post, made for a very sloppy correction because the decoy's arm absorbed a great deal of the force intended for the dog. A hard correction would simply drag both helper and dog a little closer to the handler rather than force the animal off the sleeve. The result was often that, in the end, excessive force was used in order to accomplish the out. For this reason, the back-tie method described here is actually far kinder to the dogs.

2. Forcing the out

The helper begins the process by, as always, stimulating the dog. He runs back and forth around the circle described by the dog's tether until the animal is

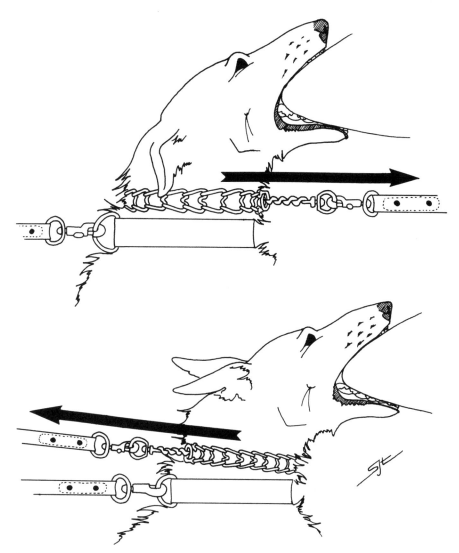

During training for the out, the correction must be made into the sleeve *(top)*. The traditional method of correcting away from the sleeve *(bottom)* stimulates the animal's opposition reflex and makes it bite down harder.

extremely excited. Meanwhile the assistant plays the line so that both decoy and dog have the freedom to move without becoming entangled. The decoy allows a bite and then he fights the animal very strongly, pulling against the tether to fix the bite. When the dog is hard on the sleeve and very much in spirit, the decoy takes three precisely timed actions:

1. He takes a very short step toward the tree, so as to drop about six inches of slack into the tether. (Never attempt to out a dog with the animal's mouth under tension. Remember, physical restraint stimulates the animal to bite harder.)
2. He then freezes, standing still with the sleeve across his torso, braced strongly against the dog's attempts to drag him to and fro.
3. When he is ready, the agitator signals to the handler with a nod.

The handler gives a crisp "Out!" command—he does not shout—and at the same instant the assistant corrects the dog sharply and with enough force that the animal instantly releases the sleeve. The assistant does not pull or tug at the dog; he delivers a snapping jerk. If the first is not enough, then he delivers another crisp and slightly stronger correction, and so on. As we have already stated, the amount of force is crucial. Therefore, the person in the club with the best "hands" and the most experience should always serve as the assistant.

The dog should out and, because of all its schooling in the hold and bark, automatically rock back and begin barking. However, if it attempts to rebite, the assistant calmly corrects it again.

The instant the dog settles and lets out a bark or two, the handler allows it another bite and a vigorous fight and then slips the sleeve for it.

In other words, we reward the animal for its out with a bite and then possession of the sleeve. Too many trainers think of the out—and all the other control exercises too—as solely forced exercises, something that the dog is only resentfully compelled to do and that it will fight against tooth and claw. But there is a way to present the out to the animal so that it is in its interest to do it, not just in order to avoid a correction, but also in order to gain a bite and then possession of the sleeve.

Remember, a good fight takes two, and when the agitator freezes he robs the dog of a great part of the gratification involved in biting the sleeve. How can the animal reactivate the agitator? By letting go of the sleeve! We teach the dog to demand the helper's participation by outing and barking. The sequence is as follows:

1. The decoy allows a bite and fights vigorously. Gratification for the dog is intense.
2. The decoy freezes. Gratification for the dog declines sharply.
3. On command, the dog outs and barks.
4. In response to the animal's barking, the decoy allows another bite, fights vigorously and then gives the sleeve to the dog.

We must make for the dog a very clear and strong connection between the act of outing and barking and being rewarded with the sleeve. We make this connection by positioning these two events very close in time. Perhaps as little as two or three seconds elapse between the moment the dog outs and the moment it has the sleeve back in its mouth again.

The mistake trainers so frequently make is to out the dog and then make it bark for two minutes in an attempt to "burn" the idea in or, even worse, to out the dog and then heel it away from the agitator in an attempt to keep it clean. This is completely wrong because it gives the dog the idea that, by outing, it gives up the agitator and the sleeve, and loses them both.

Remember, we selected the dog for precisely its tenacity and its willingness to endure a great deal in the fight to keep possession of its prey. When it does not perceive a relationship between releasing the sleeve and then immediately getting it back again, we should not be surprised if it resists all but the most extreme force in order to stay on the sleeve. Therefore, in the beginning of out training, the sequence is bite–out–bite, and this chain of events is extremely rapid.

Once the dog has the idea and the out has become somewhat habitual, we can become less concerned about rewarding the out immediately and (1) gradually extend the period of time and the number of barks between the out and the rebite, and (2) perform sequences of outs, so that the animal bites and outs several times in a row before we allow it to have the sleeve.

3. Preventing discrimination

Discrimination is the phenomenon that takes place when the dog realizes the limitations on our ability to control it. The following scenario will serve as an example.

> The out is begun with a dog and taken to the level of 60 percent reliability, meaning that the animal outs cleanly and without a correction three times out of five but requires a reminder in the form of a crack on the collar the other two times. Amazing as it seems, this is often the point at which the typical trainer takes his dog off the back tie (or whatever other device he has used for corrections) "just to see what it will do." (In dog training, anything done "to see what it will do" is premature, and therefore normally a big mistake.)
>
> The dog's behavior is still plastic, variable. The out has not yet become an inviolable habit for it. The result is that, because of the different circumstances that surround the exercise when the dog is not back tied, it disobeys. The indignant handler runs in from wherever he was watching and wrestles the animal off the sleeve, but in the meantime the dog has had the opportunity to bite for a while. And it has learned something. The rule that was in force—"out, or be corrected

TRAINING FOR THE OUT

Above: The decoy brings the dog into the spirit by agitating it vigorously.

He allows the animal to bite the sleeve and fights it strongly for a few seconds.

At right: The decoy then freezes, the assistant makes ready to deliver a correction, if necessary, and the handler commands the dog to "Out."

The dog releases the sleeve and begins to hold and bark.

After one or two barks, the decoy gives the dog another bite and . . .

. . . immediately gives the sleeve to the animal.

214

instantly''—is no longer in force when it is not tied up. The dog learns that the relationship between disobedience on the out and punishment changes according to the circumstances. It forms a new strategy to deal with the situation: ''Regardless of any commands, keep biting until my handler gets near me.''

Outraged, the handler takes the dog back to the post in order to show it ''what for.'' He trains the out on the back tie for one or two sessions and then he again takes the dog off the post too soon. And again the dog refuses to let go when commanded to ''Out!'' It steals some gratification, and winds up back on the post.

Returning the animal repeatedly to the back tie, far from correcting the problem, actually makes it worse. Each time it goes through the cycle, the dog learns more about the limitations on its handler's ability to control it. It makes the crystal-clear discrimination that it must never disobey when tied to the post, but that it can disobey in other situations, depending upon certain factors like how close to it its handler is when the command comes, whether it feels the weight of the correction collar on its neck, where the assistant is, even whether it is trial day.

This scenario shows how a true problem dog is made. Here are some common ''solutions,'' and the additional problems that result.

1. The decoy corrects the animal by striking it on the foreleg with the stick.

   The new problem: Stick corrections weaken the dog, teaching it respect for the decoy and fear of the stick. The last thing we want is for our dog to respect the decoy or fear the stick.

2. The handler stands near the dog and corrects it if it disobeys.

   The same old problem: The correction is still dependent upon the proximity of the handler. What will we do for an out at distance?

   The new problem: More seriously, this technique teaches fear and mistrust of the handler, so that the animal bites badly any time its handler is near. This, of course, is exactly the wrong state of affairs. The dog should draw strength and encouragement from its handler during bite work.

3. An electric collar is used to correct the dog on the out.

   The same old problem: Discrimination is still possible; the animal can still learn when it is wearing the ''live'' collar and when not, especially if the methods used are slipshod (as they often are when a handler buys an electric collar as a cure-all for failures in technique).

   The new problem: The electric collar is a tremendously powerful (usually too powerful) compulsive training device, and must be used with great skill and flawless technique. Unfortunately, skill and technique in the use of the electric collar must be learned at the expense of a dog or two. Therefore, few trainers really know how to use this device. In addition, because of the particular nature of electrical stimulation, the electric collar has a tendency to weaken all but very hard animals.

The fundamental reality is that we lack the ability to control the animal at all times on the field and, ultimately, we depend upon nothing more than force of habit and our strength of personality to impose our will upon it.

The solution to this fundamental problem is to keep the dog from finding us out, to *prevent discrimination*. We do so by, first, avoiding the mistakes described above and, second, by overtraining the animal. We leave it on the post so long, and perform the out in so many different ways that it is virtually locked in habit. Its behavior where the out is concerned is no longer plastic. The dog outs invariably, no matter what the context. Discrimination is prevented because, since the dog does not disobey, it never learns that sometimes we are unable to control it when it disobeys. We are, as far as it is concerned, omnipotent.

We overtrain by proofing:

1. We perform outs under very difficult, distracting or stimulating circumstances that far exceed the difficulties of a Schutzhund trial. For example:
   - out the dog off a decoy who is not frozen but actively struggling against the animal
   - out the dog off a decoy who sits in a chair or lies upon the ground
   - back tie the dog in a dark building, on a slick floor or inside a confined space and train the out
   - practice the out while the dog is surrounded by a crowd of milling spectators
2. We make the dog practice the skill perfectly many times in order to establish it as an invariable habit. Remember, practice does not make perfect; perfect practice makes perfect.

Once the animal outs flawlessly in every conceivable circumstance, no matter what the difficulty, and has done so for several weeks, during which the correction line has lain slack and unused in the assistant's hands, then it is ready to be taken off the back tie, and not before.

4. Outing the dog at distance

The training we have accomplished up to this point will suffice for all but very difficult dogs in the *front work,* the protection exercises in which the handler is relatively close to his dog for the out. However, for two reasons, the long-distance courage test outs will present problems with even an extensively overtrained and proofed dog:

1. These outs come immediately after the courage test. The dog is inspired and highly stimulated.

In order the enforce the out at a great distance from the handler, the decoy uses a short leash attached to the dog's pinch collar and corrects the animal under the sleeve.

2. During the courage test, nobody is within 100 to 200 feet of the animal, except the decoy. The unfamiliarity of the context, in addition to the dog's high level of spirit, can lead to disobedience and then discrimination.

In order to overcome these difficulties, we need a method of correcting the dog that

- does not depend upon the proximity to the dog of the handler or an assistant
- does not depend upon a cumbersome long line
- will not teach the dog respect or fear for the decoy or for the stick

The best method we have found makes use of a tight pinch collar and a short (two to three foot), very light line hanging from it. The dog drags the line with it as it goes down the field after the agitator (it has no wrist loop or knot to tangle in the animal's legs) and after the bite the helper grabs hold of it under the sleeve with his free hand. If necessary for the out, he then corrects the dog with a short, precise movement of his arm.

The agitators who are good at this technique can deliver a relatively strong correction without making it obvious to the dog from whence the compulsion comes. It is important that the decoy does not command the dog himself or threaten the animal. He acts only as a mechanical agent for the handler.

Because of limitations on leverage, and because of the physical strength of even a medium-sized dog, this technique will not work with a dog that is experienced in disobedience and determined to keep its bite. However, in the case of a well-prepared and extensively overtrained animal that is inclined to out anyway, the method is ideal.

The handler restrains the dog physically while the agitator stimulates it from a distance of twenty or thirty feet (drive phase).

Then the handler quickly releases the dog's collar, commands the dog to "Sit" and simultaneously corrects the animal into a sit with the leash (control phase).

After several repetitions, and in spite of being excited, the dog sits on command and holds its place without a correction.

The handler then sends the dog to bite with the command "Get him" (return to drive phase).

220

17

Protection:
Obedience for Bites
and the Blind Search

THE THREE MOST IMPORTANT SKILLS that the dog must master for Schutzhund protection are the hold and bark, the out and the blind search. However, there is in addition a somewhat bewildering array of minor skills that the animal must also master in order to turn in a polished performance:

- Schutzhund I attack on handler
- front transport and Schutzhund II and III attack on handler
- side transport (or side escort)
- down and search
- recall to heel from the blind

This list does not include a last aspect of the protection routine which is not one of the formal exercises but which plays a vital role in all of them. We speak, of course, of heeling—the not so simple business of moving a very excited and aggressive animal around the field with nothing but voice to control it.

Many trainers consume a great deal of their time and their dog's energy hammering in each of these minor skills as separate and distinct exercises. Yet, interestingly enough, the minor skills are often the weakest points in otherwise excellent trial performances. It is quite common to see dogs in competition that are faultless in the hold and bark and the out, and yet are still very difficult to manage on the protection field.

As a result of many years of work with biting dogs, we have developed a system that overcomes this problem by uniting all the minor skills. Once the dog has mastered a single concept, which we call *obedience for bites,* the attacks on handler, the escort, the transport, the down and search, the recall and heeling all fall naturally and even effortlessly into place.

Of course, at this stage in the dog's career, there is no need to teach it obedience. It already understands most or all the skills required. But understanding something is different than actually doing it. We must take into account the emotional and physiological context of training.

Certainly when the dog is in the mildly stimulated mood that prevails on the obedience field, it "knows" obedience and responds easily to commands. However, in the supercharged atmosphere of the protection field, obedience is another question entirely. During agitation, the dog is intensely aroused. This excitement is not only a function of its mood, but also it is a physiological phenomenon—a chemical event taking place within the animal's body. Because its bloodstream is flooded with endorphins and other hormones that considerably alter its behavior and basic characteristics, it may seem a different dog when on the protection field.

Trainers who come to Schutzhund from competitive obedience are often taken unaware by the changes that come with arousal. Because they are unaccustomed to training animals in this excited frame of mind, they do not understand that bite work is a totally different realm of behavior than obedience and that consequently different rules apply.

For example, sometimes dogs that are otherwise as sensitive and gentle as lambs become so stimulated during agitation that they turn as hard as stone, and they will endure without a blink a correction that would normally devastate them. This transformation is a normal part of bite work, and takes place to some extent in every dog. It is also very much to our advantage, because in agitation we deliberately exploit arousal in order to develop power in the dog, the kind of power that will enable it to withstand all opposition from the decoy. Unfortunately, the same power can give the dog the ability to withstand its handler's attempts to control it as well.

Arousal not only can make a dog harder than normal, it can also profoundly change its basic reactions to stimuli. For instance, sometimes physical punishment escalates an already intensely stimulated dog instead of settling it down. All the handler's efforts to control the animal only arouse it further.

What all these remarks mean to say is that obedience on the protection field is a special case. Just because the dog knows what "Heel!" means does not ensure that it will actually do it when anywhere near an agitator.

The traditional remedy for disobedience is simply to punish the animal until it does as it is told, decoy or no decoy. In the process the handler finds himself continually battling with his dog, going head-to-head against all the power that breeding and training have given the animal. For the handler this is a no win scenario. If the dog wins the battle, the handler loses because he cannot control his animal. If the dog is vanquished and forced to obey, the handler loses anyway—because in hammering the dog into submission he has wasted a great deal of time and energy, and probably killed some of his dog's character as well.

There is another way. By teaching the dog the obedience for bites concept, we can save its strength for fighting the decoy, instead of the handler.

Just like our methods for training the hold and bark and the out, obedience for bites is based upon the concept of *channeling*—diverting the animal's energy smoothly from one behavior to another while inhibiting it as little as possible. Quite simply, we teach the dog to "buy" bites with obedience skills. We make no attempt to force the exercises. Instead, we present the animal with a clear proposition: Do it, or you don't get a bite.

GOAL 1: The dog will remain focused on the handler and responsive to commands on the protection field.

Important Concepts for Meeting the Goal

1. "Coiling" the dog
2. Teaching attention with heeling
3. Teaching the minor skills of protection

1. "Coiling" the dog

Up until now, we have never asked the dog to obey any obedience commands during bite work. Except during the very brief periods when we dropped the animal into the control phase for a hold and bark or an out, the dog has spent all its time on the protection field in the drive phase. The dog burned energy at a stupendous rate, barking furiously at the agitator and straining into the leather collar that restrained it. For the dog, agitation has come to mean not just biting, but also the opportunity to *strive,* to spend itself, to vent the drive that fills it to bursting.

During training for the hold and bark and the out, we stopped the dog from striving into the collar for a few seconds at a time, taught it to channel its energy and express it by barking. Now, in obedience for bites, we will teach it to suppress its energy instead and hold it in check for gradually longer periods of time, coiling it up inside as though it were a great spring.

We cannot accomplish this by force, because the sort of harsh physical punishment that would be necessary to control the animal does not store its drive, but rather kills it. Instead, we do it by frustrating the dog, winding it tighter and tighter, and only letting it unwind when it does precisely as we ask.

The handler stands on the field with his dog at his left side, using his left hand to hold the animal back with the leather agitation collar. The dog also wears a correction collar, and the handler grips the correction leash in his right hand. We are in the drive phase.

The decoy begins agitating the dog, and the handler encourages the animal to "Get him! Get him!" The dog lunges and barks, striving against the collar.

Then, suddenly, the agitator freezes, and the handler releases his dog's leather collar and at the same time tells the dog to "Sit!" Now we are in the control phase. But the animal is, of course, far too excited to sit, and the handler will be obliged to correct it sharply into position.

Because a sit that we have to correct the dog into is no sit at all for our purposes, we repeat the exercise. The handler seizes the dog's leather collar with his left hand and commands "Get him!" The decoy stimulates the dog for five or ten seconds, freezes, and then the handler commands his dog to "Sit!"

When, after a number of repetitions of the procedure, the dog drops into a tight, coiled sit instantly upon command *and without a correction* the handler rewards it. With a quick, excited "Get him!" he drops the correction leash and sends the animal to bite the agitator.

The emphasis here is not upon brutally overcoming the dog's excitement. The leash corrections are only strong enough to sit the animal, not punish it severely. The emphasis is upon persistently denying the dog gratification until it solves the puzzle and realizes what it is that we want. Rather than controlling the animal with severe force, we rely instead upon anticipation. After several repetitions, the dog knows that another is coming and its anticipation of both the "Sit!" and the correction makes it ever more likely to obey the command. When, finally, it sits automatically and is then instantly rewarded, it begins to learn to fulfill its desire by carrying its energy into another behavior, and restraining it briefly so that the handler will allow it to bite.

After a few sessions on this kind of drill, the animal will learn to readily channel its energy into sits and downs and other obedience exercises in order to win its bite.

2. Teaching attention with heeling

We now have the animal a little in hand. It understands that the way to win bites is by responding to commands—even when it is terribly excited.

But we still lack something very important. In order to control the dog and maneuver it about the field, we need its *attention*. And this is precisely the problem because, as a result of months of agitation, the decoy has become incredibly "magnetic" to the dog. All the time that the animal is on the field its eyes remain locked on the man.

How can the handler possibly compete with the agitator for the dog's attention? Again, the classic method is to inhibit the dog—physically shock it until its level of excitement drops. As a result its orientation response to the decoy will become weaker, and it can be made to look at its handler instead. Earlier in this chapter we described this procedure as a no-win scenario because it pits the handler against the dog's desire to bite.

We have another way. Just as we taught the dog to pay for bites with sits and downs, we can also teach it to pay for bites with attention. Quite simply, if the dog looks in its handler's eyes, it gets to bite. If it looks at the agitator, it does not.

The trick is to get the animal to turn its head and look at its handler when everything in it, all the force of its instinct and its training, point it at the decoy like a compass needle pointing north. We do it by making use of heeling, an exercise in which it has already learned habitual attention.

Just as before, the helper stimulates the dog and the handler sits it. Then the handler commands it to "Heel!" then pivots smartly 180 degrees and begins walking briskly away from the decoy. As he does so he corrects his dog sharply in order to break the animal's hypnotic stare at the decoy and bring it around the turn.

The direction the handler takes is extremely important. He heels *away* from the decoy because it will be much easier to draw the dog's eye when the man is behind him instead of directly in front.

The dog, if it is any good at all, will strenuously resist being taken away and persistently try to look back over its shoulder at the agitator. The handler just strides briskly along, correcting with the leash each of the animal's attempts to turn back toward the agitator. After a few paces, the animal's eyes will, from confusion and force of habit, settle on its handler's. At that moment the handler gives the "Get him!" command.

After a few repetitions of the procedure, when the dog hears the "Heel!" command it will snap its eyes off the decoy, come smartly around to heel and lock its eyes on its handler's.

The animal has made a very important transformation. Before, it regarded the path to the bite as lying directly along its line of sight at the decoy. Now, it realizes that when it hears the command to "Heel!" its path to the bite does not lie along its line of sight. It goes first to its handler's face, and it is here that the dog now directs its energy.

Once we have the dog's attention, once it looks in its handler's eyes, then we have it under control, even on the protection field.

3. Teaching the minor skills of protection

The side transport, the recall to heel from the blind and the down and search are simply obedience exercises. Once we made the dog realize that to readily obey obedience commands on the protection field is to win bites, the dog can be taught the commands quite easily.

The attacks on handler, on the other hand, are biting exercises. At the judge's signal, the agitator suddenly attacks the handler and the dog. He charges menacingly at them and, in Schutzhund I, strikes the animal twice with the stick. However, there is no need to teach the dog to bite an attacking man. In drive work we have already accomplished it. Nor is there a need to teach the animal to out after the attack is over, for it has already learned this in field work.

The problem of the attacks on handler is *keeping control of the dog before the attacks come*. In a Schutzhund trial, whether it is Schutzhund I, II or III, there is a routine to all the exercises, and the attacks are no exception. Certain events occur, every time in the same order and the same way, that predict for the dog that the agitator is about to charge it, and that it is about to get a bite.

The front transport involves heeling on the protection field, moving a very excited and aggressive animal around the field with nothing but a voice command for control. (Susan Barwig with her first Schutzhund III dog, "Uri.")

During the side transport the dog must remain vigilant and under control. (Sandi Nethercutt and her young Schutzhund I dog with Mark Chaffin.)

The dog reads the cues, and it *anticipates* the attack. It becomes progressively more excited and more difficult to control as the moment nears. Finally, when it is nearly completely out of hand, the bite comes and rewards its anticipation. Therefore, with every attack on handler the dog will become more difficult to manage.

During training, we deal with this problem of anticipation of the attacks on handler in two ways:

1. by teaching them as obedience for bites exercises, so that the dog learns that it must heel attentively, looking directly into its handler's eyes, or there will be no attack and thus no bite.
2. by initiating the attacks *at the handler's discretion, not the decoy's.* The decoy does not simply pick his moment and attack. It is the handler who signals the bite by telling his dog to "Get him!" and he will not do so unless the animal is perfectly controlled and attentive. For his part, the decoy waits to hear the "Get him!" command and then charges at the handler and dog.

Thus, the handler's voice, face and eyes predict the bite for the dog. Like a motorist who looks up at a traffic light instead of down at the road, the animal tends now to watch its handler rather than the agitator. And when we control its eyes, we control the dog.

GOAL 2: The dog will search the field for the decoy, running around all six blinds rapidly and according to the handler's instructions.

The blind search, or revier, is in our opinion the most difficult exercise in Schutzhund protection to teach. The exercise depends upon patience and good methodology for success, and to teach it well is a slow and careful project of several months.

Success is seen in a dog that searches the blinds at a dead run, full of drive and lovely to watch, and utterly in its master's hand. More commonly we see animals that lope or trot apathetically around the first four blinds, and then gain momentum and spirit as they draw near the sixth blind, where they know that they will find an agitator. For these dogs the first five blinds are simply a duty.

Performance of this sort often arises when trainers teach the blind search as strictly an obedience exercise. On the contrary, the revier is, just as much as the hold and bark or the out, a control exercise that involves a ticklish balance between drive and responsiveness to command. The blind search should be a display of obedience driven by intense desire, of control over a dynamic and powerful force.

In our method, there are two distinct stages of training for the revier: an inductive teaching phase and a compulsive training phase.

The inductive phase we call the *shell game.* Just as the old carnival huck-

During the revier the dog must search all six blinds on the field under the handler's direction. When the dog finds the hidden agitator, the animal must detain him by barking aggressively. (Paul Hombach, background, with his Schutzhund III dog.)

sters used to confound the public with the question "Which shell is the pea under?" we confound the dog with the question "In which blind is the person?" If we do our job well, we eventually convince the animal that the only way it will find the agitator is by following its handler's directions.

By using the shell game we seek to accomplish two important objectives:

1. Teach the dog a clear understanding of and a pattern of habit for the complicated skill involved in the blind search—traveling from one side of the field to the other, crossing its handler's path and looping around six blinds in succession, starting with either the first one on the left or the first one on the right.
2. Teach the dog to move with spirit and at top speed by
   - linking the search directly to its desire to bite.
   - making the dog's expectation of a find and a bite equal for each of the six blinds, so that it goes as strongly to one as it does to the next.

In conventional, purely force-trained methods, the first five blinds are disjointed from the dog's desire to bite, because it knows that they are empty. The animal knows that it will find a decoy only in the sixth blind, and it searches the first five simply in order to avoid punishment. Only the last blind represents to it the possibility of a bite, and for this reason the dog runs at only the sixth blind with full spirit. On the other hand, when we use the shell game, and use it well, the dog believes that every one of the blinds may contain an agitator. Because each of the six blinds represents to it an equal possibility for a bite, it searches all of them diligently and with intense eagerness.

With the shell game we arrange the conditions to induce the dog to search the field without resorting to force. When the dog finds the decoy, we made it bark a few times and then we let it bite. In the process it learns not only what we expect, but also the habit of doing it in the manner we want—at top speed and with spirit.

Important Concepts for Meeting the Goal

1. Running the shell game (inducive phase)
2. Forcing the send (compulsive phase)
3. Remotivating the dog

1. Running the shell game

For the shell game we employ all six blinds set up on the field. In addition, we use a seventh blind in which to hide the dog. We put it there when we do not want it to see what happens on the field. In the beginning, however, we use only blinds 1 and 2.

We allow the dog to watch the agitator run, yelling and agitating, into blind 1. Then the handler hides the animal behind the seventh blind for about thirty seconds. While the dog's view is obstructed, the decoy moves quietly from blind 1 to blind 2.

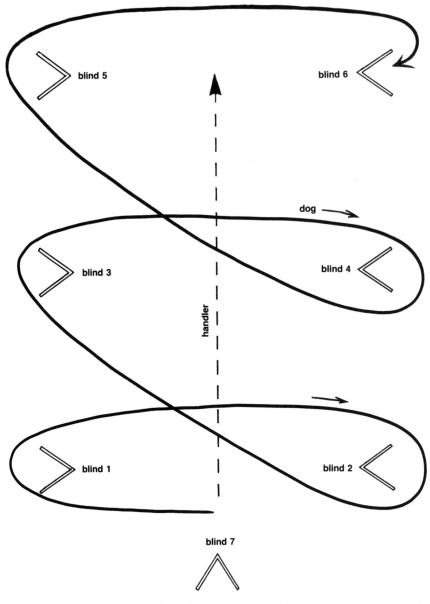

The blind search is a complicated skill. The dog must travel from one side of the field to the other, crossing the handler's path and looping around six blinds in succession, beginning with either the first one on the left or the first one on the right, according to the judge's instructions.

The handler brings his dog back out onto the field and sends it to blind 1 with a sweeping arm signal and the command "Search!" The animal runs out eagerly at the blind because it remembers seeing the agitator there half a minute earlier. The dog is therefore quite astonished to find it empty. During its moment of confusion, the handler calls it back and sends it to blind 2, where the dog finds the decoy, barks at him a few times and is then allowed to bite him.

Next time, of course, the dog will be absolutely convinced that the agitator is hiding in blind 2, because that is where it last found him. So, while the dog is hidden behind the seventh blind, we have the helper move stealthily back over to blind 1.

The handler brings his dog out and sends it to blind 2. The animal goes there willingly and finds nothing. The handler then calls it back and sends it to blind 1, where it finds the helper and gets to bite.

Eventually the dog's expectation of finding in each of the two blinds will be about equal, and this is precisely the principle of the shell game—that by keeping the dog's anticipation of finding an agitator in each blind equal for first two, then four, then all six of the blinds, we cause it to be equally willing to go to any of them. The dog does not prefer one to another, because it believes its chances are the same in each one.

As the shell game progresses, the dog also becomes increasingly mystified and distrustful of its own conclusions about where the agitator is hiding. It begins to rely unquestioningly on the handler to tell it where to go to find the decoy.

Accordingly, the dog must have no idea, when it begins a blind search, if it will find the agitator in blind 1, or 5 or 3. Consequently, it has no reason to disobey its handler. The dog does not prefer to run to blind 5 when the handler commands it to go to blind 1 because, as far as it knows, blind 5 is no more likely to be "hot" than blind 1. Since no one blind offers a greater chance of a find than another, it will go to each one the handler sends it to, all six in order, until it discovers the helper.

The result of this process of juggling the animal's expectations will be a scorchingly fast blind search, and without the use of force. However, there still remains one difficulty.

2. Forcing the send

In a Schutzhund II and III trial, the agitator is *always* found in the sixth and last blind. Consequently, after we show our dog in just a few competitions all our meticulous work on the shell game will be absolutely undone. The dog will quickly learn that in trial (a context that it easily learns to recognize) its chances of finding the decoy in all of the blinds are far from equal. It will see no point in visiting blinds 1 through 5, when it knows perfectly well that the agitator is hiding in blind 6. *Now* the dog has good reason to disobey its handler. There is only one remedy—force.

We go back to using just blinds 1 and 2. We make no attempt to fool the dog about which blind the decoy hides in. We let it see exactly where the decoy goes.

Then the handler forces the dog to go to the other blind anyway. This is much easier to do if the handler walks the animal up very close to the empty blind before sending it. Anyway, it is easy enough to accomplish because with the shell game we have already taught the dog the skill of going out to an indicated blind and searching it. Now it is just a matter of making it do it. The instant the dog rounds the empty blind, the handler praises it enthusiastically and sends it across to the other blind where the agitator is hiding.

The concept that, in order to get its bite, the dog must first run *away* from the helper is a difficult one for the dog. It must come to realize that the empty blind is an intermediate goal, that it represents the bite, and the faster the animal gets to it, the faster it will get back to the decoy in the ''hot'' blind.

Carefully, one step at a time, the handler forces the dog to search one empty blind, then two, then three, and so on, always rewarding it with a bite as soon as it completes the search. Eventually the animal will run all six blinds on command, even though the agitator stands in full view outside the sixth one.

3. Remotivating the dog

One thing still remains to be done. The dog, although still eager, probably no longer travels the blinds at its best speed.

We can easily regain its speed by again manipulating the dog's expectations, by resuming the shell game. Make no mistake, the handler still *compels* it to run all six blinds as directed, and we still place a decoy outside the sixth blind where the dog can see him. However, we also conceal one or more other agitators in blinds 1 and 5. We do this on a random basis. Thus, the animal has no idea whether it will have to run all the way to blind 6 for its bite, or whether it will suddenly come upon another, hidden decoy in the first blind it searches or the second or the third and the fifth as well.

By returning to the shell game we render the dog's expectations for a bite at each blind equal once again. Therefore, it has no reason to grudge its handler's commands to search every blind. The animal goes willingly and at top speed. As far as it knows, there is always a chance that the next blind contains a decoy.

In addition, and very importantly, the dog recognizes that it has no choice in the matter. Whether it expects a bite in the next blind or not, it knows that it must go where its handler sends it.

Conclusion

This book is just a brief look at a subject so fascinating that many thousands of people the world over, speaking a dozen or more languages and belonging to a number of different cultures and ethnic groups, are devoted to it—the working dog.

We hope to have conveyed some information, certainly, to have given the reader a grasp of theory and technique. Most of all we hope that we have communicated our devotion to, interest in and respect for brave dogs. In a way a fine, brave dog is noble, and expresses in its behavior many of the ideals that we prize in human beings—courage, fidelity, spirit, vitality and trueness of self.

All of us could pick worse company.

The Schutzhund's courage and power on the protection field arise from a steadiness of nerve. From this steadiness also arise even disposition, reliability and basic good nature. (Schutzhund III bitch with Landau children.)

Glossary of
Schutzhund Terminology

AD   The endurance degree awarded. The dog must have sufficient energy and stamina to trot beside its handler's bicycle for a twelve-mile distance. At the conclusion of the run the dog must be willing to do a few simple obedience exercises.

Agitator (helper, decoy)   Person used to sharpen and mold the dog's aggressiveness by agitating it. An agitator is needed for the protection portion of the Schutzhund Trial.

Air Scent   The airborne scent left by a person, animal or object.

AKC (American Kennel Club)   The major governing body in the United States which regulates the breeding and training of purebred dogs.

Article   The term used to describe the object first handled by the tracklayer, then dropped on the track during the tracking test. It should be neutral in color and approximately hand-sized.

"A" Stamp   German certificate that a dog's hips are of a certain quality. The dog must have an "A" stamp to be used for breeding in Germany. The dogs are given the stamp with a rating of *normal, fast normal* (almost normal) or *noch zugelassen* (acceptable).

Attack Training (protection training)   The training given to the dog so its aggressiveness toward man can be elicited under certain circumstances.

BLH (*Blindenhund*)   Guide dog for the blind.

Blind   The object or structure behind which the agitator hides during the protection portion of Schutzhund. The handler also hides behind it during the long down in the Schutzhund III routine of the obedience portion.

Body Scent   The unique aroma surrounding each individual.

BpDH I, II (*Bahnpolizeidiensthund*)   Railroad police service dog.

Bringst   Retrieve.

Bundesleistungssieger   German National Working Dog Champion.

CD (Companion Dog)   The most elementary obedience degree awarded to the dog by the AKC or CKC. The dog must be able to heel on and off leash, come when called, stand without moving while being examined by the judge, remain in a sit and down position with the handler approximately twenty-five feet in front of it.

CDX (Companion Dog Excellent)   Intermediate degree granted by the AKC or CKC. The dog must heel off leash, retrieve on the flat and over a jump, lie down on command during the recall, jump a broad jump and stay in a sit and in a down position while its handler is out of sight.

Civil Agitation   When the agitator is unarmed and unprotected, he agitates the dog using threatening body gestures, particularly hand movements and facial grimaces.

Correction   The negative inducement given to the dog to encourage an appropriate response. It should not be given for slowness in learning or inability to understand. The most effective corrections are given with the collar and leash and are followed immediately by the positive inducement of praise.

Courage   The willingness of the dog to subjugate its own personal safety in order to protect itself and/or its handler. In competition the dog's courage is rated "Pronounced," "Sufficient" or "Not Sufficient." Courage and fighting instinct are more than fearlessness. The dog must be willing to fight when threatened, even when the option to escape is present.

Cross Track   The track laid by another individual which intersects the original track in an FH or TDX tracking event.

Deep Nose   The dog's characteristic in tracking whereby it takes full scent and tracks with its nose close to the ground. This is a desirable quality.

DH (*Diensthund*)   Service dog.

Disposition   The total characteristics of the dog's ability to perform what by breed standards it is intended to do.

Dumbbell   An object, with a cylinder in the center and two end pieces, to be retrieved by the dog. The dumbbell is weighted according to the level at which the Schutzhund dog is working.

DVG (*Deutscher Verband der Gebrauchshundsportvereine*)   German Alliance for the Utility Dog Sports.

Europameister   World champion Schutzhund III dog.

FH (*Fahrtenhund*)   The most advanced tracking title awarded by the SV. The dog must follow a stranger's track approximately 1,300 paces long. The track has four articles and is intersected by cross tracks laid by another stranger and is a minimum of three hours old.

Fuss   Heel.

Gebrauchshundklasse   Adult class.

Hardness   The dog's capacity to forget unpleasant experiences during the protection phase and to demonstrate maximum courage and fighting spirit.

Hard Sleeve   A protective garment worn around the arm of the agitator. The hard sleeve is designed for the dog with a particularly hard bite and to protect the agitator from injury. It is usually constructed from heavy jute over a leather frame.

Hart, Mut und Kampftrieb ausgeprägt   Hardness, courage and fighting instincts are pronounced.

Heel   The dog walks or sits at its handler's left side, with the dog's right shoulder in line with the handler's left knee. The dog's body should be parallel with its handler's. The dog should not forge ahead or lag behind.

Henze Courage Test   The test that evaluates the dog's courage by having the agitator run at it in an aggressive way. The dog should attack the agitator aggressively.

HGH (*Herdengebrauchshund*)   Herding dog.

Hier   Come.

High Nose   The dog's characteristic in tracking whereby it tracks with its nose too high above the ground. A dog with high nose is using air scent as well as the track scent and will lose points during the tracking portion of the Schutzhund evaluation.

Hütesieger   Herding Dog Champion at the German herding dog championship.

INT1 (*Internationale Prüfungsklasse*)   International training degree.

Intelligence   The dog's ability to retain what it has learned and to profit from experience. This is an important trait in Schutzhund work.

IPO I, II, III   Schutzhund III according to the international rules.

Jugendsieger   First place winner (SG-1) in the youth class (twelve to eighteen months) at the *Sieger* show.

Junghundsieger   First place winner (SG-1) in the young dog class (eighteen to twenty-four months) at the *Sieger* show.

Kampftrieb vorhanden   Instincts present but not pronounced.

KKL I (*Korklasse I*)   Recommended for breeding.

KKL II (*Korklasse II*)   Suitable for breeding.

Landesgruppensieger   The first place winner (V-1) at the regional show in the adult class.

Lbz (*Lebenszeit*)   Breed surveyed for lifetime.

Leg   Each straight portion of a track. Also, in AKC obedience, each time a dog qualifies in an obedience competition, it earns a "leg." A dog needs three "legs" to receive a title.

Long line   A leash approximately thirty feet in length which is used during the tracking portion of Schutzhund. A heavier version is also very helpful as a training aid during the obedience and protection phase of the training.

M (*Mangelhaft*, Faulty)   Show or performance rating.

Motivation   The system of inducements given to promote desired behavior. Intangible rewards are praise and affection; these are the most effective ways to increase motivation. A tangible reward is food.

NASA (North American Schutzhund Association)   A relatively small group promoting the Americanized version of Schutzhund. It uses a modification of the VDH Schutzhund rules.

OFA (Orthopedic Foundation for Animals)   The rating from this medical group certifies that a dog's hips are of a certain quality. If the dog receives an OFA number, it is certified free of hip dysplasia. Temporary numbers may be issued by the OFA if HD-clear radiographs (X-rays) were taken when the dog was under twenty-four months of age. Permanent numbers are issued to dogs with HD-clear radiographs taken at twenty-four months or older.

PH (*Polizeihund*)   Police dog.

Platz   Down.

PSP (*Polizeischutzhundprüfung*)   Police protection dog degree.

Quartering   A dog's habit of crossing back and forth over the track, an undesirable characteristic in Schutzhund. The dog will lose points during the trial if it quarters over the track.

Revier The exercise in the protection phase of Schutzhund in which the dog is sent to a blind where the agitator is hiding. The dog is to harass and detain the agitator by aggressively barking at him from a close position. The agitator is to remain still.

Schutzhund A sport originated in Germany to evaluate a dog's ability in tracking, obedience and protection. There are three levels: A Schutzhund I degree is the most elementary and Schutzhund III is the most advanced.

SG (*Sehr gut,* Very Good) Show or performance rating.

Sharpness The sharp dog has a low threshold for sensation and has a tendency to overreact to stimuli. It often has a strong desire to bite and is sometimes a fear biter. It is not desirable in Schutzhund work if the dog's sharpness is not balanced with prey drive and good character.

Shyness Generalized avoidance behavior that shows itself as fear or desire to escape from a situation.

Sieger Grand Victor (VA-1) title at the German *Sieger* show.

Sitz Sit.

Sleeve The protective covering over the arm of the agitator used during protection training.

Spirit The zest and enthusiasm the dog shows for its work. This is a very desirable quality in Schutzhund.

Stake A dowel or other object which can be secured in the ground and is helpful in letting the tracking dog's handler know the location of the track during training. A stake is always used to indicate the start of the track during a trial.

Stick A flexible, lightweight weapon used to evaluate the dog's ability to withstand a threat. It is not meant to inflict injury.

SV (*Verein für Deutsche Schäferhunde*) The German Shepherd Dog Club of Germany, founded by Max von Stephanitz.

TD (Tracking Degree) Awarded by the AKC or CKC for dogs completing a track that is laid by a stranger and is approximately 600 paces long. A dog completes the test by locating the article dropped by the track layer at the end of the track. The track usually has three or four turns on it.

TDX (Tracking Degree Excellent) The most challenging degree awarded by the AKC and CKC in tracking, roughly equivalent to the FH.

Temperament The dog's attitude toward people. If a dog has a poor temperament, it could be shy, vicious, distrustful or nervous. Temperament can also refer to the dog's steadiness and stability.

Track Scent   The scent, left by a person, animal or object, that is produced by the change in the ground.

Training Collar   Sometimes referred to as a choke chain, this collar becomes tighter or looser on the dog's neck as pressure on the leash is applied or released. Use of this collar serves as a correction to the dog.

U (*Ungenügend*, Insufficient)   Show or performance rating.

USA (United Schutzhund Club of America)   The largest Schutzhund organization in America. It follows the SV rules and regulations.

UD (Utility Degree)   The most challenging obedience degree granted by the AKC or CKC: The dog responds to hand signals, performs scent discrimination work, and stands for examination by the judge.

V (*Vorzüglich*, Excellent)   Show or performance rating.

VA (*Vorzüglich-Auslese*, Select)   Show rating given at the Sieger show.

VH (*Vorhanden*, Sufficient)   Show or performance rating.

Viciousness   Unjustified aggression; biting without provocation.

Wall   The scaling or climbing jump which is part of the Schutzhund II and III obedience routine.

WDA (Working Dog Association)   Schutzhund organization that is a branch of the German Shepherd Dog Club of America. It follows SV rules and regulations.

Weltsieger   World Champion title at the show of the Fédération Cynologique Internationale (FCI).

Willingness   The dog's positive reaction to its handler's commands. The dog is enthusiastic and cheerful, even without a reward.

ZB (*Zuchtbewertung*)   Conformation show rating.

ZH I, II (*Zollhund I, II*)   Customs dog.

Suggested Viewing
and Reading

VIDEOTAPES

Schutzhund

Overview is designed to excite the public, the novice and the experienced Schutzhunder about the joys of the sport. It includes animated and exciting performances in all aspects of the competition, describes trial procedures and includes a basic how-to section for each phase of training.

Schutzhund Protection

Thorough enough to teach the beginner and advanced enough to appeal to the expert, these tapes are the first video series to explain, thoroughly and in depth, from beginning to end, how to train your dog for the protection phase of Schutzhund. Tapes I to III cover drive work. The tapes cover canine aggression and the art of agitation and show a step-by-step progression from the first day of training through the point at which the dog performs a hard-hitting courage test.

Protection I covers the different types of canine aggression, and explains how to mold them through agitation and how to start the puppy in bite work.

Protection II covers how to introduce puppies and young dogs to the sleeve, how to character-test the adult dog and how to teach the defense-oriented dog to make prey.

Protection III covers teaching the prey-oriented dog to bite defensively, and training the dog to bite under the stick and to do hard-hitting runaways and courage tests.

Tapes may be purchased from:

Canine Training Systems, Ltd.
7550 W. Radcliff Avenue
Littleton, Colorado 80123
(303) 973-2107

Books

Barwig, Susan, and Brenda Abbott. *The German Shepherd Book.* Wheatridge, Colo.: Hoflin Publications, 1987. (Available from Canine Training Systems.)

Fox, Michael. *Understanding Your Dog.* New York: Coward, McCann, and Geoghegan, n.d.

Johnson, Glen. *Tracking Dog: Theory and Methods.* Rome, N.Y.: Arner Publications, Inc., 1975.

Most, Colonel Konrad. *Training Dogs—A Manual.* London: Popular Dogs Publishing Co., 1951.

Pearsall, Milo, and Hugo Verbruggen. *Scent: Training to Track, Search, and Rescue.* Loveland, Colo.: Alpine Publications, 1982.

Pfaffenberger, Clarence. *The New Knowledge of Dog Behavior.* New York: Howell Book House, 1963.

Pryor, Karen. *Lads Before the Wind.* New York: Harper & Row, 1975.

Schutzhund USA published by United Schutzhund Clubs of America, St. Louis, Mo., vol. 10, no. 6.

von Stephanitz, Max. *The German Shepherd Dog in Word and Picture.* American edition revised from the original German work by J. Schwabacher, orig. publ. in 1923. (Available from Canine Training Systems.)

Bibliography

Barwig, Susan, and Brenda Abbott. *The German Shepherd Book*. Wheatridge, Colo.: Hoflin Publications, 1987.

Bergman, Goran. *Why Does Your Dog Do That?* New York: Howell Book House, 1973.

Campbell, William. *Behavior Problems in Dogs*. Santa Barbara, Calif.: American Veterinary Publications, 1975.

Davis, Wilson. *Go Find: Training Your Dog to Track*. New York: Howell Book House, n.d.

Fox, Michael. *Behavior of Wolves and Related Canids*. New York: Harper & Row, 1971.

Goldbecker, William, and Ernest Hart. *This is the German Shepherd*. Jersey City, N.J.: TFH Publications, 1957.

Johnson, Glen. *Tracking Dog: Theory and Methods*. Rome, New York: Arner Publication, 1975.

Koehler, William. *The Koehler Method of Guard Dog Training*. New York: Howell Book House, 1962.

Most, Colonel Konrad. *Training Dogs—A Manual*. London: Popular Dogs Publishing Co., 1951.

Pearsall, Milo, and Hugo Verbruggen. *Scent: Training to Track, Search, and Rescue*. Loveland, Colo.: Alpine Publications, 1982.

Pfaffenberger, Clarence. *The New Knowledge of Dog Behavior*. New York: Howell Book House, 1963.

Saunders, Blanche. *The Complete Book of Dog Obedience*. New York: Howell Book House, 1980.

Schneider-Leyer, Erich. *Der Deutsche Schäferhund*. Stuttgart: Verlag Eugen Ulmer, n.d.

Scott, John Paul, and John Fuller. *Dog Behavior: The Genetic Basis*. Chicago: University of Chicago Press, 1965.

von Stephanitz, Max. *The German Shepherd Dog in Word and Picture*. American edition revised from the original German work by J. Schwabacher, originally published in 1923.

Strickland, Winifred, and James Moses. *The German Shepherd Today*. New York: Macmillan, 1988.